Ancient Egypt
An Introduction

This book provides an introduction to one of the greatest civilisations of all time – ancient Egypt. Beginning with a geographical overview that explains the development of Egyptian belief systems as well as Egypt's subsequent political development, the book examines Egyptological methodology; the history of the discipline of Egyptology; and Egyptian religion, social organization, urban and rural life, and funerary beliefs. It also discusses how people of all ranks lived in ancient Egypt. Lavishly illustrated, with many photographs of rarely seen sites, this volume is suitable for use in introductory-level courses on ancient Egypt. It offers a variety of student-friendly features, including a glossary, a bibliography, and a list of sources for those who wish to pursue their interest in ancient Egypt.

Salima Ikram is professor of Egyptology at the American University in Cairo. An archaeologist of ancient Egypt, she is the author of several scholarly and popular books, including, most recently, *Death and Burial in Ancient Egypt*, *Divine Creatures: Animal Mummies in Ancient Egypt*, and, with A. M. Dodson, *The Tomb in Ancient Egypt* and *The Mummy in Ancient Egypt*.

Agricultural and taxation scenes from the tomb of Nefer at Saqqara. Photo Salima Ikram.

Ancient Egypt

An Introduction

Salima Ikram

American University in Cairo

CAMBRIDGE
UNIVERSITY PRESS

CAMBRIDGE UNIVERSITY PRESS
Cambridge, New York, Melbourne, Madrid, Cape Town, Singapore,
São Paulo, Delhi, Dubai, Tokyo

Cambridge University Press
32 Avenue of the Americas, New York, NY 10013-2473, USA

www.cambridge.org
Information on this title: www.cambridge.org/9780521675987

© Cambridge University Press 2010

First published 2010

Printed in Hong Kong by Golden Cup

A catalog record for this publication is available from the British Library.

Library of Congress Cataloging in Publication data
    Ikram, Salima.
    Ancient Egypt : an introduction / Salima Ikram.
        p.   cm.
    Includes bibliographical references and index.
    ISBN 978-0-521-85907-3 (hardback) – ISBN 978-0-521-67598-7 (pbk.)
    1. Egypt – Civilization – To 332 B.C.   2. Egypt – Social life and customs – To 332 B.C.   I. Title.
    DT61.I45   2009
    932–dc22   2008040753

ISBN 978-0-521-85907-3 Hardback
ISBN 978-0-521-67598-7 Paperback

To Barbara Mertz for feeding the heart, mind, imagination, soul, and stomach,
and
to Aidan Dodson for his constant friendship and support, even at 3:21 AM

Contents

Acknowledgements

A book of this sort depends on the work of many, and I am indebted to all my colleagues, past and present, who have contributed to the field and who have made their opinions and discoveries available through the last century and a half. I am also obliged to those who have taught me and whose modes of instruction have influenced me – for the good, I hope. More specifically, I am very grateful to Janet Richards for suggesting that I write this book (and for her invaluable suggestions after reading a draft, above and beyond the call of friendship) and to Beatrice Rehl for encouraging me to do so. I am also grateful to John Swanson, Fayza Haikal, Lisa Sabbahy, Janice Kamrin, Aidan Dodson, Peter Lacovara, and a slew of other colleagues for our discussions about various aspects of ancient Egypt. I am particularly indebted to Janice, Janet, Nicholas Warner, Barbara Mertz, and Dyan Hilton for reading various versions of the manuscript – any mistakes that remain are (sadly) my own. I am very grateful to Meredith Brand for indexing aid. Most of all, I am grateful to all the students whom I have taught for helping me to form what is written in the following pages.

Preface

The civilisation of ancient Egypt is one of the most compelling in this world and has attracted attention, both popular and scholarly, throughout the ages. Perhaps this is due to its awesome monumental architecture, its beautiful tomb paintings, or its beliefs in the continuity of life after death that resulted in the invention of mummification. Many specialist books have been written about different aspects of Egypt and its culture, but few books furnish a broad overview that makes all aspects of Egyptian civilisation accessible at a fundamental level. This book aims to provide readers with an introduction to ancient Egypt, setting the stage for their further study and investigation. It starts by introducing the reader to the geography and geology of the country and explaining how these have influenced Egypt's culture and history, and then it proceeds to chronicle the history of Egyptology and the methodologies employed by scholars to unravel Egypt's past. Subsequent chapters cover Egyptian religion, history, and social organization; the daily lives of Egypt's inhabitants; and, finally, Egyptian funerary customs. A chronology, glossary, list of Egyptological resources, and select bibliography provide further tools for an understanding and exploration of ancient Egypt. I hope that this book will give its readers a basic knowledge of one of the world's most fascinating cultures and will lead them to read more widely and deeply on the subject.

Cairo, Luxor, and New York

Chronology

Horus or Throne Name	Personal Name	Regnal Dates
PREDYNASTIC PERIOD (5000–3050 BC)		
Badarian Culture		5000–4000
Naqada I (Amratian) Culture		4000–3500
Naqada II (Gerzian) Culture		3500–3150
Naqada III Culture/Dynasty 0		3150–3050
EARLY DYNASTIC/ARCHAIC PERIOD (3050–2663; DYNASTIES 1–2)		
Dynasty 1		
Horus Narmer		
Horus Aha		3050–
Horus Djer	Itit	
Horus Djet	Iti	
Horus Den	Semti	
Horus Adjib	Merpibia	
Horus Semerkhet	Irinetjer	
Horus Qaa	Qebh	–2813
Dynasty 2		
Horus Hetepsekhemwy	Baunetjer	2813–
Horus Nebre	Kakau	
Horus Ninetjer	Ninetjer	
?	Weneg	
?	Sened	
Horus Sekhemib/ Seth Peribsen	Perenmaat	–2709

Horus or Throne Name	Personal Name	Regnal Dates
EARLY DYNASTIC/ARCHAIC PERIOD (3050–2663; DYNASTIES 1–2)		
Dynasty 2 (continued)		
?	Neferkasokar	2709–2701
?	?	2701–2690
Horus and Seth		
Khasekhemwy	Nebwyhetepimyef	2690–2663
OLD KINGDOM (2663–2160; DYNASTIES 3–8)		
Dynasty 3		
Horus Sanakht	Nebka	2663–2654
Horus Netjerykhet	Djoser	2654–2635
Horus Sekhemkhet	Djoser-ti	2635–2629
Horus Khaba	Teti?	2629–2623
Nebkare	Seth?ka	2623–2621
Horus Qahedjet?	Huni	2621–2597
Dynasty 4		
Horus Nebmaat	Senefru	2597–2547
Horus Medjedu	Khufu	2547–2524
Horus Kheper	Djedefre	2524–2516
Horus Userib	Khafre	2516–2493
Horus Kakhet	Menkaure	2493–2475
Horus Shepseskhet	Shepseskaf	2475–2471
Dynasty 5		
Horus Irimaat	Userkaf	2471–2464
Horus Nebkhau	Sahure	2464–2452
Neferirkare	Kakai	2452–2442
Shepseskare	Isi	2442–2435
Horus Neferkhau	Neferefre	2435–2432
Niuserre	Ini	2432–2421
Menkauhor	Ikauhor	2421–2413
Djedkare	Isesi	2413–2385
Horus Wadjtawy	Unas	2385–2355
Dynasty 6		
Horus Seheteptawy	Teti	2355–2343
Nefersahor/Meryre	Pepy I	2343–2297

OLD KINGDOM (2663–2160; DYNASTIES 3–8)

Dynasty 6 (continued)

Horus or Throne Name	Personal Name	Regnal Dates
Merenre	Nemtyemsaf I	2297–2290
Neferkare	Pepy II	2290–2196
Merenre?	Nemtyemsaf II	2196–2195

Dynasty 7/8

Netjerkare	?	2195–
Menkare	Nitokris	
Neferkare	?	
Neferkare	Neby	
Djedkare	Shemay	
Neferkare	Khendu	
Merenhor	?	
Nikare	?	
Neferkare	Tereru	
Neferkahor	?	
Neferkare	Pepysonbe	
Neferkamin	Anu	
Qakare	Ibi	
Neferkaure	?	
Neferkauhor	Khuihapy	
Neferirkare	?	–2160

FIRST INTERMEDIATE PERIOD (2160–2066; DYNASTIES 9–MID-11)

Dynasties 9/10 (Herakleopolitan)

Meryibre	Akhtoy I	2160–
Neferkare	?	
Wahkare	Akhtoy II	
?	Senenen …	
Neferkare	Akhtoy III	
Mery…	Akhtoy IV	
(Various)	(Various)	
?	Meryhathor	
Nebkaure	Akhtoy V	
Merykare	?	
?	?	–2040

Horus or Throne Name	Personal Name	Regnal Dates

FIRST INTERMEDIATE PERIOD (2160–2066; DYNASTIES 9–MID-11) (CONTINUED)

Dynasty 11a (Theban)

Horus or Throne Name	Personal Name	Regnal Dates
Horus Tepya	Mentuhotep I	2160–
Horus Sehertawy	Inyotef I	–2123
Horus Wahankh	Inyotef II	2123–2074
Horus Nakhtnebtepnefer	Inyotef III	2074–2066

MIDDLE KINGDOM (2066–1650; DYNASTIES MID-11–14)

Dynasty 11b

Nebhepetre	Mentuhotep II	2066–2014
Sankhkare	Mentuhotep III	2014–2001
Nebtawyre	Mentuhotep IV	2001–1994

Dynasty 12

Sehetepibre	Amenemhat I	1994–1964
Kheperkare	Senusert I	1974–1929
Nubkhaure	Amenemhat II	1932–1896
Khakheperre	Senusert II	1900–1880
Khakaure	Senusert III	1881–1840
Nimaatre	Amenemhat III	1842–1794
Maekherure	Amenemhat IV	1798–1785
Sobkkare	Sobekneferu	1785–1781

Dynasty 13

Khutawire	Wegaf	1781–
Sekhemkare	Sonbef	
Nerikare	? Amenemhat V	
Sehetepibre	Qemau	
Sankhibre	Amenemhat VI	
Smenkare	Nebnuni	
Hetepibre	Hornedjhiryotef-sa-Qemau	
Swadjkare	?	
Nedjemibre	?	
Khaankhre	Sobkhotep I	
?	Renisonbe	
Auibre	Hor	
Sedjefakare	Kay-Amenemhat VII	
Sekhemre-khutawi	Amenemhat VIII-Sobkhotep II	

MIDDLE KINGDOM (2066–1650; DYNASTIES MID-11–14)

Dynasty 13 (continued)

Horus or Throne Name	Personal Name	Regnal Dates
Userkare/Nikhanimaatre	Khendjer	
Smenkhkare	Imyromesha	
Sehotepkare	Inyotef IV	
Sekhemre-swadjtawi	Sobkhotep III	
Khasekhemre	Neferhotep I	
?	Sihathor	
Khaneferre	Sobkhotep IV	
Khahetepre	Sobkhotep V	
Wahibre	Iaib	
Merneferre	Ay	
Merhetepre	Sobkhotep VI	
Mersekhemre	Neferhotep	
Merkaure	Sobkhotep VII	
Djedneferre	Dedumose	
Seheqaenre	Sankhptahi	
Swahenre	Senebmiu	–1650

Dynasty 14

Unclear; possibly located in the Delta and precursor of Hyksos

SECOND INTERMEDIATE PERIOD (1650–1549; DYNASTIES 15–17)

Dynasty 15 (Hyksos)

Horus or Throne Name	Personal Name	Regnal Dates
Maaibre	Sheshi	1650–
Meruserre	Yakobher	
Seuserenre	Khyan	
Nebkhepeshre/ Aqenenre/Auserre	Apophis	1585–1545
?	Khamudy	1545–1535

Dynasty 16

?

Dynasty 17 (Theban)

Horus or Throne Name	Personal Name	Regnal Dates
Sekhemre-wahkhau	Rahotep	1650–
Sekhemre-smentawi	Djehuty	
Sankhenre	Mentuhotep VII	
Swedjenre	Nebiriau I	

SECOND INTERMEDIATE PERIOD (1650–1549; DYNASTIES 15–17)

Dynasty 17 (Theban) (continued)

Horus or Throne Name	Personal Name	Regnal Dates
Neferkare	Nebiriau II	
Sekhemre-shedtawi	Sobkemsaf I	
Sekhemre-wepmaat	Inyotef V	
Nubkheperre	Inyotef VI	
Sekhemre-heruhirmaat	Inyotef VII	
Sekhemre-wadjkhau	Sobkemsaf II	
Senakhtenre	Taa I	–1558
Seqenenre	Taa II	1558–1553
Wadjkheperre	Kamose	1553–1549

NEW KINGDOM (1549–1069; DYNASTIES 18–20)

Dynasty 18

Horus or Throne Name	Personal Name	Regnal Dates
Nebpehtire	Ahmose	1549–1524
Djeserkare	Amenhotep I	1524–1503
Akheperkare	Thutmose I	1503–1491
Akheperenre	Thutmose II	1491–1479
Menkheper(en)re	Thutmose III	1479–1424
Maatkare	Hatshepsut	1472–1457
Akheperure	Amenhotep II	1424–1398
Menkheperure	Thutmose IV	1398–1388
Nebmaatre	Amenhotep III	1388–1348
Neferkheperure-waenre	Amenhotep IV/ Akhenaten	1352–1335
Ankhkheperure	Smenkhkare	1339
Neferneferuaten		1338–1332
Nebkheperre	Tutankhamun	1335–1325
Kheperkheperure	Ay	1333–1328
Djeserkheperure-setpenre	Horemheb	1328–1298

Dynasty 19

Horus or Throne Name	Personal Name	Regnal Dates
Menpehtire	Ramesses I	1298–1296
Menmaatre	Seti I	1296–1279
Usermaatre-setpenre	Ramesses II	1279–1212
Banenre	Merenptah	1212–1201
Userkheperure	Seti II	1201–1195

NEW KINGDOM (1549–1069; DYNASTIES 18–20)

Dynasty 19 (continued)

Horus or Throne Name	Personal Name	Regnal Dates
Menmire-setpenre	Amenmesse	1200–1196
Sekhaenre/Akheperre	Siptah	1195–1189
Sitre-merenamun	Tawosret	1189–1187

Dynasty 20

Horus or Throne Name	Personal Name	Regnal Dates
Userkhaure	Sethnakhte	1187–1185
Usermaatre-meryamun	Ramesses III	1185–1153
User/Heqamaatre-setpenamun	Ramesses IV	1153–1146
Usermaatre-sekheperenre	Ramesses V/ Amenhirkopshef I	1146–1141
Nebmaatre-meryamun	Ramesses VI/ Amenhirkopshef II	1141–1133
Usermaatre-setpenre-meryamun	Ramesses VII/ Itamun	1133–1125
Usermaatre-akhenamun	Ramesses VIII/ Sethhirkopshef	1125–1123
Neferkare-setpenre	Ramesses IX/ Khaemwaset I	1123–1104
Khepermaatre-setpenre	Ramesses X/ Amenhirkopshef III	1104–1094
Menmaatre-setpenptah	Ramesses XI/ Khaemwaset II	1094–1064
Hemnetjertepyenamun	Herihor	1075–1069

THIRD INTERMEDIATE PERIOD (1064–656; DYNASTIES 21–25)

Dynasty 21

Horus or Throne Name	Personal Name	Regnal Dates
Hedjkheperre-setpenre	Smendes	1064–1038
Neferkare-heqawaset	Amenemnesu	1038–1034
Kheperkhare-setpenamun	Pinudjem I	1049–1026
Akheperre-setpenamun	Psusennes I	1034–981
Usermaatre-setpenamun	Amenemopet	984–974
Akheperre-setpenre	Osokhor	974–968
Netjerkheperre-meryamun	Siamun	968–948
Tyetkheperure-setpenre	Psusennes II	945–940

THIRD INTERMEDIATE PERIOD (1064–656; DYNASTIES 21–25) (CONTINUED)

Dynasty 22

Horus or Throne Name	Personal Name	Regnal Dates
Hedjkheperre-setpenre	Shoshenq I	948–927
Sekhemkheperre-setpenre	Osorkon I	927–892
Heqakheperre-setpenre	Shoshenq II	895–895
Hedjkheprre-setpenre	Takelot I	892–877
Usermaatre-setpenamun	Osorkon II	877–838
Usermaatre-setpenre	Shoshenq III	838–798
Hedjkheperre-setpenre	Shoshenq IV	798–786
Usermaatre-setpenamun	Pimay	786–780
Akheperre	Shoshenq V	780–743

Theban Dynasty 23

Horus or Throne Name	Personal Name	Regnal Dates
Hedjkheperre-setpenamun	Harsiese	867–857
Hedjkheperre-setpenre	Takelot II	841–815
Usermaatre-setpenamun	Pedubast I	830–805
?	Iuput I	815–813
Usermaatre-setpenamun	Osorkon III	796–769
Usermaatre	Takelot III	774–759
Usermaatre-setpenamun	Rudamun	759–739
?	Iny	739–734
Neferkare	Peftjauawybast	734–724

Dynasty 23

Horus or Throne Name	Personal Name	Regnal Dates
Sehetepibenre	Pedubast II	743–733
Akheperre-setpenamun	Osorkon IV	733–715

Dynasty 24 (Kushite)

Horus or Throne Name	Personal Name	Regnal Dates
Shepsesre	Tefnakhte	735–727
Wahkare	Bokkhoris	727–721

Dynasty 25

Horus or Throne Name	Personal Name	Regnal Dates
Seneferre	Piye	752–721
Neferkare	Shabaka	721–707
Djedkare	Shabataka	707–690
Khunefertumre	Taharqa	690–664
Bakare	Tanutamen	664–656

Horus or Throne Name	Personal Name	Regnal Dates

LATE PERIOD (664–332; DYNASTIES 26–31)
SAITE DYNASTY/PERIOD (664–525; DYNASTY 26)

Dynasty 26

Horus or Throne Name	Personal Name	Regnal Dates
Wahibre	Psamtek I	664–610
Wehemibre	Nekho II	610–595
Neferibre	Psamtek II	595–589
Haaibre	Apries	589–570
Khnemibre	Amasis	570–526
Ankhka(en)re	Psamtek III	526–525

Dynasty 27 (Persian)

Horus or Throne Name	Personal Name	Regnal Dates
Mesutire	Kambyses	525–522
Setutre	Darius I	521–486
?	Xerxes I	486–465
?	Artaxerxes I	465–424

Dynasty 28

Horus or Throne Name	Personal Name	Regnal Dates
?	Amyrtaios	404–399

LATE PERIOD (664–332; DYNASTIES 26–31)

Dynasty 29

Horus or Throne Name	Personal Name	Regnal Dates
Baenre-merynetjeru	Nepherites I	399–393
Usermaatre-setpenptah	Psamuthis	393
Khnemmaatre	Akhoris	393–380
?	Nepherites II	380

Dynasty 30

Horus or Throne Name	Personal Name	Regnal Dates
Kheperkare	Nektanebo I	380–362
Irimaatenre	Teos	365–360
Senedjemibre-setpenanhur	Nektanebo II	360–342

Dynasty 31 (Persian)

Horus or Throne Name	Personal Name	Regnal Dates
	Artaxerxes III	
	Okhos	342–338
	Arses	338–336
	Darius III	335–332

MACEDONIAN DYNASTY & PTOLEMAIC PERIOD (332–30)
Macedonian Dynasty

Horus or Throne Name	Personal Name	Regnal Dates
Setpenre-meryamun	Alexander (III/I)	332–323

Horus or Throne Name	Personal Name	Regnal Dates

MACEDONIAN DYNASTY & PTOLEMAIC PERIOD (332–30)

Macedonian Dynasty (continued)

Horus or Throne Name	Personal Name	Regnal Dates
Setepkaenre-meryamun	Philippos Arrhidaeos	323–317
Haaibre	Alexander (IV/II)	317–310

Ptolemaic Dynasty

Horus or Throne Name	Personal Name	Regnal Dates
Setpenre-meryamun	Ptolemy I Soter	310–282
Userka(en)re-meryamun	Ptolemy II Philadelphos	285–246
Iwaennetjerwysenwy-setpenre-sekhemankhen-amun	Ptolemy III Euergetes I	246–222
Iwaennetjerwymenekhwy-setpenptah-userkare-sekhemankhenamun	Ptolemy IV Philopator	222–205
Iwaennetjerwy-merwyyot-setpenptah-userkare-sekhemankhenamun	Ptolemy V Epiphanes	205–180
Iwaennetjerwyperwy-setpenptahkhepri-irimaatamunre	Ptolemy VI Philometor	180–164
Iwaennetjerwyperwy-setpenptah-irimaatre-sekhemankenamun	Ptolemy VIII Euergetes II	170–163
	Ptolemy VI (again)	163–145
?	Ptolemy VII Neos Philopator	145
Iwaennetjermenekh-netjeretmerymutesnedjet-sepenptah-merymaatre-sekhemankhamun	Ptolemy VIII (again)	145–116
Iwaennetjermenekh-netjeretmenekhsatre-setpenptah-irimaatre-senenankhenamun	Ptolemy IX Soter II	116–110
	Ptolemy X Alexander I	110–109
	Ptolemy IX (again)	109–107
	Ptolemy X (again)	107–88
	Ptolemy IX (again)	88–80
	Berenike III	80

Horus or Throne Name	Personal Name	Regnal Dates
	MACEDONIAN DYNASTY & PTOLEMAIC PERIOD (332–30)	
	Ptolemaic Dynasty (continued)	
?	Ptolemy XI	80
Iwaenpanetjerentinehem- setpenptah-merymaatenre		
sekhemankhamun	Ptolemy XII Neos Dionysos	80–58
	Ptolemy XII (again)	55–51
	Kleopatra VI	58–57
	Berenike IV	58–55
	Ptolemy XII (again)	
	Kleopatra VII Philopator	51–30
?	Ptolemy XIII	51–57
?	Ptolemy XIV	47–44

Iwaenpanetjerentinehem-
  setpenptah-irimeryre-
  sekhemankhamun
	Ptolemy XV Kaisaros	41–30

ROMAN PERIOD (30 BC–AD 395)
BYZANTINE PERIOD (395–640)
ARAB PERIOD (640–1517)
OTTOMAN PERIOD (1517–1805)

A scene from a Ramesside tomb in the Valley of the Kings showing the progress of the sun barque at night. Photo Salima Ikram.

The 5th Dynasty pyramid of Userkaf, with the 3rd Dynasty pyramid of Djoser in the background, at Saqqara. Photo Salima Ikram.

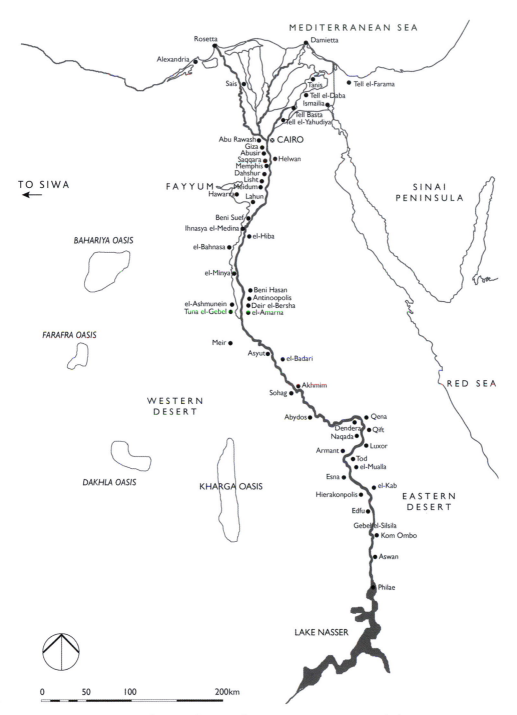

MEDITERRANEAN SEA

Rosetta
Damietta
Alexandria
Sais
Tanis
Tell el-Farama
Tell el-Daba
Ismailia
Tell Basta
Tell el-Yahudiya
Abu Rawash
CAIRO
Giza
Abusir
Helwan
Saqqara
Memphis
Dahshur
Lisht
Meidum
FAYYUM
Hawarra
Lahun
TO SIWA
Beni Suef
Ihnasya el-Medina
el-Hiba
BAHARIYA OASIS
el-Bahnasa
el-Minya
Beni Hasan
Antinoopolis
el-Ashmunein
Deir el-Bersha
Tuna el-Gebel
el-Amarna
FARAFRA OASIS
Meir
Asyut
el-Badari
Akhmim
WESTERN DESERT
Sohag
Abydos
Qena
Dendera
Qift
Naqada
Luxor
Armant
Tod
el-Mualla
Esna
el-Kab
DAKHLA OASIS
KHARGA OASIS
Hierakonpolis
EASTERN DESERT
Edfu
Gebel el-Silsila
Kom Ombo
Aswan
Philae

SINAI PENINSULA

RED SEA

LAKE NASSER

0   50   100   200km

Figure 1. Map of Egypt showing the main sites. Drawing Nicholas Warner.

1

The Black and the Red

Geography and Environment

The Greek historian and traveller Herodotus famously described Egypt as the gift of the Nile. Although this description was particularly true at the time of Herodotus's visit to Egypt in the fifth century BC, there was far more to the country's prosperity than just the Nile River with its attendant annual floods. Egypt's natural boundaries of deserts, seas, and boulder-strewn river rapids helped to protect the country from invaders and allowed its culture to flourish in relative security. Its geographic location as a crossroads between Africa and Asia, where it served as a cultural and economic bridge between the two continents, made it an important entrepôt. Ideas, objects, and people travelled across Egypt, providing its people with a rich material and cultural life. Its borders on the Mediterranean Sea to the north and the Red Sea to the east offered access, respectively, to Europe, the Levant, Arabia, and India. Egypt's geographic location played a critical role in its social, cultural, and economic development, as well as in its interaction with other areas of the ancient world, and contributed to its diverse history and heterogeneous population. Of all the ancient cultures,

1

Egypt is perhaps unique in having maintained roughly the same boundaries throughout its history. (Fig. 1.)

Brief Geological History

The land that the country of Egypt now occupies emerged during the Cenozoic period (some 65 million years ago), when the current configuration of continents was being formed. For several million years geological forces were at work, forming the topographical features that were the precursors of what we see today. For hundreds of thousands of years Egypt was covered by a vast ocean, called Tethys by geologists, that gradually drained off to form what is now known as the Mediterranean Sea, leaving a land consisting of layers of granite covered by layers of sandstone and limestone. Many of the sea creatures that were denizens of the ocean were trapped in these newly formed rock layers and became fossilized. It was perhaps the discovery of such fossils that helped engender ancient peoples' views of mythological beasts and divine creatures.

The early part of the Cenozoic era (starting about 30 million years ago and continuing through about 500,000 years ago) can be characterised as a time of dramatic climatic variation, with torrential rainfalls feeding precursors of the modern Nile River, and carving up parts of the land, creating the *wadis* (valleys) that riddle the surface of Egypt today. About 10 million years ago in the late Miocene, a deep north to south furrow cut through the land and formed the first Nile, known as the Eonile. Over time, the river became known as the Paleonile (c. 300,000–180,000 BP), the Prenile (c. 800,000–400,000 BP), and, finally, the Nile as we know it (from c. 12,000 BP to the present). These earlier phases of the Nile did not follow the same physical course as the current Nile, and might even be considered to have been three different rivers.

The groove carved through the landscape by the Nile reveals the different rock formations that had been created over time. Most of Egypt, from north to south, consists of limestone beds. At Gebel Silsilah, near Aswan, this morphology changes to sandstone, with granite emerging at Aswan and along the Red Sea coast. In these early periods of Egyptian history the bed of the Nile was much higher than it is at present, and the Delta was tiny although it was gradually extended by deposits of soil brought from Upper Egypt by successive Nile floods.

Egypt's climate varied, with wet intervals alternating with dry ones. This oscillation in rainfall affected the path of the Nile, creating a terraced effect on both sides of the river as its levels fluctuated and its course changed. Prior to c. 90,000 BP, the whole of Egypt was a much wetter and greener place than it is today. Much more of the country was habitable then, not just the areas along both sides of the Nile and around the oases, as became true later. The land supported a more diverse flora and fauna than is seen today, with acacia forests and different species of grasses, reeds, rushes, and flowering plants, and a vast range of animals, including lions and leopards, monkeys, elephants, hippopotami, rhinoceri, giraffes, foxes, hyenae, wolves, several kinds of antelope, and wild cattle, and hundreds of species of fish and birds, including ostriches. Many of these species persisted well beyond the Pharaonic period (c. 3050–30 BC), with, for example, hippopotami becoming completely extinct in Egypt only in the late 1800s!

During the course of the Palaeolithic period (between 90,000 and 10,000 BP) the Egyptian environment changed further, and the land became a savannah-like plain similar to what is seen in parts of East Africa today, becoming decreasingly green over time. The Nile ran through the country, and fed by the rains in the highlands of modern Ethiopia and Uganda, the river flooded annually. Gradually, starting from 30,000 BC, and increasingly around 8000 BC, because of continuing climate change, hunter-gatherer populations started to settle closer to the Nile as it provided a more stable source of water, although other areas continued to be exploited as well. These early inhabitants of Egypt left their traces in the form of stone tools,

Egypt's Name

Ancient Egyptians called their country *Kmt*, meaning the Black Land, after the colour of the fertile soil deposited annually by the Nile floods. Egypt was also known as *Tawy*, or the Two Lands, referring to Upper and Lower Egypt, as well as perhaps to the 'black land' of the Nile Valley and the 'red land' of the surrounding deserts. Another designation for Egypt was the 'Two Banks', referring to both sides of the river, as well as to the desert and the flood plain. The word *Egypt* is derived from the area's Greek name, *Aegyptos*, which may have had its origins in the mispronunciation of the ancient Egyptian name for the city of Memphis, *hwt-ka-Ptah* (the dwelling of the soul of the god Ptah). As a result of the Greeks' habit of pronouncing only some of its letters, the ancient name for Memphis may have morphed into *Aegyptos*. The modern Arabic name for Egypt is *Misr*, which means land or fortress and refers to the fortifications on Egyptian soil near Cairo.

crude shelters, and rock art, found on the higher terraces along the Nile and in the oases. By 5000 BC, there was a further push by early people to settle along the river as outlying areas became increasingly desiccated, although still able to support considerable wildlife. This movement of hitherto nomadic hunter-gatherers to the Nile Valley presaged a new and settled lifestyle, one based on agriculture and domesticated livestock, such as sheep, goats, and cattle. It was during this period of its history that much of Egypt's culture was conceived and established. Egypt's now essentially dry climate remained fairly stable throughout most of the Old Kingdom (c. 2663–2160 BC), after which time there were further intermittent climatic fluctuation.

The Areas of Egypt

Geographically, Egypt can be divided into five main regions that are defined by their relationship to the Nile River: the Nile Valley, the Delta, the Eastern Desert, the Western Desert, and the Sinai Peninsula. Each has a unique character based on its geography, which has influenced not only the development of each area but also the history of Egypt as a whole.

The Nile River

The river Nile, the longest river in the world, dominates the Egyptian landscape today as it did in the past. The ancient Egyptians called it simply *Itrw*, or 'the River', as it was the only river that they knew. In the ancient world the Nile River was regarded as unique in flowing from the higher ground in the south and emptying into the sea in the north; thus the southern part of Egypt is known as Upper Egypt, and the northern part as Lower Egypt. The hieroglyphic sign that indicates going north (downstream) is a boat with furled sails, showing that it is going with the flow of the current, whereas the hieroglyphic sign for travel to the south is a boat with an unfurled sail, using what the Egyptians called 'the sweet breeze of the north'. (Fig. 2.)

The current Egyptian Nile is a combination of the waters of the Blue Nile flowing from the Lake Tana in Ethiopia and of the White Nile originating in Lake Victoria in Uganda, which unite at Khartoum. Further on, in northern Sudan, other, smaller, tributaries, such as the Atbara River, add to the Nile's flow. Within the borders of modern Egypt the river measures about sixteen hundred kilometres (some 1,000 miles), running from Aswan to the

Figure 2. The Nile is bordered by fertile black soil that supports lush vegetation. Beyond the margins of this soil is the 'red land', or desert, that is inhospitable to humans and most animals. It is possible to put one foot upon the black fertile soil and the other on the barren desert sand. Stark limestone cliffs enclose the Nile Valley and the low desert on either side, providing a natural boundary for those living within the Valley. Photo Salima Ikram.

Mediterranean Sea. Until the development of seafaring, the Mediterranean acted as a natural boundary, and even after, because of its tides, currents, and winds, the Nile could be navigated only with care. The Egyptian name for the Mediterranean Sea was *wadj-wer*, meaning 'the Great Green', or *'shen-wer'*, translated as 'the Great Encircler'.

At Aswan, the Nile meets with the First Cataract, an outcropping of large granite boulders that creates dramatic rapids, making navigation impossible for about ten kilometres. This cataract generally marked Egypt's southern boundary, although throughout its history the land that Egypt has controlled has included more southern areas, including parts of what is now Sudan. Five additional cataracts punctuate the river between Aswan and Khartoum. (Fig. 3.)

From Aswan, the river continues through Egypt, with a narrow flood plain; it makes a sharp turn in the area known as the Qena Bend, just to

Figure 3. The tip of Elephantine Island at Aswan with a felucca steering around the island. Just further south of Elephantine lie the densely scattered treacherous granite rocks of the First Cataract, which marks the southern boundary of Egypt. Photo Salima Ikram.

the north of Luxor, and the flood plain enlarges dramatically. North, in the Delta, the Nile diverges into several branches and sub-branches before emptying into the sea. During the Graeco-Roman period seven major branches are recorded; now only two of these (Rosetta or Rashid, and Damietta or Damyat) survive.

Owing to the torrential rains of the African highlands, the Nile flooded annually, its rising waters reaching Egypt in late June and finally abating in September in Aswan, and by the end of October farther to the north. The peak flood months in Egypt were late July to early September. On average, the Nile used to carry 200 million cubic metres of water, until the time of the flood, when the volume increased to 700 million cubic metres a day. The flood deposited rich black silt in its wake, a minimum of 10 centimetres every century, thus providing the Egyptians with fresh arable land on an annual basis, as well as supplying the country with reserves of water that could be distributed by canals and stored in reservoirs for use later in the year. The deposits of earth and minerals not only enriched the flood plain but also

Figure 4. The inundation at Dahshur, with the village encircled by the flood and the pyramids in the background. Photo courtesy of Lehnert and Landrock.

helped build up the Delta and provide nutrients at its edge, thus supporting a rich variety of marine life near the shores of the Mediterranean Sea that could be exploited by fishermen. The inundation further aided agriculture by regularly washing the salt from the soil that was omnipresent from the time when an ocean had once covered Egypt. (Fig. 4.)

The rich, fertile, black soil that the Nile deposited in the flood plain gave Egypt its ancient Egyptian name, *Kmt*, referring to the black land that together with *Deshret*, the desert or red land, made up ancient Egypt. Although alien and threatening, the desert was nonetheless a part of Egypt, providing a contrast and balance to the flood plain, as well as a source of mineral wealth. Not only was the silt from the Nile useful in agriculture but it also provided the Egyptians with the raw material for their ceramic industry and for the mud bricks that were the main component of their domestic architecture. Of course, care had to be exercised to keep the settlements along the Nile well out of the reach of the floods. Villages were frequently located either away from the river or on the natural high dikes constituting the Nile's bank, and cemeteries were located in the desert, well beyond the flood plain. As will be discussed, in the Delta the problem was avoided by founding towns and cities on high parcels of ground that effectively became islands during the annual inundations.

The rhythm of the Nile also directed the Egyptian year. The Egyptian calendar was based on the inundation, with the year being divided into three basic seasons: *akhet* or 'inundation', which lasted from June through September/October; *peret* or 'coming forth' or 'growing', when the land emerged from the water and could be tilled, lasting from October to mid-February; and *shemu* or 'drought', when the crops ripened and were harvested, lasting approximately from February to June. The New Year festival coincided with the advent of the flood. This event was linked to the very bright star, Sothis (probably modern Sirius, the dog star), which vanished from the sky for a period of seventy days in the late spring and whose reappearance in the sky marked the arrival of the inundation. The Nile also defined the Egyptians' sense of direction: they viewed their origins as coming from the south, the source of the Nile, and so they considered the south to be a 'head' for the country.

The Nile River provided the Egyptians with their water for drinking, irrigation, and washing, and was the main conduit for the transportation of people, technology, objects, and information. (Fig. 5.) It supported a vast variety of birds and fish that were a mainstay of the diet of the ancient

Figure 5. Boats transported people, animals, and goods along the length of the Nile until quite recently. This 5th Dynasty scene from a tomb at Saqqara shows boats loaded with pottery vessels and sacks. Photo Salima Ikram.

Egyptians. The plants that grew alongside the river, such as papyrus, reeds, lotus, and lily, all contributed to the Egyptian economy. (Fig. 6.) Parts of the papyrus and lotus could be used for food; additionally, papyrus became the source for papermaking. Reeds and rushes, together with papyrus, were the raw materials the Egyptians used for building houses, shelters, and boats and for making baskets, mats, and sandals.

Egyptian theology and iconography were also derived from the Nile. The inundation that renewed the land was a symbol for rebirth and re-creation, and the river itself was part of the divine landscape. The lush growth of papyrus in the wetlands of Lower Egypt made it that region's titular plant, while the lotus and the lily became associated with Upper Egypt, where they were commonly found; thus each half of the country was identified by the riverine growth common to it.

Controlling the River

During the last one hundred years or so, with the construction of a series of dams and barrages in the area of Aswan, and with an ever-increasing population, the climate and geography of Egypt have been in flux. The dams have saved Egypt from famine and provided it with the power and electricity vital to economic growth. Even though the Nile still rises, the river no longer floods the land and washes out the salts in the soil. Large amounts of fertilizer must now be added for the land to be productive. The Delta suffers, as there is no reinforcement of the land by fresh silt deposits, and its marine life has less to sustain it. Salts in the soil dissolve and rise up through the groundwater, decreasing the land's fertility. The salts also cause problems for Egypt's ancient monuments. The stones of the ancient temples absorb the salts, and as the stones dry in the sun, the salt precipitates, leaving a deposit that ultimately undermines the strength of the rock and destroys the reliefs and paintings that may decorate it. Archaeologists are struggling to record and to conserve monuments whilst they can, and environmentalists are seeking ways to balance the needs of Egypt's heritage and its living population.

The Nile Valley

Egypt's Nile Valley encompasses an area that starts at Aswan and ends roughly at Cairo. For political, practical, and theological purposes, the ancient Egyptians divided their country according to its geography, with the Nile Valley proper being regarded as the land of Upper Egypt, or *Ta Shemaw*

Figure 6. Lotus, or lilies, and papyrus used to be commonly found in Egypt. They have both been reintroduced, and the latter is used to make sheets of papyrus. Photo Salima Ikram.

to the ancient Egyptians, and the Delta as *Ta-mehu* (see the next section), its complement. In modern terms, Upper Egypt is the area south of Beni Suef, and Lower Egypt is the area north of Beni Suef, although in ancient times the division between the two parts of the country lay further north near ancient Memphis. Physically, the Nile Valley is characterised by its narrowness: it is rarely wider than five kilometres, and at some points it is reduced to the river itself and a narrow strip of cultivation adjoining the river's course. Generally, in southern Upper Egypt the wider flood plain is located on the east bank and the more narrow area is on the west. This fact may have contributed to the Egyptians' decision to found the majority of their settlements in Upper Egypt on the eastern side of the river, although there are also metaphysical reasons for this choice (see Chapters 5, 7, and 9).

Upper Egypt can be divided into two sections, one more northern than the other, which is sometimes called Middle Egypt today. The northern part of Upper Egypt is the area between Asyut and Cairo. This section of the Nile Valley is rich agricultural land and is broader than areas further south, measuring from 15 to 25 kilometres or more in width. In contrast to Upper Egypt, in Middle Egypt the majority of arable land lies to the west of the river. Perhaps this is why some of the settlements in this area were established in the west rather than in the east.

The most substantial flood plain in southern Upper Egypt is now called the Qena Bend, named after the Upper Egyptian town of Qena. Here the river almost doubles back on itself, creating a huge cultivable area that is a great source of local wealth. This area also has access to trade routes to the Red Sea and to many of the rich mineral resources of the Eastern Desert. This wealthy locale has been a home to many political and military leaders who have influenced the course of Egyptian history.

At Aswan, the river is punctuated by the red granite boulders of the First Cataract and is flanked by sandstone cliffs that peter out north of Gebel el-Silsilah, where they yield to the limestone cliffs that delineate the edges of the escarpment in most of the region. It is these stone cliffs that provided the building blocks for most of Egypt's monuments, be they tombs or temples. The flood plain narrows until Aswan, where it nearly disappears, leading the way into the barrenness of Egyptian Nubia and essentially protecting Egypt from major invasions from the south.

The Delta

The area north of Cairo is generally known as Lower Egypt, called *Ta-mehu* by the ancient Egyptians. Nowadays the Delta is one of the largest and most heavily populated parts of Egypt; however, this was not always the case, as during earlier periods of Egyptian history it had less area, its waters were more brackish, and its soil was less arable. Near Cairo, the Nile Valley is some 40 kilometres wide, its edges marked by limestone cliffs. The Delta starts some 20 kilometres north of Cairo, where the cliffs vanish and the Nile divides into two main branches, the western Rosetta or Rashid branch, and the eastern Damietta or Damyat branch. At one time, these major branches divided into several more meandering branches, before they all emptied into the Mediterranean Sea, some 200 kilometres to the north. Along the way these tributaries created a large flood plain measuring 400 kilometres from east to west and forming a large triangle. Thus the Greeks named this area after their triangular-shaped letter 'delta'.

The number of branches of the Nile that traverse the Delta to the Mediterranean has varied between two and seven as the climate and the flow of the Nile changed. During most of the Pharaonic period, three main branches of the Nile dominated the area: the waters of Pre (the Classical period's Pelusiac branch), which went far to the east, the waters of Ptah (the Sebennytic branch), which was more central, and the waters of Amun (the

Upper Egypt and Lower Egypt

For historical, political, practical, and theological reasons, the ancient Egyptians divided their country into complementary doubles, thus creating the two lands of Upper Egypt and Lower Egypt that united to form the whole of Egypt.

Each part of Egypt was symbolised by icons derived from the environment that characterised it. The floral icon for the more barren Upper Egypt was the blue Egyptian lily, sometimes called the Egyptian lotus (*Nymphae coerulea*), whereas Lower Egypt was denoted by the papyrus (*Cyperus papyrus*) because of the lush papyrus swamps that dominated that region.

The Egyptian vulture, a bird that soared over the commanding limestone cliffs of Upper Egypt, symbolised the region. This bird was also associated with the goddess Nekhbet, who was the main goddess of el-Kab and Hierakonpolis or Nekhen, important early sites in the area. Lower Egypt's symbol was the cobra, the most dangerous and magical creature found in the area and the totem of the goddess Wadjet, who was linked to Buto, or Pe, the chief religious and political site of the region.

The Egyptians also divided Egypt into the fertile black land of the Nile flood plain and the barren red desert, *Kmt* and *Deshret*, respectively. Each half of the country and its tutelary deities had a vital role to fulfil in Egypt's history and religion. Thus, metaphorically, whether Egypt was divided between the north and the south, or between the red and the black, it remained a united duality, the *Tawy*, or 'Two Lands'. (Figs. 7 and 8.)

Canopic branch), which was further to the west. Currently, only two main branches survive, both of which are named for the modern towns located where the water empties into the sea: the Rosetta (*Rashid*, in Arabic) in the west, and the Damietta (*Damyat*, in Arabic) in the east.

Early in Egypt's history, the Delta was a salty marshland, particularly in the area north of the modern city of Tanta. Now this sort of ecosystem is to be found only along the coastal strip of the Delta and features a chain of large, shallow, saline lakes parallel to the Mediterrean Sea: Lake Manzala in the east, and Lake Burullus, Lake Idku, and Lake Maryut in the west. In antiquity, cultivation was limited to the non-saline areas, and habitation was really possible only on islands called 'turtlebacks', or *guzur* (sing. *gezira*) in Arabic, which were deposits of sand and soil that stood from 1 to 12 metres above the water level and were most commonly found in the eastern Delta. Dry land was limited, and settlements developed on one or

Figure 7. The lotus, or more correctly the lily (right), and papyrus (left) were the titulary plants of Upper and Lower Egypt, respectively. These pillars are in Karnak Temple, and their iconography provides an internal geography for the temple. Photo Salima Ikram.

a series of turtlebacks, with houses and shelters constructed of the easily available reeds daubed with mud plaster. In addition to limited agriculture, the Nile and the Mediterranean Sea provided settlers with avian and piscian food.

Over time, the number of marshes and waterways that once characterised the Delta has decreased, making it a significant area for agricultural activity as well as habitation. As seafaring developed, the Delta's access to the Mediterranean contributed dramatically to the region's economy through trade and exchange with Europe and the Aegean Islands, as well as with the Eastern Mediterranean. The Delta's physical connection, through the Sinai, with the Near East provided it with further cultural and economic links that led to the development of ancient Egypt.

Figure 8. This image of Wadjet and Nekhbet, the two titular deities of Lower and Upper Egypt, respectively, comes from Hibis Temple. Wadjet, the cobra goddess who ruled over Lower Egypt, is shown wearing the Red Crown and is balanced upon a papyrus plant, the plant symbolic of her domain. Nekhbet, the vulture goddess who presided over Upper Egypt, wears the White Crown and is balanced upon a lily/lotus, the plant that symbolised Upper Egypt. Each goddess holds out ankh signs to the names of the king, giving him eternal life. Photo Salima Ikram.

The Western Desert and Its Oases

The desert that lies to the west of the Nile is known as the Western, or Libyan, Desert and is part of the great African Sahara. It is the most arid region of Egypt and has some of its most spectacular desert scenery. Other than hosting six oases, it is now an enormous inhospitable tract of land, although as late as the Neolithic period it was a more savannah-like and welcoming space than it is today. The Western Desert is actually a vast plateau that slopes gradually downward from the Sudanese border in the south to the Mediterranean coast in the north and consists of sandstone in the south and limestone from the latitude of Luxor north. About one-third of the Western Desert is covered with sand dunes, including the famed Great Sand Sea, which runs from Siwa Oasis in the north to the Gilf al-Kabir, a high desert plateau located in the south-west corner of Egypt. The Gilf al-Kabir

Figure 9. A rock art panel in Egypt's Western Desert shows a mother and baby giraffes on leads held by men, and two elephants. The environment here in earlier times was clearly wetter and could support diverse wildlife such as elephants, giraffes, and several types of antelope. Photo Salima Ikram.

gradually rises to the massif of Gebel Uwaynat, also nestled in the southwest corner of Egypt. The highest peaks of Gebel Uwaynat approach two thousand metres above sea level and are home to a series of extraordinarily rich painted rock art sites created by some of the earliest inhabitants of the area. (Fig. 9.) Indeed, many parts of the Western Desert provide evidence of early Palaeolithic inhabitants (700,000 BC onward) in the form of stone tools and rock art. However, from about 3000 BC onward, the area was probably much as it is today – a vast, harsh, sandy tract of desert that is difficult to traverse and, unless one knows its routes, is a natural barrier between Egypt and the rest of Africa. (Fig. 10.)

One curious feature stands out in the Western Desert – many areas contain aquifers that are trapped between the limestone and sandstone rock strata. Although no one is sure as to the origins of this groundwater, geologists posit that it is rain water that filters into the strata from western Sudan and equatorial Africa. Regardless of its origins, this phenomenon has helped make cultivation possible in the desert's oases; indeed, the oases were assiduously exploited throughout the Roman period.

Figure 10. *Most of the Western Desert consists of beautiful but bleak sandscapes. Kharga Oasis, once a lush, verdant place, is now mainly barren and sandy. Photo Salima Ikram.*

There are six main oases in the Western Desert: Siwa, Bahariya, Fayyum, Farafra, Dakhla, and Kharga. The oases occupy natural depressions that lie within the desert. Their levels situate them closer to the trapped aquifers, making cultivation easier. Several of these oases show evidence for the presence of lakes, which would have supported a diverse ecosystem in the Prehistoric period. (Fig. 11.) The Fayyum, which was the oasis closest to the Nile Valley, was probably the most heavily exploited of the oases of the Western Desert, particularly during the Roman period, when it was intensively cultivated and new towns were founded within its confines. It is unique in being linked to the Nile by a canal, called the Bahr Yusuf, or Joseph's Canal. This canal probably follows a natural watercourse that was enhanced during the Pharaonic era (Middle Kingdom [2066–1650 BC]), making the Fayyum one of Egypt's most agriculturally productive oases, as well as one that had abundant fish, birds, wild boar, and other game.

Although the oases were inhabited throughout the Pharaonic period, and were administered by the Egyptian state, we are only now learning about their precise relationship with Egypt's central government, as new excavations and discoveries take place. During Egypt's early history, the oases served as outposts that protected Egypt against invaders from the west. However, their main function remained agricultural; they produced grain

Figure 11. Lake Moeris in the Fayyum is salty, but it provides an excellent habitat for a diverse population of birds and fish. Some of the earliest Neolithic settlements in Egypt were situated along the north shore of this lake, which may have been less saline in earlier periods of Egyptian history. Photo Salima Ikram.

and fruit, and were even noted for their wine, which was exported throughout the Eastern Mediterranean. The oases also supplied some of Egypt's stone and mineral wealth, in the form of hard stones like basalt and dolerite for building, making tools, and carving vessels; gypsum for plaster; natron for mummification; alum for medicine, mummification, tanning leather, and dyeing cloth; ochres for paint and dyes; and perhaps even, on a small scale, iron. Iron deposits were only marginally exploited during dynastic times – as pigment sources and fluxing agents for copper smelting; few tools were made out of this metal until the first millennium BC. The oases were also lynchpins on the caravan routes used in trans-Saharan trade, with Kharga providing a land link into ancient Nubia/Kush, the area that is now Sudan, and perhaps even what is now Chad, and Siwa providing a stopping place or entrepôt for trade with the diverse inhabitants of what is now Libya.

The Sinai Peninsula, the Eastern Desert, and the Red Sea

The Sinai Peninsula is a curious and vital part of Egypt's geography. Along the north, this triangular piece of land links Egypt to the Near East, and elsewhere it provides access to ports along the Red Sea. It is topographically diverse: the north consists of a flat desert plain covered by dunes and sandy soil, with a few water sources. This area provided the main route connecting Egypt with its north-eastern neighbours. The centre of the Sinai consists of a series of limestone plateaus, punctuated by springs that support bands of nomads. The south is characterised by the forbidding red-granite mountains (including Mount Moses, where the Ten Commandments are said to have been delivered to Moses by God) that lead down to the Red Sea. (Fig. 12.) This area receives a limited amount of rainfall and can support small-scale agriculture, although nothing compared to what can be achieved in the Western Desert.

The Sinai has been an important source of mineral wealth for Egypt. Time and again it has been penetrated by expeditions seeking stones such as granite, schist, and diorite, as well as semi-precious stones in the form of turquoise and malachite, together with copper for metalworking.

The area east of the Nile's flood plain marks Egypt's Eastern Desert, which occupies the area from the Nile Valley to the Red Sea, and from the Mediterranean coast to the Sudanese border. Although it might seem to be an eastward continuation of the Sahara, the Eastern Desert does not resemble its Western neighbour. Its geological composition is different; its landscape is dominated by red granite near the Red Sea and the remainder made up of limestone, with little dune activity. Because of the height of the Red Sea Mountains, the Eastern Desert actually sees some precipitation in the winter. Thus there is enough moisture in parts of the desert to make it semi-arid

Figure 12. The Red Sea hills border the sea as well as penetrating inland to the Eastern Desert. In some places, particularly in the Sinai, the granite hills give way to small, cultivable areas. Photo courtesy Dirk Huyge.

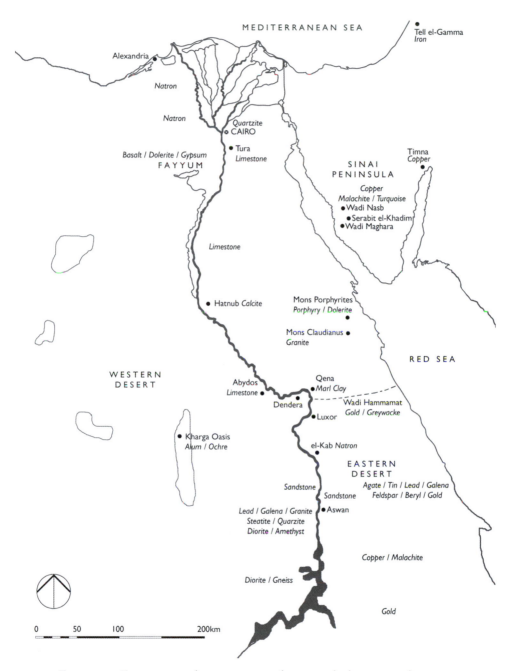

MEDITERRANEAN SEA

Tell el-Gamma
Iron

Alexandria

Natron

Natron

Quartzite
CAIRO

• Tura
Limestone

Basalt / Dolerite / Gypsum
FAYYUM

SINAI
PENINSULA

Timna
Copper

Copper
Malachite / Turquoise
• Wadi Nasb
• Serabit el-Khadim
• Wadi Maghara

Limestone

• Hatnub *Calcite*

Mons Porphyrites
Porphyry / Dolerite

Mons Claudianus
Granite

RED SEA

WESTERN
DESERT

Abydos
Limestone

Qena
Marl Clay

Dendera

Wadi Hammamat
Gold / Greywacke

• Luxor

• Kharga Oasis
Alum / Ochre

el-Kab *Natron*

EASTERN
DESERT

Sandstone

Agate / Tin / Lead / Galena
Feldspar / Beryl / Gold

Sandstone

Lead / Galena / Granite
Steatite / Quartzite
Diorite / Amethyst

• Aswan

Copper / Malachite

Diorite / Gneiss

Gold

0   50   100   200km

*Figure 13. Egypt was rich in raw materials, particularly stone and copper.
Drawing Nicholas Warner.*

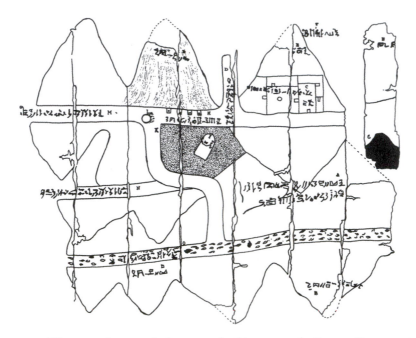

Figure 14. This map showing the location of gold mines in the Eastern Desert region of Wadi Hammamat was drawn on papyrus and is now in the Turin Egyptian Museum. This is probably the world's oldest map, and it is a clear indication that the Egyptians charted their world and had a clear idea as to how to exploit its natural resources. Drawing Keli Alberts.

rather than arid, offering a supportive environment for sparse vegetation, wildlife such as gazelle and ibex, and the pastoralists who have been active in the region from at least 10,000 BC until today.

Like the Sinai, the Eastern Desert has been a rich source of natural resources for Egypt throughout its history. Quarries for quartzite, porphyry, greywacke, alabaster, and different sorts of granite are found in the area. The Eastern Desert has also provided Egypt with copper, lead, galena, a little tin, and much of its gold. In fact, a map leading to gold mines in the Wadi Hammamat is thought to be one of the world's earliest maps. The Red Sea coast at the edge of the desert has also provided places for the extraction of bitumen, a form of petroleum used in mummification, as well as being employed as a sealant for all kinds of objects. Semi-precious stones such as jasper, amethyst, and malachite, as well as beryl and crude emeralds, were mined here during the Roman period. (Fig. 13.)

The red-granite mountains of the Red Sea are punctuated by deep valleys (*wadi, pl. wadian*), that link the sea to the Nile River and were part of important trade-routes in ancient times, as well as more recently. These include the Wadi Hammamat route that connects ancient Koptos (Qift) to the area near the port of Quseir on the Red Sea, the Wadi Abbad route that goes to the Ptolemaic city of Berenike on the Red Sea, and the Wadi Gasus route that connects to Safaga on the coast. A minor route, the Wadi Araba, that departs some 80 kilometres south of Cairo connects this area to the Gulf of Suez, as did the more frequently used northern link through the Wadi Tumulat, the location of the modern Ismailia Canal. In antiquity, several other ports punctuated the coast of the Red Sea, serving as points for the departure and arrival of vessels that plied the east coast of Africa, the Arabian Gulf, and points as far as India. Even though the Red Sea Mountains provided *wadi*-routes to the Red Sea, both the Eastern Desert and the Red Sea kept the Nile Valley isolated and protected from possible encroachment from the east without precluding the possibility of limited contact between the Egyptians and the peoples of the East. (Fig. 14.)

2

Travellers, Thieves, and Scholars
The History of Egyptology and Egyptomania

What can be considered the Western scientific study of ancient Egypt did not begin until the mid-nineteenth century AD with the decipherment of hieroglyphics. However, ancient Egypt has fascinated people since antiquity, and many have written about the country throughout the ages, observing its history, geography, flora and fauna, and customs. The Egyptians themselves were very conscious of their past and its links to their present. By the New Kingdom (1549–1069 BC), people were visiting the pyramids of the Old Kingdom, not just to revere those early kings of Egypt but also to view their immense and curious burial places. The graffiti left by these early visitors at Saqqara and Dahshur is still visible today. At Saqqara, for example, a scribe called Hadnakht records taking a pleasure trip west of Memphis where he saw the wondrous tomb of King Djoser – a pyramid that was already well over a thousand years old when he visited it. As numerous travellers' accounts from the Hellenistic and Roman eras attest, Pharaonic monuments were a source of national pride and identity, propaganda, curiosity, and tourist revenue.

Figure 15. Prince Khaemwese, the fourth son of King Ramesses II, worked extensively on restoring and studying the monuments of earlier kings of Egypt. The pyramid of King Unas of the 5th Dynasty at Saqqara was one building that the prince restored, inscribing the south face with a text that provided details of his achievement. Photo Salima Ikram.

The first formal record we have of someone caring for and maintaining Egypt's past simply for the sake of preserving history dates to the Ramesside period, specifically to the reign of Ramesses II (1279–1212 BC). Prince Khaemwese, the High Priest of Ptah at Memphis and the fourth son of Ramesses II, took charge of documenting, studying, and restoring the monuments of his ancestors, thus making him the first Egyptologist in history. Later revered for his wisdom and magical powers, Khaemwese left an inscription on the south face of the 5th Dynasty pyramid of King Unas at Saqqara describing how he had restored the collapsing pyramid. (Fig. 15.) He also managed the labyrinthine subterranean burials of the sacred Apis bulls at Saqqara and, with it, was involved in the cult of divine kingship. Ironically, at the same time as the prince was seeking to preserve monuments, his father's workmen were using other venerable structures as quarries for new buildings. Earlier kings of the Middle Kingdom also excavated and refurbished some of the tombs belonging to the first kings at Abydos, but, unlike Khaemwese, they did not leave monumental inscriptions recording their deeds.

To some extent, the kings of the 26th Dynasty (Saite period [664–525 BC]) also preserved the past, but they did so mainly for propaganda reasons. When Egypt's supremacy was seriously challenged by other powers in the Near East and Africa, the 26th Dynasty kings conserved monuments from earlier periods and resurrected older styles of artistic representation in order to link themselves to their more powerful and successful ancestors and invoke the glorious past. They even took their restoration work seriously enough to provide the 4th Dynasty king Menkaure with a new coffin.

The very powers that were contesting Egypt's authority were enthralled by its history and its reputation for magic and healing. The Nubians (southerners who conquered Egypt in c. 752 BC) had long since appropriated the Egyptian pantheon and made Egypt their religious or spiritual focus. The Assyrians and others in the Near East adopted aspects of Egyptian religion, borrowed images of Egypt's divinities to help magically cure illnesses, and considered Egypt's magicians amongst the most powerful in the world. This idea of Egypt as a land filled with magic and esoteric knowledge persists today, as is attested to by the tourists who still come to pray at Egyptian temples and to gain 'powers' by entering the burial chamber in the Great Pyramid of Khufu at Giza.

Greek and Roman Scholars and Travellers

By the sixth century BC, Greeks were coming to Egypt in droves, not only to trade but also to study. Their numbers included, allegedly, such luminaries as the mathematician and philosopher Thales, the poet and statesman Solon, the philosopher Plato, and the philosopher and mathematician Pythagoras. Indeed, the first foreigners to document Egypt are from this era. The most famous of these is Herodotus of Halicarnassus (c. 484–430 BC). In Book II of his *Histories*, Herodotus writes in detail about his travels in Egypt and records historical and cultural information about the country, its people, and its monuments. Despite the inclusion of hearsay and rumour, this work has been a standard reference work for all students of ancient Egypt. However, Herodotus was probably not the first Greek to write about Egypt. Some of Herodotus's work may have been based on that of Hekataios of Miletus (sixth century BC), whose own book was lost save as quotations in other sources.

Subsequently, the second king of the Ptolemaic dynasty, Ptolemy II (285–246 BC), commissioned a full history of Egypt, the *Aegyptiaca*, from one Manetho, a priest of Re from Sebennytos (modern Samanud in the Delta).

To a large extent, this history was written to connect the Ptolemaic dynasty to the earlier kings of Egypt and thus give them legitimacy. Manetho wrote his book in Greek, presumably using both historical records that graced temple walls and more detailed records written on papyrus and stored in temple and state archives. Manetho's work, however, is lost to us, save as fragments quoted by later scholars such as Josephus in the mid-first century AD, Sextus Julius Africanus (AD 220), Eusebiaus (AD 320), and most recently by the monk George, known as Syncellus (AD 800). Sadly, many of these sources do not agree on what Manetho actually wrote. In addition to providing some basic historical documentation, Manetho's greatest legacy is his organization of Egyptian history into dynasties, or ruling families similar to the more modern Tudors, Bourbons, Hapsburgs, Ming, and Han; these dynastic designations are still being used by scholars today. However, unlike most modern dynasties, which follow a father–son succession, Manetho's divisions sometimes have a single family straddling two dynasties (e.g., Dynasties 3 and 4 or 17 and 18) and, occasionally, a distant relation (even by marriage) of the ruling royal house taking control mid-dynasty. Some dynasties, such as the 13th, seem to show little in the way of familial ties; instead, they seem to be groups of monarchs who are unrelated save through temporal proximity.

The next extant record of Egypt appears in Book I of Diodorus Siculus's *Biblioteca Historica* (c. 59 BC). This work is similar to that of Herodotus, and indeed borrows from it, although it contains different details and emphases. Diodorus discusses the origins of humans in Egypt, Egyptian mythology and religion, the geography and geology of the land, and Egypt's flora and fauna, society, and culture. Hard on the heels of this work came the *Geographica* of Strabo (64 BC–AD 22). Strabo was a Greek-speaking native of Pontus who lived in Alexandria and accompanied the Roman prefect Aelius Gallus to the First Cataract in 25–24 BC. Book 17 of Strabo's opus deals primarily with the country's geography and natural curiosities, summing it all up with a rather disparaging, 'So much for Egypt'.

Subsequent reference works on Egypt are Pliny the Elder's (AD 23–79) multi-volume *Historia Naturalis* and Claudius Ptolemaeus's (AD 87–150) *Geography*. As their titles suggest, the former deals with the sorts of animals that lived in Egypt then, with reliable as well as fanciful descriptions of their habits, and the latter explains the basic layout of the country, lists its main cities, and describes the course of the Nile. The majority of classical writers on Egypt tended to focus on its physical description, main tourist attractions, and oddities. Pliny's account of sites is particularly noteworthy as he was the first person to describe the Sphinx at Giza.

A focus on Egyptian religious beliefs is found in Plutarch's (AD 50–120) *Moralia*, which contains the most complete, albeit Romanized, version of the myth of Isis and Osiris. This work was probably one of the main conduits through which the highly attractive ideas of rebirth and resurrection that were key elements of the Egyptian religion were disseminated throughout the Roman Empire. To some extent, these beliefs syncretised ancient Egypt's more optimistic promise of eternal existence with the Greek (and later Roman) Mystery Religions featuring Bacchus and Ceres, replacing the more traditional grim view of an eternal shadowy existence in the realm of Pluto. Thus, the cults of Egyptian divinities such as Isis spread as far west as Roman Britain, as well as to the eastern ends of the Roman Empire. During and after the Renaissance, Plutarch's text provided scholars with an insight into Egyptian religious beliefs, as did, to a lesser extent, Apuleius's (c. AD 123–180) book *Metamorphoses*, which stresses the power of the Isis cult. These works continued to propagate the image of Egypt as a land filled with esoteric knowledge.

From at least the time of Herodotus, tourists and traders (particularly Greeks and Romans) had been coming to Egypt. Presumably, some of these travellers used Herodotus's works as guidebooks, while others relied on locals to take them around, as tourists continue to be guided at archaeological sites in Egypt today. Many of these early visitors paid homage to the grandeur of the ancient Egyptian civilisation by composing poems inspired by the awesome sights that they beheld. According to Herodotus and other writers, the outer casings of the pyramids were covered with travellers' graffiti. Unfortunately, starting in the tenth century AD, the pyramid casings were removed and used to build the city of Cairo, so these testimonials have been lost. However, the poems and graffiti inscribed by such visitors on the legs of the colossi of Memnon (Amenhotep III) at Thebes still remain. (Fig. 16.) Many tourists were inspired not only by the sheer size of the statues but also by the fact that a fault in the rock from an earthquake (c. 27 BC) caused the northern one to 'sing' at dawn if the wind blew from a particular direction. Regrettably, the singing stopped in AD 202 when the Emperor Septimius Severus restored the head and shoulders of the statue with new blocks. (Fig. 17.)

The Romans were keen not only to visit the monuments of Egypt but also to acquire souvenirs and collect antiquities. Today, there are more standing obelisks (pillar-like monuments capped with a small pyramid) in Italy than

Figure 16. The colossi of Memnon, actually quartzite statues of King Amenhotep III, had cracked in antiquity so that they 'sang' when the wind blew through them. Many Greek and Roman travellers experienced this marvel, and inscribed the feet and legs of the statues with graffiti with their names and impressions, and sometimes even with poems of great beauty and literary merit. Photo Salima Ikram.

there are in Egypt. Huge numbers of statues, blocks from temples, and other memorabilia were removed from Egypt during this time. Given the interest in the Isis/Osiris cult, large numbers of statues of these deities made their way across the seas. Later, the presence of these objects in Europe served to re-establish a Western interest in Egypt during the Renaissance.

With the advent of Christianity ancient Egyptian ways were slowly discarded. The Edict of Theodosius (AD 391) ordered the closure of pagan temples throughout the Roman Empire, of which Egypt was a part. In AD 397, a mob of fanatical monks stormed the temple to the god Serapis, the Serapeum, in Alexandria and razed it to the ground. Many other Egyptian temples suffered a similar fate, as did portions of the great Library of Alexandria. In AD 580, the emperor Justinian had the oracular temple of Amun at Siwa closed, and the last remaining priests of Isis at Philae arrested. These actions effectively marked the official end of ancient Egyptian religion and culture, save for vestigial remains in vernacular traditions and in some of the

Figure 17. Sadly, inscribing one's name has always been irresistible to people. This graffito in Philae Temple was created in two parts. First, B. Mure visited and inscribed his name, and then someone else wrote 'stultus est' beneath it, meaning 'is stupid'. Photo Salima Ikram.

words and grammar of Coptic, the language of Egypt's Christian population. (Fig. 18.)

The interest in Egypt's antiquity did not end with Christianity, however; it now focussed on a different theme: Egypt's relation to biblical history. One of the first Christian travel writers to discuss Egypt, albeit briefly, was Lady Egeria, either of Gaul or northern Spain, a nun who journeyed to Egypt in the fourth century AD to trace its biblical past. Possibly going as far south as Thebes (Luxor), she identified (whether rightly or wrongly is still debated) several sites with those mentioned in the Bible.

Arab Interest in Ancient Egypt

By the Arab period (post–AD 640), the ancient monuments of Egypt had fallen into disrepair and many tombs were being used as monastic cells by Christians,

Figure 18. Temples and tombs were often taken over by Coptic Christians, who converted them into churches. A part of Philae Temple was turned into a church, and a cross was carved over the face of a goddess. In some instances, the Christians whitewashed over the ancient images; however, it was more common to smash, chisel out, or disfigure the forms of the ancient gods and thus destroy their power. Photo Salima Ikram.

while temples had become homes for peasants or served as quarries for the construction of the new metropolis of Cairo and other cities throughout the land. (Fig. 19.) However, some Arab scholars were intrigued by the antiquity of Egypt and travelled through the country examining and recording the ancient monuments, sometimes obtaining information from Coptic monks and their monastic libraries or from the writings of classical scholars.

One notable Arab scholar interested in ancient Egypt and its denizens was Abd al-Latif (d. 1231), a doctor from Baghdad. He spent some time at Memphis, studying the remains of the innumerable temples that littered the area. He also visited Giza, where his description of the Sphinx suggests that it still retained much of the original red paint on its face and that its nose and

Figure 19. Many blocks from ancient monuments were reused in the building of Cairo. This granite threshold from Baybars al-Jashankir's funerary complex in Cairo retains some of its original hieroglyphic text, on part of which is superimposed the engraved image of a lion, the symbol of another, more famous Baybars. Photo Nicholas Warner.

beard were still intact. By the time of the historian al-Maqrizi (d. 1440), the Sphinx had lost its nose. Writing in the first volume of his *Khitat*, al-Maqrizi describes how a Sufi fanatic, Mohammed Sa'im al-Dahr, had shot the nose off (other accounts record that he used a crowbar) in 1378, although this is debated. The geographer al-Idrisi (d. 1251) was responsible for a volume on the pyramids at Giza that included a complete architectural description of the site with measurements (the first book to do so), as well as a description of the activities that were then taking place in its environs. He glossed over the Sphinx after making a bad-tempered remark about there already being too many stories about it in circulation. Al-Idrisi also concerned himself with the decipherment of hieroglyphs, as did Ibn Wahshiyah (ninth/tenth century), al-Qalqashandi (d. 1418), and other Arab scholars. Both al-Idrisi and al-Qalqashandi thought (correctly) that Coptic could be linked to ancient Egyptian and that it might aid in that language's decipherment. Although some of these scholars came close to a basic understanding of Egyptian hieroglyphs, ultimately it was Jean-François Champollion, a Frenchman, who successfully deciphered them (see box on deciphering hieroglyphs).[1]

The Crusades and Later

The Crusades (1095–1272, intermittently) marked an increase in interaction between the West and Egypt in the form of religious tourism, for Egypt figured prominently in both the Old and the New Testaments. Egypt not only was part of an embattled region during the Crusades but also became a place for sacred and secular tourism. Biblical sites were firmly tied to the geography of Egypt. The Giza pyramids were identified with the seven famous granaries built by Joseph (despite there being more than seven pyramids on the Giza plateau), and various sites that the Holy Family had purportedly visited (many of which had once been sacred sites of the pagan Egyptians) gained importance and became part of an established itinerary thought to contribute to the pilgrim's ultimate salvation. After the Turks conquered Egypt in 1517, tourism enjoyed a further increase, with a large number of religious, scientific, or simply curious visitors flocking to Egypt.

Travel accounts of Egypt also became popular starting in the fourteenth century. One of the most popular fourteenth-century travel books to include Egypt was *The Voiage and Travaile of Sir John Mandeville, Knight*. This book, translated into several languages and a best-seller in its own time, was supposed to be a first-hand account of the author's adventures on his way to Jerusalem. Perhaps the curiosities that he mentions, such as the miraculous phoenix that lived in Heliopolis, the half-goat/half-human or wolf-headed creatures of the desert, or the Ethiopian one-legged men who lay on their backs and used their feet for shade at midday, contributed to the book's popularity. It seems, however, that the Sir John described in the book never existed. The actual author was probably one Jean d'Outremeuse of Liège, who concocted this book out of several other works on Egypt and indeed may never even have travelled beyond his native France. Nonetheless, John Mandeville's account of Egypt served as a basis and an inspiration for many subsequent works on Egypt, including those of the Dominican monk Wilhelm von Boldinsel and the Spaniard Pero Tafur. Certainly, it helped to fuel the idea, already in circulation, that Egypt was a land of esoterica and exotica.[2]

The theme of Egypt as a rich and unique source of curiosities, as well as a font of hidden knowledge, continued well into the Renaissance. Perhaps this idea was spurred by the memory of Ptolemy II's Museion and Library at Alexandria, where scholars from all over the Mediterranean had flocked to benefit from one another's expertise and from the knowledge left by the ancient Egyptians. These houses of learning were destroyed in stages, generally by fire, beginning with the Roman domination of Egypt. The vast number of monuments inscribed with hieroglyphs scattered throughout

Italy convinced scholars of the 'secret' wisdom of the ancient Egyptians. This belief intensified with the fifteenth-century republication of a fourth-century work, *The Hieroglyphica* of Horapollo. This study of hieroglyphs categorically stated that Egyptian was a symbolic language rather than one based on letters or sounds. Athanasius Kircher (1601–1680), a German Jesuit, continued to foster this belief, and also claimed that Egypt was the main source for the world's esoteric knowledge. Kircher pointed out that Egyptian religious and philosophical thought had inspired the Greeks and reiterated that Plato depended on Egyptian wisdom. Although Kircher's attempts at deciphering hieroglyphs were fundamentally flawed, he did correctly postulate that Coptic was the surviving form of the ancient language.

During the Graeco-Roman period and later, the Egyptians were also credited with great knowledge of astronomy (many thought that the Great Pyramid at Giza was a giant sundial) and of medicine (because of their mummy making). The quest to unlock the secrets of Egypt's 'hidden secret knowledge' began in earnest during the Renaissance. The Masons and other secret groups in the West identified with the Egyptians and incorporated ancient symbols such as the Eye of Horus, pyramids, and obelisks into their iconography and rituals. Many allusions to the Masons and to ancient Egypt can be found in Mozart's 'The Magic Flute'. Manifestations of this influence can also be seen in the iconography surrounding the establishment of the United States, many of whose founders were Masons; for example, the dollar bill is adorned with a pyramid and the 'all seeing eye', and the Washington Monument has the form of an obelisk. Many of the European traders and travellers who visited Egypt and carried back with them animal or human mummies and other artefacts as souvenirs also tended to focus on Egypt's oddness rather than on its reality.

The sixteenth and seventeenth centuries saw an increase in the number of travellers to Egypt, some of whom, such as André Thévet, the chaplain of Catherine de Medici of France, had read Herodotus and could correctly identify the pyramids of Giza as tombs of the pharaohs. Although Thévet, like others, failed to understand the role of the Sphinx as a guardian statue, he did explore it sufficiently to find the 26th Dynasty shafts in the neck and posterior that gave access to the area behind its head and under its body. These spaces later became associated with (imaginary) secret libraries and temples for initiating people into cults of immortality.

The Mummy Trade

Many mummies have had an unquiet rest. This is not only because people have robbed them of the gold and amulets that they wore, burned them as fuel, or collected them as macabre souvenirs, but also because they have been used as a form of medicine. Because the Arab physicians who extolled the benefits of *mum/mumia*, a black mineral pitch resembling bitumen, as a medication for diseases associated with blood, joints, and internal organs mistakenly thought that this pitch was used to embalm bodies, they ground up mummies to obtain the *mumia* for their cures. This cure became popular in Europe, and mummies were exported by the score to Europe to be pulverized and eaten. Ingesting mummy was thought to cure diseases of the blood and joints, to stop bleeding, and to improve general health. King Francis I of France, for example, always carried with him a small packet of mummy powder, allegedly mixed with rhubarb, in case of an attempt to assassinate him by stabbing or poison. Such beliefs were slow to fade, and the trade in mummy as a *materia medica* continued well into the ninteenth century. (Fig. 20.)

Figure 20. Mummies were ground up for medicine, burned as fuel, or sold to tourists as macabre souvenirs of Egypt. Photo private collection.

Scholars and *Savants*

In the late seventeenth century, a slightly more sedate and scholarly view of Egypt began to emerge. This was tied to the exploration of Egypt and Africa, particularly the search for the source of the Nile. At this time, not only geographers and travellers but also embassies and special missions from Europe were collecting Egyptian antiquities to be displayed in the continent's palaces and curiosity cabinets. These objects became the core of Europe's great national collections of Egyptian antiquities. A number of scholars were active during this time, including the Englishman John Greaves, who studied the pyramids of Giza. Greaves published his *Pyramidographia* in 1646 and in this work correctly identified the owners of the three main pyramids on the plateau. Another Englishman, Bishop Richard Pococke (1704–1765), recognised that canopic jars were used for the storage of mummified organs. He also made the first plea for the conservation of Egyptian monuments when he indignantly deplored how 'pillars were being hewn into millstones'. Pococke's *A Description of the East and Some Other Countries* (published in 1743) remains a valuable resource to this day. One of the greatest contributors to the study of ancient Egypt at this time was a Jesuit priest, Father Claude Sicard, who travelled and worked in Egypt between 1707 and 1726. His maps and notes were exceptionally advanced and reliable for the time, and they still provide us with information on long-destroyed sites. He was the first person to correctly locate and identify ancient Thebes (Luxor) and to identify and describe a temple of Isis in the Delta at Behbet el-Hagar; additionally, he located 24 temples, 20 pyramids, and more than 50 decorated tombs. Captain Frederik Ludvig Norden's *Travels in Egypt and Nubia* (published in 1741) is also a rich source of maps, plans, and images of now-vanished Egyptian sites.

The true origins of the orderly and scientific study of ancient Egypt can be attributed to Napoleon Bonaparte and his team of *savants* (scholars). In order to wrest the trade-route to India from the British, the French government sent Bonaparte to conquer Egypt and cut a canal from the Isthmus of Suez to the Mediterranean. In April 1798, modelling himself on Alexander the Great, Napoleon took a group of *savants* with him to 'seize' Egypt intellectually, along with an army of forty thousand soldiers to take physical control. This group of one hundred and fifty or so historians, artists, zoologists, naturalists, chemists, geologists, geographers, historians, linguists, doctors, and engineers was instructed to document the country, both past and present. To help these scholars, as well as to spread propaganda, Bonaparte brought to

Egypt its first printing press, which he commandeered from the Vatican, that could print in both Latin and Arabic scripts. As members of the newly formed Institut de l'Égypte in Cairo, the *savants* set about collecting and recording all things Egyptian: crafts, customs, flora and fauna, geology, and most important for Egyptology, monuments and artefacts from the Pharaonic, Coptic, and Islamic periods.

Although Bonaparte failed militarily when his troops were forced by the British to withdraw from Egypt in 1801, the intellectual legacy of his mission was enormous. Virtually all of the extensive collection of artefacts made by the French, amongst which was the bilingual Rosetta Stone, were ceded to the British in September 1801 as spoils of war, and now can be visited in the British Museum. But their notes, drawings, and paintings remained with the French and, between 1809 and 1813, were published in a twenty-four-volume work entitled *Description de l'Égypte*. These tomes, which include images not only of Egypt's antiquities but also of its flora, fauna, and technologies, allow us to see Egypt as it was in the early nineteenth century. This is particularly valuable in light of subsequent site disintegration from natural causes, the hand of time, vandalism, and the press of urban expansion.

One of the main contributors to the visual record of Bonaparte's expedition and the *Description* was Dominique Vivant Denon (1747–1825). A premier draftsman who came to Egypt with the *savants*, Denon not only contributed to the *Description* but also stole a march on it by publishing his own illustrated memoirs of his time in Egypt, *Voyage dans la Haute et la Basse Égypte*, in 1802. He was tremendously taken with Egyptian art and architecture, and impressed that the Egyptians had invented so many forms so far in advance of the Greeks. Denon's dedication to his craft was so great that he ran out of pencils and charcoal, and had to melt bullets for the lead to make new pencils.

In terms of the history of Egyptology, the most important prize that the French secured – and surrendered to the British – was the Rosetta Stone. This large, inscribed fragment from a granite stela was discovered by Pierre François Xavier Bouchard, an engineer in the French army, at the site of Fort Jullien at Rashid (Rosetta) in August 1799. The inscription was divided into three parts, each written in a different script: the top was engraved in hieroglyphs, the middle section in demotic (a form of cursive hieroglyphs used from around 660 BC onward, with a greater variety of phonetic forms than the earlier hieratic), and the bottom section in Greek. Although the British seized the actual stone, rubbings of its text were kept by the French and circulated amongst the European scholarly community. This text ultimately served as the key to the decipherment of hieroglyphs by the Frenchman Jean-François Champollion (1790–1832), who beat the Englishman Thomas Young (1773–1829) to this end by a hairsbreadth. Champollion was a linguistic genius who had mastered at least eighteen languages by the time he was seventeen. Using his own research in Coptic (the language of Christian Egypt) and Greek, his observations of hieroglyphs, and the findings of other scholars involved in similar research (see box on deciphering hieroglyphs), Champollion managed to establish the correct values of individual signs on one line of the stone. He sent these results to his brother in August 1808. In 1822, having reached a better understanding of the Egyptian writing system, he published his famous 'Lettre à Monsieur Dacier' wherein he outlined his conclusions about the hieroglyphic writing system. The decipherment of hieroglyphs, when the words of the ancient Egyptians could once again be read, marks the start of scientific Egyptology. (Fig. 21.)

Deciphering Hieroglyphs

The Rosetta Stone, a bilingual text that allowed the French scholar Jean-François Champollion (1790–1832), using demotic, to associate hieroglyphic signs with Greek, provided the key to the decipherment of hieroglyphs. Unlike many other scholars of the early 1800s, Champollion believed that Coptic was a later development of demotic; thus, by working backward one could understand hieroglyphs. He also thought that hieroglyphs might be phonetic, which meant that its symbols could be correlated to sounds, which then could be attached to Greek letters. Using the name of Ptolemy that appeared on the Rosetta Stone and was enclosed in a cartouche in the Egyptian, Champollion succeeded in tentatively assigning sounds to symbols. Fortunately, he could check his results, and extend his knowledge of hieroglyphs, using another bilingual text (although inscribed in both Greek and Egyptian, the text itself was different), the Bankes obelisk, at Kingston Lacey in Dorset, England. This monument was engraved with the names of Ptolemy and Kleopatra in Greek on the base and within cartouches on the obelisk itself. Thus Champollion could identify the letters *P*, *O*, and *L* precisely and, extrapolating from these, could get the remaining letters. Champollion's work yielded thirteen alphabetic signs, which allowed him to identify the names of Alexander the Great and the Ptolemaic queen, Berenike, as well as of several Roman emperors, thereby adding to his repertoire and the beginning of Egyptology as a proper discipline.

Researchers had been working to decipher hieroglyphs and to collect inscribed Egyptian antiquities prior to Champollion's successful decipher-

Figure 21. This reconstruction of the Rosetta Stone shows the fragment found by Napoleon's soldiers set into the original stela. The royal cartouches on this stone, together with the Greek text, helped Jean-François Champollion to decipher the hieroglyphics. Reconstruction of the Rosetta Stone by Mike Neilson; courtesy of and copyright The British Museum.

ment. One such scholar was the Englishman Sir John Gardner Wilkinson (1797–1875). Wilkinson moved to Egypt in 1821 and lived there for twelve years, thereafter returning to the country intermittently until 1856. Whilst living in Egypt he became fast friends with the Orientalist Edward William Lane (1801–1876). The two men collected antiquities and contributed significantly to an understanding of the daily life of the Egyptians, both ancient and contemporary. Wilkinson's three-volume *The Manners and Customs of the Ancient Egyptians* (1837) chronicled the daily life of the ancients using tomb reliefs as the basis for his interpretation. This work is still valuable today for its detailed insights into the minutiae of Egyptian life, while Wilkinson's book on the geography of Thebes, *Topography of Thebes, and General View of Egypt* (1835), remains a standard reference for our understanding of the

Giovanni Battista Belzoni

Giovanni Battista Belzoni (1778–1823) was an engineer, some 6'8" in height, who left his native Italy for England, where he ultimately worked as a circus strongman. After pursuing his circus career for some time, he and his British wife, Sarah, travelled to Egypt to make their fortune. Belzoni hoped to interest Muhammed Ali Pasha, the ruler of Egypt, in an engineering scheme to build a machine to raise water from the Nile. Belzoni had a successful interview with the pasha, and proceeded to construct his machine. But when the time came for Belzoni to demonstrate the machine's efficacy to the pasha, the demonstration went poorly and also resulted in an injury to a young Egyptian, which caused the pasha to withdraw his support for the entire project as well as for Belzoni personally.

Stranded in Egypt, Belzoni turned his attention to an interest that he had developed during his time in the country: collecting antiquities. Working both independently and on behalf of the British consul Henry Salt, Belzoni set about acquiring antiquities and exploring Egypt. In 1818, he became the first westerner to enter the pyramid of Khafre at Giza, a fact attested to by graffiti that can still be seen written in soot in the burial chamber. He also explored the tomb of Seti I, and he cleared Ramesses II's temple at Abu Simbel of sand. Using his skills as an engineer, he was able to move enormous stone statues, including one of the monumental figures of Ramesses II (2.67 m in height and 7.5 tons in weight) from the Ramesseum; an obelisk from Philae; the granite sarcophagus of Ramesses III; and the alabaster sarcophagus of Seti I. Much of his collection is now in the British Museum.

Belzoni did not just collect: he also sponsored displays and published extensively. He made two models of the tomb of Seti I, which he displayed in Paris and in London in 1821. His models and displays of Egyptian antiquities made Egypt accessible to the general public in the West. His work, *Narrative of the Operations and Recent Discoveries in Egypt and Nubia*, published in 1820, provides a vibrant record of his adventures in Egypt. It is also a detailed account of his excavations, giving the exact locations for his discoveries, a degree of precision unknown to most of his contemporaries, who deemed it adequate in terms of provenance to say that an object had come from 'Thebes'. (Fig. 22.)

monuments in that area. Published a year earlier than the Wilkinson volumes, Lane's *The Manners and Customs of the Modern Egyptians* (1836) provides ethnographic insights into the lives of the Egyptians of the nineteenth century and is also useful in the study of the Egyptians' ancestors. Another notable Egyptologist was the Swiss scholar John Lewis Burckhardt (1784–1817). Burckhardt had studied Arabic at Cambridge University and wished to travel in the East. He was the first westerner to visit and to record the site of Petra

Figure 22. *Giovanni Battista Belzoni often dressed in the Arab fashion as he journeyed through Egypt exploring little known sites and gathering antiquities for Henry Salt or for himself. Engraving, private collection.*

(now in Jordan), later described by the cleric-poet Dean Burgen as the 'rose red city half as old as time'. In 1813, he became the first westerner to visit the temple of Ramesses II at Abu Simbel. Later he told Giovanni Battista Belzoni (1778–1823; see box) about the site, and the latter went on to excavate this astonishing rock-cut edifice.

A Plague of Plunderers

The publication of the *Description* started a rage for all things Egyptian in Europe and marked the post-Renaissance rebirth of Egyptomania, characterised by the use of Pharaonic motifs in art, architecture, furniture, and clothing. Such an upsurge of Pharaonic inspiration in design matters did not reoccur until the 1920s with the discovery of Tutankhamun's tomb. The *Description* also sparked what was akin to a gold rush in Egypt, with the prize being antiquities rather than gold. The renewed European fascination with Egypt, coupled with the newfound understanding of hieroglyphs, resulted in a series of expeditions to Egypt with the sole aim of acquiring that country's past. Some of these undertakings purported to be scientific, while others were clearly mercenary. Many wealthy tourists engaged in smaller-scale forays in obtaining antiquities. Because of this craze, Egyptian peasants and antiquities dealers pandered to collectors by illicitly digging in tombs to extract objects or chiselling out pieces of reliefs or statue fragments to sell. This activity not only destroyed many monuments, but it also separated the objects and fragments from their contexts, decreasing the amount of information that they could convey. A full-scale European rivalry to procure the largest collection of Egyptian antiquities ensued, with the French and the British taking the lead. The French were represented by their consul, Bernardino Drovetti (1776–1852), and the British by their consul, Henry Salt (1780–1827), and by his agents, who included Giovanni Belzoni amongst their number.

Large-scale rivalries involving subterfuge, violence, bribery, and stealth characterise this period of collecting. The story of the Zodiac of Dendera typifies collection methods of this time. At Dendera, the French and the English contended (sometimes under cover of night) over possession of the carved stone roof block from the temple, using bribery, corruption, and brute force. A Frenchman ultimately employed gunpowder to facilitate the block's extraction, and the marks from this blast are still visible in the temple. The Zodiac was finally brought to the Louvre Museum in Paris, where it can be seen today. The rulers of Egypt at this time were content to aid and abet these foreigners as long as they had obtained legal permission and paid a fee to the government to 'hunt' antiquities. In some instances, officials offered foreigners antiquities in exchange for their technological expertise to help make Egypt competitive in an increasingly industrialised age.

Egyptian monuments did not suffer only from commerce in antiquities. Because many Egyptians believed that the ancient monuments marked sites where the Pharaohs had buried huge deposits of gold, they often engaged in large-scale hunts for gold and treasure. Before embarking on their search, they would burn incense and chant spells to help them gain access to this hidden wealth. These hunts by Egyptians became such a big business that manuals for treasure hunters were written and quickly became best-sellers. In an effort to stop large-scale destruction, Gaston Maspero, who was the director of the Egyptian Antiquities Service (see Saviours and Scholars section), reissued one such favourite, the *Book of Hidden Pearls and Precious Mystery Concerning the Indication of Hiding-Places, Findings and Treasures*, in 1907, for the risible price of a few piastres. He hoped that people would realise that if access to the supposed treasures came so easily and so cheaply, then the treasures (if they had ever existed) must surely be long gone.[3]

The Great Expeditions

In addition to these independent diggings, a series of state-sponsored archaeological expeditions began in 1828 with one led by Champollion for the French king and joined with another, sponsored by the grand duke of Tuscany, led by Ippolito Rosellini. The two men recorded scenes and inscriptions and collected antiquities, as well as churlishly engraving their own names on monuments such as the Ramesseum. Champollion's collections of artefacts included reliefs from the tomb of Seti I that he claimed he was saving for posterity by taking them to a French museum. In addition to gathering their collections, Champollion and Rosellini published entertaining accounts of their travels and provided a wealth of images of Egypt's monuments as they were at the time.

Between 1842 and 1845, Karl Richard Lepsius (1810–1884) led a Prussian expedition to Egypt and Nubia. Perhaps one of the best-equipped expeditions to work in Egypt, Lepsius and his team spent their time surveying monuments, gathering objects, and carrying out excavations. Lepsius's excavations at the Labyrinth (mortuary temple of Amenemhat III) at Hawara in the Fayyum was one of the earliest proper scientific digs, with good record-keeping and section drawings. Ultimately, fifteen thousand antiquities and plaster casts made their way from Egypt to the museum in Berlin. The information garnered during the expedition was published in Lepsius's twelve-volume *Denkmäler aus Aegypten und Aethiopien* in 1859. As these books did not contain all the material that Lepsius had gathered, a further five volumes were published after his death between 1897 and 1913. Lepsius's work perhaps inspired the establishment of the earliest journal dedicated to Egyptology, the *Zeitschrift für Ägyptische Sprache*, which was founded in Berlin in 1863.

Saviours and Scholars

The middle of the nineteenth century witnessed not only the plundering of Egypt's antiquities but also the start of their salvation. The founder of the

Figure 23. Auguste Mariette was buried near his museum at Boulaq in a sarcophagus that was eventually moved to the new museum at Tahrir Square. Mariette's remains and his statue dominate the western side of the museum's garden. Photo Salima Ikram.

Egyptian Antiquities Service, Auguste Mariette (1821–1881), was one saviour. (Fig. 23.) This Frenchman arrived in Egypt in 1850 to collect Coptic, Ethiopic, and Syriac manuscripts for the Louvre Museum. While engaged in this work he became fascinated by ancient Egypt and started digging in Saqqara. During his Saqqara excavations, aided by his able and trusted foreman Hamzouni, Mariette discovered the avenue of sphinxes leading to the Serapeum, and the Serapeum itself, that is, the labyrinthine tombs of the sacred Apis bulls. At Giza, in 1853, he discovered the Valley Temple of King Khafre.

Said Pasha, who was then the ruler of Egypt, was so impressed by Mariette's work and by his dedication to the country that in June 1858, on the recommendation of the Suez Canal's engineer, Ferdinand de Lesseps, he named Mariette director of Egyptian monuments. This post was to some extent a revival of an earlier organisation, the first Antiquities Service, directed by

Yusuf Zia. Mariette was intent on formulating regulations for the Antiquities Service governing concessions (who dug where), excavation (documentation rather than pure extraction of objects), and division of the finds (the better artefacts to remain in Egypt, and any object that left had to have an export permit). He also broadly divided the country into different regions, assigning 'inspectors' to check on the antiquities and excavations in each area. Thus Mariette established the Antiquities Service's core rules, many of which are still in force today. Throughout his varied career, Mariette excavated all over the Nile Valley, discovering many new monuments and publishing extensively on them. Not all his publications dealt with excavations, however; he was even responsible for the ideas behind, as well as some of the text for, the libretto for Verdi's opera *Aida*; this perhaps owed something to Mariette's early life as a writer of historical fiction.

After starting a collection of antiquities on behalf of the Egyptian state in 1858, in 1863 Mariette founded the Bulaq Museum of Egyptian Antiquities in Cairo. It was named for the port area where it was located, conveniently situated on the river so that heavy objects could be transported to the museum with ease. This was not the first antiquities museum in Egypt. The earliest antiquities museum was a khedival museum created by Pasha Mohammed Ali's decree of 15 August 1835. Rifaa al-Tahtawi, a sheikh who was interested in ancient Egypt and wrote one of the earliest histories in Arabic of ancient Egypt also played a key role in founding the first Egyptian museum, while Joseph Hekekyan was responsible for its design and construction.[4] The museum itself was headed by the scholar Yousuf Zia and located near the chic al-Azbakiya Lake in Cairo. Zia also had responsibility for inspecting archaeological sites in Upper Egypt annually in an effort to prevent their being despoiled – a largely unsuccessful effort to stop the pillage of Egypt's antiquities. Unfortunately, much of the royal collection that was kept in the museum was slowly gifted away.[5] In 1855 the khedive Said gave what remained of the collection to the archduke Maximillian of Austria to encourage him to provide technical aid to Egypt and to support him diplomatically,[6] effectively closing this particular incarnation of the museum. Most of the khedival museum's contents are now in the Kunsthistorischesmuseum in Vienna.

Unlike the original khedival museum, the Bulaq Museum was meant to be open to the public. Initially, it contained a new royal collection, as well as objects that were purchased and, soon thereafter, objects that were excavated. Mariette, who had even more power than the khedive in museum matters, strove to retain the objects in his museum. When the French empress

Eugenie saw the recently discovered gold jewellery of Queen Ahhotep on display at the Bulaq Museum in 1869 and intimated to Ismail Pasha that such a parure was worthy of an empress, the pasha, who had already bestowed gifts aplenty on the empress, turned to Mariette, a citizen of France, and stated, 'A higher authority than mine rules in the Bulaq Museum'. Mariette gracefully refused the empress, stressing that the treasures of Egypt should remain there. Needless to say, this refusal did not endear him to the empress.[7] The museum was Mariette's pride and joy, and when he died (18 January 1881) his remains were interred in a granite sarcophagus in the museum's garden. When the museum moved to its new location in what is now Tahrir Square in 1902, Mariette's sarcophagus was moved with it, and can still be visited.

After Mariette, all directors of the Antiquities Service were French, until 1952, when Mustafa Amer replaced Etienne Drioton. One of Mariette's most notable successors was Gaston Maspero, who directed the museum from 1881 to 1886, and again from 1899 to 1914. Under Maspero's direction, Egypt was further divided into several sections or inspectorates, each run by a chief inspector responsible for the upkeep of the monuments in his area, theft prevention, new excavations, and site management for tourism.

The Egyptian Museum was at first run by Europeans. The museum's curators represented many nationalities – Egyptian, Italian, English, German, and Belgian – until the 1920s, after which Egyptians progressively took over all positions. One Egyptian pioneer of Egyptology was Ahmed Kamal (1851–1923). Kamal first worked in the Antiquities Service and later as an assistant curator in the museum. (Fig. 24.) He excavated throughout Egypt, and, in 1910, founded and directed the School of Egyptology for Egyptian students. Among his most well-known students were Mahmoud Hamza (1890–1980), who succeeded the Englishman Rex Engelbach as director of the Egyptian Museum in 1941, and the archaeologist Selim Hassan (1893–1961). Kamal was at the point of establishing a College of Archaeology in 1923 when he died; the college was absorbed into the larger Egyptian University, where Egyptian archaeology is still taught today.

Egyptology Established

Another key figure in the history of Egyptology is Amelia Edwards (1831–1892). Born into a wealthy English family, Edwards wrote fiction and worked as a journalist. Like many Europeans of means, Edwards visited Egypt. During her tour, in 1873–74, she fell in love with the country, its culture, and its

Figure 24. Ahmed Kamal was among the first Egyptian Egyptologists to head the Egyptian Museum in Cairo. His bust has been placed with those of other eminent Egyptologists in the museum's garden. Photo Aidan Dodson.

antiquities. Her classic travel memoir, *A Thousand Miles Up the Nile*, first published in 1877, recounts her first journey to Egypt and how the country and its antiquities captured her imagination and attention. For example, while visiting the temple of Abu Simbel, she found residual white plaster attached to the face of the northernmost statue of Ramesses II from casts made by Robert Hay and Joseph Bonomi in the late 1820s or early 1830s. Edwards was greatly distressed by this disfigurement of the magnificent statue, and she decided to have it cleaned. Under the direction of her boat's captain, Reis Hassan, the crew climbed a scaffolding of oars and wood that they constructed over the statue and removed the white plaster chunks. Those pieces that they could not remove without causing damage to the face, they dyed with specially brewed thick coffee. Edwards writes that 'the coffee proved a capital match for the sandstone; and though it was not possible wholly to

Figure 25. Amelia Edwards's tomb in Henbury Church. The obelisk and the ankh *sign are a tribute to her dedication to the study of ancient Egypt. Photo Aidan Dodson.*

restore the uniformity of the original surface, we at least succeeded in obliterating those ghastly splotches, which for so many years have marred this beautiful face as with the unsightliness of leprosy.[8]

Edwards was so enamoured of ancient Egypt that she devoted all her attention and wealth to its study and to the furthering of Egyptological research. She funded many excavations and, in 1882, established the Egypt Exploration Fund (later Society). This association is still the main British research institute for Egyptology and has funded many archaeological excavations in Egypt through the years. Under the terms of her will, Edwards established the first chair of Egyptian Archaeology and Philology at University College London and also bequeathed her library and collection of antiquities to the university. (Fig. 25.)

The first incumbent of the Edwards chair at University College was the noted archaeologist William Matthews Flinders Petrie (1853–1942), who held the position until 1933. Before (and after) Petrie's time, many people excavated in Egypt, but most had little or no scientific grounding in archaeology. Their aim was to acquire beautiful objects, which they would then try to interpret, rather than to conduct controlled stratified excavations in which the provenance of an object was as important an element as the object itself. Petrie, however, unlike most of his contemporaries, was thorough in his methods and paid as much attention to the humblest object as he did to the most magnificent. For his time, he was one of the finest excavators to work in Egypt.

The origins of Petrie's interest in ancient Egypt were somewhat unorthodox. The source of his interest was a book called *Our Inheritance in the Great Pyramid* (1864), written by the Astronomer Royal of Scotland, Charles Piazzi Smyth (1819–1900). Smyth's rather fantastical book stated that the measurements of the Great Pyramid at Giza encoded divine messages relating to the history of the world and encapsulated all mathematical and astronomical knowledge. Petrie, who trained as a surveyor, first travelled to Egypt in 1881 to survey the pyramids and to check the veracity of these theories. Once there, he found Smyth's theories to be completely false, but he was so smitten with learning about the ancient Egyptians that he returned to Egypt regularly, both as an independent scholar and with the Egypt Exploration Fund. Petrie probably worked at more sites in Egypt than any other Egyptologist before him or since. His contributions to Egyptology, in terms of both methodology and discoveries, are enormous.

Petrie's interest in the minutiae of excavation led to his greatest contribution to Egyptology: seriation, or sequence-relative dating of objects. This method does not give absolute dates; rather, it provides a chronological sequence of objects. The idea behind it is that styles evolve in certain ways, and by documenting their stylistic evolution, one can arrange the objects into a relative chronology. Later, more precise dates can be attached to the sequence through further excavation and chemical dating (see Chapter 3). Petrie worked out his sequences by studying grave goods from a vast number of burials. He established typologies of pottery, figurines, slate palettes, and flint tools by recording the objects from each grave, as well as their groupings. He focussed on the most plentiful objects – ceramics – and arranged these in a relative sequence, assigning to those styles that he could distinguish numbers ranging from 30 to 80, leaving numbers free at the beginning and at the end of the sequence for objects that are found later. According to Petrie, the styles numbered in the 30s were the earliest objects, and those in the 70s the latest. By comparing Petrie's sequence to their own finds, other excavators could date their objects or could refine Petrie's typologies and sequences, as was done by the German archaeologist Werner Kaiser in the 1950s. Using his own method Petrie cross-dated imported pottery and artefacts of Minoan, Mycenaean, and Aegean origins with those of the Egyptians. Petrie's method of sequence dating is still used today, although new dating methods have also been developed.

Another of Petrie's contributions to the field of Egyptian archaeology that continues to this day was the training of the first *Guftis*. Petrie recruited people from the village of *Guft* (Koptos) in Upper Egypt and taught them archaeological techniques. His original workers passed on this knowledge to subsequent generations, with each generation adding to the archaeological information that is passed down. Nowadays these immensely gifted excavators are the most prized diggers (and site managers) in Egypt, and they work on sites throughout the country.

Although Petrie's work in Egypt was, for the most part, exemplary, he was a difficult and eccentric colleague, with some rather unfortunate socio-political views. He was absolutely devoted to his research, spending every penny he had on it, and he did not suffer fools gladly; he constantly fought with other archaeologists on matters of method and theory. Moreover, to keep curious (and annoying) tourists at bay while he worked at the Giza pyramids he dressed only in his underwear, a sure-fire way of offending the Victorian sensibilities of his would-be visitors. He was hard on his staff, making them build their own accommodation out of mud brick, and keeping them on a strict and limited diet of canned foods, particularly sardines. Petrie was none too modest, and he thought himself something of a genius, as did his wife, Hilda. When Petrie died of malaria in Jerusalem on 28 July 1942, in accordance with his wishes, Hilda severed his head from his body and transported it to London. There the head was given to the Royal College of Surgeons so that his brain could be examined and his skull kept as an example of the skull of a British man of extreme intelligence.[9]

Besides Petrie, another major British contributor to early Egyptology was the chemist Sir Robert Mond (1867–1938), who financed the excavation of monuments in Thebes and publication of the findings into the 1920s. Mond is notable for his intensive photo-documentation of tombs. He designed a special carriage for his camera so that it moved smoothly on a single plane, making it easy to photograph an entire wall. He also experimented with colour photographs.

Figure 26. Egyptians use Pharaonic Egypt as a unifying point for the diverse religious and ethnic groups that constitute the state of modern Egypt. Indeed, archaeology and history have been used for political purposes throughout the world. The mausoleum of Saad Zaghloul, one of Egypt's great nationalists, was constructed in the modern Pharaonic style and is located near the parliament building in Cairo. Photo Salima Ikram.

George Andrew Reisner (1867–1942), an important American excavator, also made extensive use of photography, in addition to drawings, and is known for his detailed recording of objects. He worked in Egypt and in Nubia, discovering sites in both areas. He contributed significantly to the study of object types and the evolution of tomb architecture. Another American, James Henry Breasted (1865–1935) of the Oriental Institute in Chicago, contributed to Egyptology enormously by founding Chicago House, the University of Chicago's outpost in Luxor, and instigating a programme to copy the inscriptions and scenes on the various Theban temples. He was the first holder of a chair in Egyptology in the United States. In Egypt, the first Egyptian to hold the title of professor of Egyptology was Selim Hassan, who was on the faculty of Cairo University. He worked extensively at Giza, as well as in Nubia. Another notable Egyptian scholar was Ahmed Fakhry (1905–1973), whose many accomplishments included bringing the study of Egypt's oases into mainstream Egyptology. (Fig. 26.)

The many scholars who have contributed to Egyptology have focussed their attention on diverse subjects including state formation, settlement archaeology, urbanism, the history of specific sites, philology, architecture, art, religion, economy and trade, objects of daily life, technology, human remains, funerary customs, and the ancient environment. Early scientific analysis of materials carried out by Alfred Lucas (1867–1945) and Zaki Iskander (1916–1979) has contributed to our understanding of the material culture of the Egyptians. Major discoveries such as a cache of royal mummies in Deir el-Bahari in the nineteenth century; intact royal tombs, like those of the pharaohs of the 21st Dynasty at Tanis, discovered by Pierre Montet, or Tutankhamun's in the Valley of the Kings, discovered by Howard Carter; the tombs and houses of the workers at Deir el-Medina; or entire towns, such as Tell el-Amarna, all contribute to our knowledge of ancient Egypt. But today it is not just archaeological discoveries that augment our information about Egypt; to these must be added new scientific methodologies involving magnetometry and ground penetrating radar to view what is buried below the surface, as well as Carbon-14 and thermoluminescence to date the age of objects (see Chapter 3). Trade relations, in terms of the origins of the materials traded, can now be determined by gas spectrometry, and mummified remains can be viewed without destroying them through the use of computed axial tomography (CAT or CT scans) and other non-invasive imaging. All these new technologies with their attendant experts are invaluable aids in our study of the ancient Egyptians and in our understanding of their history and their lives.

3

Re=creating Ancient Egypt
Sources and Methodologies

Despite the number of texts, monuments, and artefacts that the Egyptians left behind, the study of ancient Egypt is still challenging, and ultimately we have only a fragmentary view of the past. Indeed, we should remember that any 'view' that we may have of ancient Egypt is, to a large extent, conditional upon temporal or personal factors – a twenty-first-century person's experiences of and ideas about ancient Egypt are vastly different from those of someone living in the eighteenth century. Each individual's constructed reality of Egypt is based on the limited amount of evidence that has survived and is biased by how we gather the evidence and how we process it through our subjective filters. Much of what we have is an accident of archaeological survival or discovery, a result of what and where one excavates and how carefully one digs. Thus, our picture of the past is necessarily filled with lacunae, and a re-creation of this picture will vary from person to person. These multiple views of what ancient Egypt and Egyptians may have been like can be regarded as equally valid, providing that we consider all of the available evidence fairly and, as much as possible, without bias.

The sources of our evidence about ancient Egypt are varied. The most important of these are the primary sources: landscape, monuments, artefacts, and the texts created by the Egyptians themselves. The next tier of evidence is secondary source material. There are gradations in this: what was written in antiquity, such as the reports of people who visited or lived in Egypt during the time of the Pharaohs (e.g., Herodotus), and what has been written subsequent to the Pharaonic period by later visitors and scholars; of course, all of these accounts are very subjective. One should also be wary of using evidence from one moment in Egyptian history and extrapolating it across the three thousand years of Egypt's Pharaonic past. Egyptian society and culture evolved over time, and one should not expect the systems to function in an identical fashion at different times.

Each type of evidence has problems that need to be taken into account when evaluating it. For example, the preponderance of evidence that we have comes from temples and tombs because such monuments are the best preserved as they were generally located in the desert or at its edge and thus were protected by the sand. As these monuments were being built for eternity, they were made out of stone, whereas palaces and houses were made out of more perishable mud brick. This material has not only deteriorated under the stress of time and the environment, but it has also been attacked by the *sebbakhin*, the diggers of fertilizer (*sebbakh*) who use the crushed bricks to increase the yield of arable land. These villagers have decimated ancient settlement sites and temple enclosure walls in their quest for the nutrient-rich black soil that was used to make ancient Egyptian bricks. A further complication is that a site thought to be a good place to inhabit in antiquity tends to continue to be viewed as a desirable area in which to build, and, as a consequence, old settlement sites are often buried under new ones. These many layers of settlements create mounds known as *koms* or *tells* (examples of these can be found at Edfu or Akhmim). (Fig. 27.) *Tells* are potentially rich sources of information about Egyptian town life, but because they are frequently covered over by living towns, they are inaccessible. The dramatic post–nineteenth-century increase in Egypt's population makes it increasingly difficult to access ancient settlement areas and threatens other sites as well.

In addition to the vagaries of preservation, temples and tombs have received a great deal of attention from a majority of Egyptologists for other reasons. In the early days of archaeology, scholarly interest was focussed not so much on the minutiae of daily life as on spectacular monuments that could be displayed in national (or personal) museum collections. Thus,

Figure 27. This small hillock is the tell, or kom, that marks the ancient site of Mendes in the Delta. The town once covered several square kilometres and was the location of an important temple dedicated to the ram-headed god Bannerdjeb. Photo Salima Ikram.

most excavators chose to work on temples and tombs, where statues, reliefs, inscriptions, and objects were guaranteed, rather than on settlement sites, where artefacts were both scarcer and less spectacular. Only a handful of Pharaonic settlement sites have been excavated, including el-Amarna, Kom el-Hisn, Deir el-Medina, Tell el-Dab'a, Elephantine, Malqata, el-Lahun, parts of Abydos, and the Workmen's Village at Giza, although there is now a concerted effort being made to redress the imbalance. Settlement sites of the Graeco-Roman period that are now in the desert have fared better and are being actively documented, particularly as they too are being threatened by expanding agricultural programmes.

Primary Sources

Egyptian monuments should be studied as an integrated entity as that is, presumably, how the ancient Egyptians planned them. This would include studying the building's position and location in the landscape and its relationship to other monuments, as well as its architecture, decoration, texts, and when possible and applicable, its contents. Such studies require diverse skills, and the results are often the fruits of the collaboration of many different experts.

Through both their texts and images, tombs and temples elucidate Egyptian religious and funerary beliefs and, to a lesser extent, Egypt's history and politics. They obviously also provide information about ancient art, architecture, and building technology. Tombs also reflect social stratification and wealth by virtue of their size, location, and decoration, and often provide personal information concerning the individual buried within, through texts, artefacts, and the body of the deceased.

The exterior walls of temples tend to be decorated with images of a pharaoh carrying out deeds of valour against Egypt's enemies or against fierce animals. The accompanying texts detail the king's bravery in battle and often highlight specific campaigns against Nubians, Syrians, Libyans, or other enemies of Egypt. One might think that these texts and images would provide a vast amount of first-hand information about Egyptian history, but careful study calls their accuracy into question. In fact, these reliefs and texts are often propagandistic, showing the king in the best, but not always the truest, light. Also, many scenes where the pharaoh is smiting a foreign foe are really stock iconographic images of what a ruler *ought* to do to be considered a good, brave, and just king of Egypt, rather than representations of what any one king actually did do. Many Egyptian reliefs and inscriptions therefore depict an ideal rather than reality.

Even texts that appear to be factual, such as King Lists (registers of rulers, sometimes including the lengths of their reigns and important events), are biased. (Fig. 28.) Often King Lists exclude kings who were unacceptable to those who compiled the list. Thus, the kings of the religiously revolutionary Amarna period and later, including Tutankhamun, are excluded from King Lists, as are many female rulers, such as Hatshepsut (18th Dynasty) or Sobekneferu (13th Dynasty), as they do not fit the canon of Egyptian kingship. The names of kings also engender confusion. An Egyptian king could have as many as five different names, and sometimes different ones appear in different King Lists. The Greek transliteration of some of these names, such as those that appear in Manetho's history, also obfuscate the issue as they are sometimes difficult to correlate with the Egyptian spellings.

Most internal walls of temples bear fairly standard religious texts and images. These can include images showing the king making offerings to different gods and the gods in return validating the king's reign. The images provide insight into the Egyptian belief system and liturgies, but by no means explain them with any great clarity or depth.

Figure 28. The Abydos King List, inscribed in the Seti I temple to Osiris, is one of the most complete King Lists that we have. It is notable that the names of the Amarna pharaohs, amongst other rulers, are not included. This list linked the 19th Dynasty with its predecessors and gave the dynasty added legitimacy. Photo Nicholas Warner.

Tombs contain a greater variety of texts than do temples; these can be religious texts, biographical texts, or captions. This last group of texts, which is found in the decorated tombs of the elite and consists of short inscriptions written above or next to figures shown engaged in their daily work, functions rather like a modern comic book. These texts give us an insight into the daily life of the ancient Egyptians. Religious texts on tomb walls were considered protective and, along with funerary goods such as sarcophagi and coffins, can illustrate the ancient Egyptians' funerary beliefs. The most important texts found in tombs are those that name the deceased and identify him or her further through the individual's genealogy and titles. These help us to understand social organization, rank, and wealth. Titles are varied, and their meanings can be obscure; they include: Director of Embalmers of the Great House, Inspector of Scribes of the Royal Granary, Herdsman of the White Bull, Steward of the Great Estate, Overseer of the King's Works, Secretary of the Toilet-House, and Fan Bearer to the King. Possibly the individuals who occupied these positions did not actually, physically, carry out some of the jobs, but they did reap the benefits in payment and status conferred on them by the titles.

Autobiographical texts are also often associated with tombs. Frequently, autobiographical inscriptions contain standard phrases that present an ideal sort of person, rather than the real individual. Naturally, if one wants to project an image of oneself for eternity, perfection would be preferable to the real, flawed individual (and far more impressive). Nevertheless, these idealized texts are useful as an indication of what the Egyptians thought of as perfection and of what they aspired to. Occasionally, the autobiographical texts in a tomb relate incidents specific to the deceased or historical events that really happened. Examples of such tomb texts include a description of the nobleman Amenemhab (TT85) rescuing King Thutmose III from a rampaging elephant by severing its trunk; the letter that the eight- or nine-year-old King Pepy II sent to the Governor Harkhuf thanking him for carrying out a successful expedition to Africa and for safely bringing home a pygmy for him to play with was inscribed on Harkhuf's tomb wall at Kubbet el-Hawa, Aswan, as a mark of royal favour; the detailed description of his duties as a vizier that Rekhmire included in his tomb (TT100); and the inscription in the tomb of Ineni (TT81) that records excavating and preparing a secret and hidden tomb for King Thutmose I, possibly KV20 in the Valley of the Kings.

The majority of ancient texts found in Egypt tend to be those inscribed on temple or tomb walls. The number of papyrus documents that have come down to us is surprisingly small given the number that must have been written in the highly bureaucratic society of Pharaonic Egypt. Kinds of textual material recorded on papyrus include historical, tax, legal (land ownership, water rights, wills, contracts); personal (letters, both between living correspondents and between the living and the dead), literary (stories and poems), religious (hymns, prayers, and, more commonly found in tombs than in temples, funerary texts), and didactic (the ancient equivalent of Emily Post's rules of etiquette, moral codes, and advice on how to advance in life). However, only limited numbers of each genre survive, because of the fragility of their organic materials. Moreover, many of these documents

Figure 29. An ostrakon, now in the Munich Museum, inscribed in hieratic with a portion of the Maxims of Prince Hordjedef. The text gives advice on provisioning one's tomb and sustaining its upkeep. On ostraka as well as on papyrus, headings, punctuation, and important points were highlighted in red ink, with the bulk of the text written in black ink. Photo Salima Ikram.

would have been kept in towns and cities, and few of these sites have been excavated. Settlement sites such as Lahun and Deir el-Medina provide us with the bulk of this evidence from the Pharaonic period. In addition, some Graeco-Roman settlement sites that are now in the desert have yielded significant amounts of papyrological evidence.

Papyrus deteriorates because of environmental factors – it crumbles when it is too dry, and it dissolves when it is too wet. In addition, papyrus was often reused in a variety of ways. Old pieces of papyrus were scraped and rein-scribed, and papyrus was also used to make cartonnage, an ancient Egyptian form of papier mâché used for mummy masks and coverings, amongst other objects. In the post-Pharaonic period, papyrus was also burnt for fuel. Some less formal texts, mainly accounts and some artists' sketches, were inscribed on ostraka (*sing*. ostrakon), which are pieces of broken pottery or flakes of limestone. These are most commonly found in settlements and therefore are not as plentiful as we would like. (Fig. 29.)

Artistic evidence is another source of information for interpreting Egypt's past. Egypt is rich in both two- and three-dimensional art. Again, much of this art comes to us from tombs and temples, as more of these than settle-ments have been excavated. However, some settlements and palaces have been investigated, and their decoration also gives us insight into Egyptian aesthetics and beliefs. Tomb art in particular provides a window into what the Egyptians viewed as a 'perfect' eternal existence, one that they hoped to inhabit after their deaths. Thus tomb art is not always wholly accurate – just because there are no flies or mosquitoes drawn on tomb walls does not mean that the ancient Egyptians were not plagued by these insects.

Tomb art was probably meant to be interpreted on a number of levels. The most basic was for its literal depiction of daily life: scenes of harvest provide details about agriculture, images of fishing and fowling show food acquisition and sport, vignettes of banquets show the foods eaten and the clothes and jewellery worn by the early Egyptians. Additionally, these representations can be read as metaphors: harvest scenes show the eternal cycle of death, rebirth, and resurrection, and fishing and fowling scenes demonstrate the tomb owner's triumph over the chaotic aspects of nature and the ability to restore *maat* (order or balance). Thus, these renderings provide both practical and metaphorical insights into the lives and belief system of the ancient Egyptians. However, it is not guaranteed that our readings of the allegories and allusions are accurate, as we come to the images with very different backgrounds from the ancient Egyptians', thus our interpretation of Egyptian art should be tempered with caution.

Although many details of Egyptian daily life are depicted in tomb art, whether as images on tomb walls or through the intricately carved wooden models often included as grave goods, these do not necessarily show every step of a process, be it the brewing of beer, butchering of cattle, or baking of bread. Instead, they illustrate the most recognizable highlights of these processes, with the understanding that the audience could fill in the gaps. Naturally, ancient viewers would have been able to do this, as the images and activities depicted were familiar to them, but the modern audience will have a harder time. Ethnoarchaeology, that is, using ethnological data from living groups as an analogy for understanding people and activity patterns of the past, and experimental archaeology, attempting to replicate and understand ancient technologies and their by-products, are particularly useful tools in interpreting technological history. They can help fill in the blanks in tomb depictions and aid in identifying enigmatic artefacts and archaeological deposits. (Fig. 30.)

The vast array of artefacts excavated from different sites all over Egypt help to elucidate the culture and history of the past. Many different types of

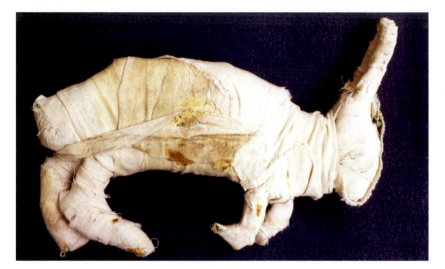

Figure 30. Experimental archaeology can be used to better understand the process of mummification. This rabbit mummy (Peter Cottontail) was prepared by the author and her students in Cairo in 2000 in an effort to re-create ancient mummification methods. To date, the mummification is successful. Photo Francis Dzikowski.

objects have been dug up, including pottery, furniture, tools, weapons, statues, jewellery, clothing, boxes and baskets, boats, chariots, as well as human (often mummies), animal (mummies and food), and plant remains. Not only do the items themselves have significance but also their provenance or findspots. Having a context for an object helps us to understand the role it originally played in antiquity. Certain pots had very specific functions, such as housing pigeons or storing liquids, and by finding these objects in situ their use becomes clearer. Furthermore, knowing whether a statue comes from a temple, a tomb, or a house is significant, as statues had different roles in each locale. (Fig. 31.)

The primary evidence is not always straightforward. Often rulers usurped one another's monuments, erasing earlier cartouches and replacing them with their own. They also demolished earlier structures and reused portions of these in new buildings, as the Middle Kingdom kings did with blocks from Old Kingdom pyramid complexes. Ironically, this sometimes saved the older monuments as the blocks were preserved by being buried or reused. This reuse also occurred in the private funerary (elite) sphere, where people's names were erased, sometimes to eradicate their existence or merely to replace

Figure 31. Antiquities theft is a serious problem for archaeologists. If the robbers succeed it means that the artefacts are removed and their contexts lost forever. Whether the robbers succeed or not, looting damages not only the targeted artefact but also the surrounding areas. The thieves who tried to steal part of this relief from Hibis Temple at Kharga were apprehended before they had extracted the piece; however, they destroyed a large portion of the wall. Photo Salima Ikram.

them with someone else's name. Some objects might be inscribed with three or more names. One example is a group of sphinxes of Amenemhat III that travelled widely through the country. (Fig. 32.) Originally erected by the king in Fayyum, these were probably moved to Pi-Ramesses (modern Qantir in the Eastern Delta) and reinscribed for Ramesses II, before being taken to Tanis (in the Western Delta) in the 21st Dynasty with the cartouches of kings from that period added to them. Such usurpation was not limited to statuary, but was extended to monuments. One of the worst offenders was Ramesses II, which explains why he has left behind such a huge corpus of sculpture and buildings, most of which he usurped from earlier rulers.

The Antiquities Trade

The reuse of Egyptian antiquities over time and in a variety of ways has destroyed important evidence of the past and obliterated significant parts of Egyptian history and culture. Once an object loses its provenence, it loses much of its meaning. A de-contextualized artefact cannot convey the information that an excavated object, whose location, date, and function are known, can.

Some precious objects were destroyed to obtain gold, wooden objects were burnt as fuel, stone was reused as building material in subsequent constructions, and limestone was burnt to make lime. Many objects also fell prey to antiquities thieves and collectors. People have long collected Egyptian artefacts as curiosities, with the heyday of large-scale governmental collections occurring in the nineteenth century. Auguste Mariette (see Chapter 2), and Egypt's khedive worked to prevent large-scale acquisition of Egyptian remains by individuals and foreign nations. A decree of 17 November 1851 prohibited excavations without a permit issued by the general director of museums and excavations and his committee. Legitimate excavators could dig, but their finds had to be shared equally with the Egyptian Museum. In 1880 a series of decrees forbade the export of antiquities without a permit. These and other decrees were articulated in 1897 as a law, one of the earliest to be passed against the illegal exportation of antiquities. In 1912 this law was further refined to say that Egyptian antiquities were the property of the state and could not leave Egypt without government permission. Legitimate sales of antiquities, often through registered dealers or shops, were permitted. Nevertheless, illegal export continued, prompting passage of another, similar, law in 1951, but with more severe punishments.

Ultimately, in 1983, the Egyptian government passed a law (number 117) that forbade *all* export of antiquities abroad. Unfortunately, antiquities are still being smuggled out of Egypt, destroying monuments and leading to the loss of valuable data. Currently, Egypt's government and Supreme Council of Antiquities (SCA) are working to eradicate the antiquities trade and to trace and recover Egypt's stolen antiquities.

Secondary Sources

In addition to the texts, buildings, and objects that the ancient Egyptians have left behind, travellers' accounts, such as those of Hekataios and Herodotus (see Chapter 2), are sources for information about the history and culture of the ancient Egyptians. The Egyptians themselves did not (as far as we know) write narrative history. In their accounts, these classical authors were describing what they, as foreigners, saw when (and if) they visited Egypt, so

Figure 32. These leonine sphinxes carved for Amenemhat III were moved from site to site and reinscribed for several different kings. They were finally deposited at Tanis and are now in the Egyptian Museum, Cairo. Stylistically they fit into the corpus of Amenemhat's statuary and emphasize the leonine and solar aspects of the king rather than his human attributes. Photo private collection.

the information is filtered through their eyes. Also, they are describing Egypt in the sixth and fifth centuries BC, and things that were true then might not have been so in the twenty-fifth century BC. Furthermore, the reliability of what these observers wrote about ancient Egypt also depended on whether they correctly remembered and understood what they had seen or had been told. Even Manetho, the Egyptian priest who wrote a history of Egypt for the Ptolemaic kings, may have adapted his writings to link his patrons to the earlier pharaohs, and thus appease them.

The value of secondary sources such as travel accounts, as well as encyclopaedic works such as the multi-volume *Description de l'Égypte* (1809–13) or Lepsius's *Denkmäler* (1859), is in their verbal or drawn images that convey what their authors had experienced as contemporary Egypt. They are particularly valuable because many of the sites they describe have since been vandalized by antiquities hunters, builders, or *sebbakhin*, or have fallen prey to

Figure 33. This nineteenth-century photograph shows the Coptic monastery that was built over the temple of Hatshepsut at Deir el-Bahari. When archaeologists became interested in the temple, they dismantled the monastery rather hastily, losing valuable information. Photo Antonio Beato, private collection.

the ravages of time and nature. These books give us an idea of what the intact monuments looked like and are also helpful in reconstructing the provenance of stolen objects or of objects that are now in museums. The work of excavators, art historians, and philologists, amongst others, has also yielded books and articles that flesh out the Egyptian past. (Fig. 33.)

New Technologies

The different primary sources provide the main body of information concerning ancient Egypt. In the past, most of this data came from excavations; now, however, new techniques and technologies are being used to find and map sites, to analyse objects, and to interpret the past. Instead of large-scale excavations, geophysical surveys using remote sensing (magnetometry, resistivity, or radar) and satellite photography are being carried out so that buried structures can be mapped without digging, or with limited, targeted test excavations. Such surveys are very significant: because so many sites are being lost owing to Egypt's ever-increasing population and its attendant needs for shelter, nourishment, and employment.

Instead of relying only on seriation or relative chronologies (see Chapter 2) for dating, new technologies are being employed to provide absolute dating for excavated objects. Carbon 14 (C-14) testing and dendrochrology are used for dating organic materials, potassium-argon for dating ancient minerals, and thermoluminescence (TL) and archaeomagnetic for dating ceramics. All these technologies are helping to make the chronology of ancient Egypt more precise and can be used in conjunction with more traditional methods of dating, such as sequence dating for objects or stratigraphy for sites.

New ways of analysing pottery are being pioneered. The Vienna system (named for the city that hosted the conference where the system was invented) analyses the fabric of a pot. Thus, in addition to using its form to gain information about a vessel, the pot's material, its method of manufacture, and the possible sources for the pot's material are explored. Additional tools, such as thin-sectioning, also shed light on pottery manufacture.

Data can be extracted from objects using other new scientific technologies as well. Instead of unwrapping mummies, today's scholars study them using X-rays, CT scans, and MRI images, and work is slowly being done to establish familial and ethnic relationships with the improved interpretation of ancient DNA material. (Fig. 34.) The components of the ancient environment and diet can be identified by isotope analyses on human and animal remains, and through analysis of archaeozoological, archaeobotanical, and pollen remains. Paints, resins, oils, residues, and other substances can be studied chemically or by using scanning electron microscopy (SEM), archaeometric tools, or gas spectrometry (GS), thus shedding light on the technology, trade, and economy of ancient Egypt.

Modern technologies are also revolutionizing how archaeologists record their finds. New databases are used on excavations to connect objects to one another and to place them in their archaeological context. Global Information Systems (GIS) are particularly useful in archaeology as they permit researchers to link objects and features on different strata for recording and analysis. When GIS is used together with Global Positioning Satellites (GPS), even very large sites can be mapped quickly and accurately.

Digital photography, computer-drawing programs, and photogrammetry (measuring through photographs) have helped to expedite the recording of temple and tomb walls, a task that can take several decades,

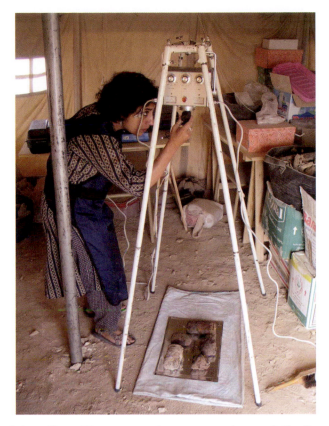

Figure 34. Salima Ikram X-rays animal mummies at the site of Abu Rawash using a portable X-ray machine. The radiographs permit one to view the contents of the mummy bundles without destroying the wrapped packages. Photo Alain Charron.

depending on the monument's size and complexity. By using different kinds of light sources (such as UV) in photography or imaging, the layers or faint vestiges of paint or ink can also be revealed. Digital photography also helps with kite aerial photography (KAP) so that researchers can check their results almost immediately. (Fig. 35.) Satellite images help to locate sites and map them, and are particularly useful for tracking ancient roads. Mapping sites and buildings no longer requires painful days with tape measures – total stations, electronic optical instruments that combine an ability to calculate height and distance, and are linked to a computer, are faster and far more accurate. These tools are just a few of those being adopted by archaeologists to improve the way in which information concerning ancient Egypt can be extracted from the available evidence.

Re-creating Ancient Egypt

Figure 35. Tomek Herbich and his assistant set up a grid to conduct a resistivity survey in the Western Desert. This technology allows archaeologists to see what lies below the surface without having to excavate. Photo Nicholas Warner.

Of course, financial constraints must also be considered – Egyptologists work within severely limited budgets; sadly, this does influence our results.

Ultimately, the study of ancient Egypt requires that the results of researchers be published. The failure to publish excavation reports, surveys, or documentation about temples and tombs is akin to tomb robbery because it means that none of the information extracted from the material can be accessed by either scholars or the public.

Working in Egypt

Current access to primary source material on ancient Eygpt is gained either through the study of museum collections or through excavations. Whether carried out by Egyptian or by foreign missions, all excavations are conducted under the auspices of the Supreme Council of Antiquities (SCA), the most recent manifestation of Egypt's Antiquities Service. Excavators submit proposals to the SCA explaining where they want to work and why; a committee of Egyptian specialists than reviews the request and if they approve, the project can begin. The SCA emphasizes conservation and preservation of sites, and it focuses on getting researchers to work in the Delta or at other sites that are particularly endangered by human activity or by nature. Under Director General Zahi Hawass, the chief of the SCA at this writing, the SCA rule that excavators must publish their results within five years of excavation is strictly enforced; if they do not, they can lose their sites (concessions).

Shadows in the Sand

Egypt's Past

Despite the fact that the ancient Egyptians left so many inscribed monuments, there is really no complete history of ancient Egypt written by the Egyptians themselves. Only fragments of ancient records of events inscribed on stone or written on papyrus have come down to us, and it is these, together with the archaeological evidence (see Chapter 3), that allow us to reconstruct Egypt's history. With each new discovery or translation of a text, Egypt's history is revised and rewritten.

Scholars divide most of Egyptian history by convention into different eras known as 'kingdoms' and 'periods'. The former describe eras of stability and unity, and these alternate with times of instability and fragmentation called 'intermediate periods'. Each such period is divided further into 'dynasties', which refer to the groups of rulers of that era. The idea of Egyptian dynasties has come down to us through Manetho's (now incomplete) history (see Chapter 3). Generally, 'dynasty' implies a succession of rulers all belonging to one family, but this is not true for Egypt. Often, under Manetho's designations, a single family spans more than one dynasty, and there is no clear indication as to why Manetho changed dynasties at any given point.

Egypt's history comprises thirty-one dynasties, preceded by 'Dynasty 0', when Egypt was at the brink of being unified under a single ruler. After these thirty-one dynasties, the country came under the control of the Ptolemaic Dynasty, following which it was subsumed into the Roman Empire. According to both the Turin Canon, or Turin King List, composed during the reign of Ramesses II and inscribed on papyrus, and the Palermo Stone (composed in the 5th Dynasty), the history of Egypt began when the gods ruled the earth, with Osiris being Egypt's first king. As with many countries' mythologies, this Golden Age was replaced by a time of human rule, which is when the more recordable history of a country was perceived to begin.

Although Egypt's history as a complex society, with settlements and an established agricultural tradition, started in about 5000 BC, what we regard as true Pharaonic culture, or the Dynastic period, characterised by a unified state, a ruling family, an administration, a religion, and an artistic style, did not emerge until approximately 3100 BC. The time prior to that is described as the Predynastic period.

The Predynastic Period (5000–3050/3000 BC)

In the Predynastic period, Egypt was not a single unified country, but an array of disparate towns and cities with individual rulers. During the sub-periods into which the Predynastic is divided, the rulers of these different areas presumably fought with one another, or made alliances, with some rulers successfully extending their hegemony to create larger polities. By the end of the Predynastic period, the country was divided into at least two major areas, one in the north and the other in the south. Ultimately, presumably through a mixture of conquest and diplomacy, Egypt was united. Also during this time, different political, religious, technical and technological traditions developed. Indeed, the first evidence of writing in Egypt appears around 3150 BC, near the end of this era, at the site of Abydos in Upper Egypt. Presumably, early records such as these were created to keep track of commodities, as well as of land and water ownership. The invention of writing to track commodoties and ownership of land and water set the stage for a more complex bureaucracy and laid the foundations for Egyptian civilisation.

Predynastic cultures were not the same in the north and the south. Doubtless, each society was partially formed in response to its particular environment and to external factors such as settlers from and trade with the Near East or from more southern portions of Africa. Each area showed distinct cultural traditions until c. 3250 BC, after which time the entire country manifested an increased uniformity in material culture, culminating not only in a complete merger of cultural systems but also in political unification. (Fig. 36.)

Throughout the history of Egyptology, different phases of the Predynastic period have enjoyed a variety of names. These originated from the locations where the material cultures of each phase was first identified, both in the north and in the south. This is owing to the marked difference in the cultural sequence between the various areas of Egypt until the late Naqada II (c. 3300 BC) period, when the more southern of the two cultures became dominant and spread throughout the country. This shift may have resulted from a combination of interactions between the two major areas: for example, warfare; political alliances cemented through marriage; and improved transportation resulting in an increase in trade and traffic between the two regions. Both the material and the metaphysical cultures of the two areas originally differed, and separate culture names for the two parts of the country were used prior to the Naqada I period. Today, there is a relatively uniform nomenclature employed for the whole country based on the Upper Egyptian site of Naqada, about 80 kilometres (50 miles) north of Luxor, which shows an evolution in phasing that gives us the Naqada I (4000–3500 BC), Naqada II (3500–3200 BC), and Naqada III (3200–3000 BC) cultures.

Nomenclature for the Predynastic

The names for the divisions of the Predynastic period have changed during the course of Egyptological history. The chart that follows gives the names used in older books, the accompanying dates for each period, and the geographical areas to which the names were most closely attached. The different eras were named for the sites where these cultural assemblages were first identified by their material remains.

Date (c.)	Old Term	Upper Egypt	Lower Egypt
5300–4000	Fayyum A, B		Neolithic
4400–4000	Badarian	Badarian	Neolithic
4000–3500	Amratian	Naqada I	Omari A/Maadi Cultural complex
3500–3200	Gerzean	Naqada II	Maadi/Buto Cultural complex
3200–3000	Semaian	Naqada III/Dynasty 0	All Egypt

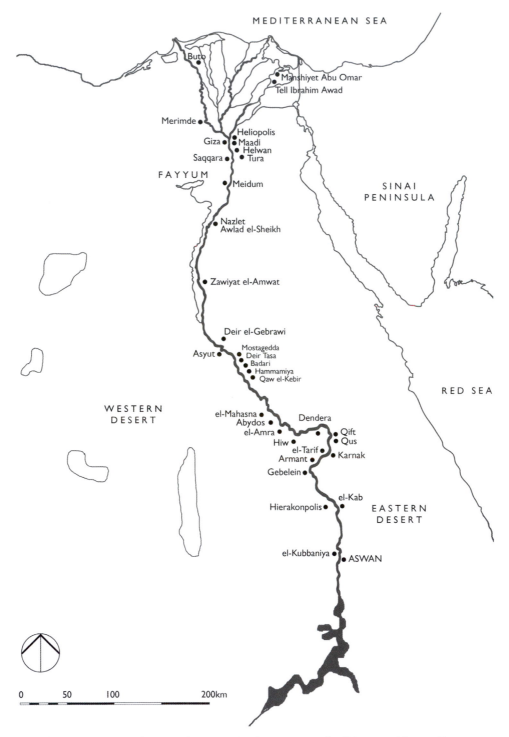

MEDITERRANEAN SEA

Buto

Manshiyet Abu Omar
Tell Ibrahim Awad

Merimde

Heliopolis
Giza
Maadi
Helwan
Saqqara
Tura

FAYYUM

SINAI
PENINSULA

Meidum

Nazlet
Awlad el-Sheikh

Zawiyat el-Amwat

Deir el-Gebrawi

Mostagedda
Deir Tasa
Asyut
Badari
Hammamiya
Qaw el-Kebir

RED SEA

WESTERN
DESERT

el-Mahasna
Abydos
el-Amra
Hiw
el-Tarif
Armant
Gebelein

Dendera

Qift
Qus

Karnak

el-Kab

Hierakonpolis

EASTERN
DESERT

el-Kubbaniya
ASWAN

0   50   100   200km

*Figure 36. Map showing the major Predynastic sites for Upper and Lower Egypt.
Drawing Nicholas Warner.*

The culture that predates the Naqada I period in the south is known as the Badarian, named after the site of Badari where the material culture that typifies this period was first identified. Several other sites in Upper Egypt that were subsequently excavated share this material culture and were all active during this time. Badarian settlements typically consisted of simple mud-brick structures with palm-wood and reed-mat roofs; cooking hearths were often within dwellings. Cemeteries were located at some distance from the settlement. The bodies, which were buried in a foetal position, with their heads pointing to the south and their faces turned to the west, were placed in baskets or skins and sometimes dressed in linen clothes. Grave goods for both men and women included skin and leather clothing; jewellery, such as bracelets and beads made of ivory, horn, wood, and shell; pottery vessels; ivory figurines; and rectangular stone palettes for grinding cosmetics. Excavations in the many cemeteries and the more limited settled areas of the Badarian culture reveal that most objects were of local manufacture. Imported goods and even items imitating foreign goods, particularly ceramics, are few, perhaps because of the relative physical isolation of this part of Egypt.

The Badarian was concurrent with both the late Neolithic and the Maadi Cultural Complex, or the Maadi/Buto culture, in Lower Egypt. These people built circular or oval houses of woven reed, sometimes strengthened by mud or mud brick, with conical or pitched roofs supported by a wooden pole. Many houses were not purely surface built; their interior floors were sunk into the ground to a depth of about 40 centimetres or more, in a way that is more typical of dwellings found in southern Palestine. Unique to Egypt, particularly at the site of Merimde, are the steps leading down to the houses: these were made of hippopotamus tibiae (thigh bones). Many of the Lower Egyptian sites seem to have in-settlement or near-settlement burials, perhaps due to the absence of desert areas or stone cliffs to house cemeteries. The houses as well as the burial traditions seem to be closer to Near Eastern traditions than to those of Upper Egypt. Indeed, many of the ceramics found at Lower Egyptian sites dating to this period seem to have originated in Palestine or were copying prototypes that originated there. Clearly, settlers from or trade with the neighbouring Near Eastern cultures, together with a shared geography, strongly influenced the culture and tradition of Lower Egypt.

The Naqada I period in the south was contemporary with the pure Maadi Cultural complex in the north. The southern culture continued the tradition of locating cemeteries away from settlements, with more complicated tombs

Figure 37. This vessel dates to the Naqada II period and is now in the Egyptian Museum Cairo. It is typically decorated with an image of what is probably a boat and a group of animals and humans, the latter in positions of praise or mourning. Photo Salima Ikram.

containing different amounts of grave goods that seem to reflect an increasing social hierarchy as well as technological advances in the production of stone and ceramic goods. In addition to the types of grave goods found in earlier periods, stone vessels and bone and ivory combs surmounted by images of birds or animals have also been found. Houses became larger and multi-chambered and increasingly dependent on mud brick for their construction. The northern tradition remained relatively static, but shows some advances in technology, as well as some mud-brick production for dwellings, although reeds remained a construction mainstay. The tradition of burials in or near the settlement was maintained, and social stratification through differentiated grave goods is not very apparent. Trade and exchange with the Near East continued.

The real change in the Predynastic Egypt began in the Naqada II period, when goods and objects from the south started appearing in the north, and, to a lesser extent, objects imported from the Near East, or copies thereof, were found in the south. This might have been due in part to an advance in boat-building technology. A significant number of images of boats appear as petroglyphs, on pottery, and in tomb decoration, clearly indicating a notable innovation. (Fig. 37.) This suggests that in Egypt a cultural and artefactual union preceded the political one. Quite probably there were also improvements in artificial irrigation technology, which meant that the control of water and land became increasingly vital and that throughout Egypt bureaucracies and hierarchies proliferated to deal with this issue. The settlements at

Naqada and Hierakonpolis, to name but two, increased in size, and there is evidence for the spread of settlements and people throughout Egypt during this time. Archaeological data suggests that Hierakonpolis was then the most important southern town, if not a city, and that Buto played a similar role in the north. Excavations show that these towns contained not only dwellings and cemeteries but also temples and administrative areas, as well as locales for different craft specialities. Nubians also seem to have been part of the scene, living separately but peacefully amongst the Egyptians. Quite possibly not all the intercourse between the different parts of Egypt was peaceful at this time; likely, expansionist tendencies might have been expressed in a warlike way by many of the rulers of the existing city-states.

The Naqada III era preceded the unification of Egypt. By this time, the entire country shared not only the same material culture, including complex burials containing vast varieties of grave goods and multi-chambered houses, but also many ideas concerning government, society, and religion. (Fig. 38.)

Unification and the Early Dynastic Period

The unification of Egypt under a single ruler marks the start of the Dynastic period. The time during which this transition took place is known as Dynasty 0 (in earlier publications, the Protodynastic period), and is a somewhat shadowy era between the end of the Naqada III period and the beginning of Dynasty 1. (Fig. 39.) It seems to have been a time of warfare amongst the rulers of strong city-states, culminating in a struggle for control by two of the rulers, one from the north and the other from the south. The triumph of the southern ruler is commemorated on a few artefacts, the best known being the Narmer Palette, a ceremonial stone palette used to grind make-up depicting a ruler of the south, Narmer, smiting his northern enemies. (See Fig. 125.) There is some debate as to which king actually unified the country. According to Manetho and the Abydos King List, Menes was the first king of a unified Egypt, but scholars dispute whether he is to be identified with Narmer, or with Narmer's immediate successor, Aha.

The early history of the united Egypt was not smooth. The new rulers had to set up a complex government with an accompanying bureaucracy that functioned in both the north and the south and was loyal to the new king, establish boundaries for provinces that reflected the new order, and combine social and religious traditions to knit together a new country. The southern rulers moved their administrative centre northward, to the strategic point

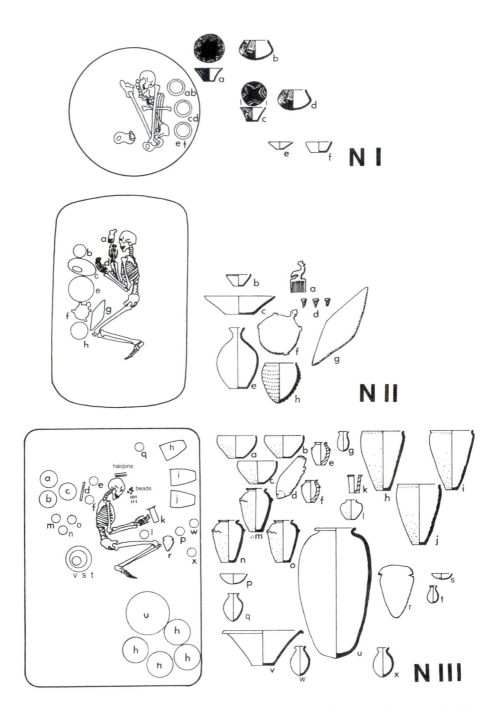

Figure 38. These three images depict burials from the Naqada I, II, and III periods. They illustrate the different tomb shapes, body orientations and poses, and grave goods typical for each period. Drawing courtesy of Helena Jaeschke, from Predynastic Egypt, Shire Publications Ltd, 1988.

Figure 39. These bone labels come from the Abydos tomb (Uj) of King Scorpion (c. 3150 BC), one of the first rulers of Egypt, and are amongst the earliest examples of writing. The labels were threaded onto a linen string or a leather thong and then tied around storage jars. These labels indicate that the jar's contents came from the area of Basta (Bubastis in Greek). The bird has the sound, 'ba', and the throne, 'st', in hieroglyphics. Photo courtesy Guenter Dreyer and the Deutsches Archaeologisches Institut Kairo.

where the limestone cliffs of Upper Egypt give way to the verdant plain of the Delta. This city, just south of modern Cairo, was called Ineb-hedj ('White Wall'), or Memphis, by the Greeks, and remained the administrative capital of the country throughout most of its history. It also was a significant religious centre, although the southern city of Abydos was equally important in this regard, as eleven of the kings of the 1st and 2nd Dynasties were buried there. The remaining Dynasty 2 kings and many of the elite of this period were buried at Saqqara and Helwan, both necropoleis that were in sight of Memphis.

The Early Dynastic period (Dynasties 1–2) is also known as the Archaic, or Thinite, period. Manetho called the first two dynasties Thinite because the rulers of this period supposedly came from the town of This, near Abydos. During this time the Egyptian state established itself: the bureaucracy flourished, large-scale irrigation and architectural projects were launched, basic religious and funerary beliefs were clarified, and the artistic canon was

established. Moreover, an economic system involving both temples and the king was instituted. Royally sponsored expeditions for trade or mining set out to the Eastern and the Western deserts, as well as to the Sinai. Occasional battles with Egypt's Asiatic neighbours also took place during this period, securing the north-eastern border.

As far as we know, the course of Dynasty 1 was a relatively smooth one; however, there is evidence of a civil war during Dynasty 2 that was ended only by the last king, Khasekhemwy. His son, Djoser, was to be the first major ruler of the Old Kingdom and the first king of Egypt to be buried in a pyramid.

Nomes, or Provinces

In order to maintain control over the country and to better oversee its organization, Egypt was divided into a series of provinces, or nomes (from the Greek), called *sepat* in Egyptian. Some of these divisions reflected pre-unification city-state borders, but most were probably re-surveyed areas roughly equal in size, with access to enough land and water to sustain their populations. The earliest reference to a nome dates to the 3rd Dynasty, but doubtless they existed well before that time. The governors of these provinces, called nomarchs, administered the nomes like mini-kingdoms, although they were responsible to the central authority and the king. Each nome had an identifying emblem, most of which pre-dated unification. The number of nomes varied somewhat throughout Egyptian history, but, for the most part, the country was divided into a total of forty-two nomes, twenty-two in Upper Egypt and twenty in Lower Egypt. (Fig.40.)

Old Kingdom (2663–2160 BC)

The Old Kingdom, the most centralized and stable period in ancient Egyptian history, consisted of Dynasties 3 through 8. This was perhaps the grandest epoch in Egyptian history, marked by technological innovations

---

Figure 40. This triad shows King Menkaure clad in a shendyt kilt and wearing the White Crown, flanked by the goddess Hathor with her headdress of horns and sun-disk, and by the nome deity of the area, which roughly corresponds to the modern-day Asyut governerate. The nome standard of a couchant canid rises above the nome deity's head. The goddesses have their arms around the king, indicating their support for the king and his rule. Photo courtesy Sandro Vannini and Egyptian Museum, Cairo.

Figure 41. The Step Pyramid complex is enclosed by a limestone wall. The complex might well be a simulacrum, or skeuomorph, of a ritual complex at Memphis. It includes the pyramid itself; the Southern Tomb, which probably served as a cenotaph; a funerary temple to the north; and two small edifices known as the House of the North and the House of the South, as well as a heb-sed *course and court, and a place for the king to refresh himself and prepare for the necessary rituals accompanying the* heb-sed. *Photo Salima Ikram.*

to improve irrigation and by the construction of awesome architecture in the form of pyramids, together with their dependent temples and towns. The Step Pyramid, the first major stone architecture ever produced in the world, was constructed for King Djoser-Netjerykhet during this time. This pyramid form remained the structure of choice for royal burials for the next thousand years. (Fig. 41.) During this period, the logistics involved with the construction of numerous stone pyramids and temples (organizing the work schedules, food, lodging, transport, and care of the workers and providing the raw materials needed for the buildings) attest to Egypt's wealth, complex bureaucracy, and stability.

At probably no other time in Egyptian history was the king's divine nature as pronounced as it was during the 4th Dynasty (see Chapter 5). The king ruled supreme as a god on earth, the son of the sun god Re, and the anthropomorphic manifestation of the god Horus. His tomb was enormous; obviously, to build it he had to wield a huge amount of economic, political, and religious power. His courtiers schemed to be buried near him so that they might join him in the Afterlife and continue to reap rewards there as they had on earth. Members of the royal family occupied important government and religious positions, giving persons of royal blood dominion over all others. In subsequent dynasties, when there seems to have been some problem with the succession, the king's role was not as sacrosanct. Thus, fabricated stories, such as those recorded in the Westcar Papyrus (see box), had to be constructed to bolster the legitimacy and divinity of the rulers of Dynasty 5. During this time, an increasing number of non-royals were elevated to important positions in the bureaucracy, and the priests of the god Re, who were related to the kings of this dynasty, were given ever-increasing amounts of power and wealth. The 6th Dynasty saw a continuing upsurge in the strength and wealth of provincial nobility and the nomarchs, as well as of the priesthood. As one might expect, this trend diminished royal power and control, and, possibly coupled with problematic environmental factors, laid the foundation for the First Intermediate Period.

For the most part, Egypt's borders were secure during the Old Kingdom, permitting large-scale royal expeditions for exploration, mining, quarrying, and trade. The diorite quarries that lay in the desert south-west of Aswan were tapped to provide stone for royal statuary. Donkey caravans penetrated deep into the Western Desert in search of minerals and new trade routes to Libya, Chad, and the Sudan. Turquoise, malachite, and copper were extracted from the Sinai, and gold from the Wadi Hammamat. Trade with areas comprising modern-day Lebanon and Syria supplied Egypt with materials that were unavailable locally: massive trunks of cedar and juniper wood with which to make furniture, boats, buildings, and temple doors, and resins to be used in practical objects and in religious rituals to anoint images or to burn as incense.

Some military activity took place during the Old Kingdom, mainly against Libyan nomads. Egypt's western boundaries were less well established than they are today, and Libyans regularly encroached on what the Egyptians considered 'their' soil. The Egyptians generally emerged victorious their battles with the Libyans, acquiring livestock, grain, and prisoners of war.

The Nubians and the Egyptians also engaged in skirmishes during this time, which, according to Egyptian accounts, were all won by the Egyptians.

Towards the end of the Old Kingdom the Egyptians tried to establish better trade relations with the Nubians, possibly with the aim of expanding into and controlling Nubia. Several Egyptian expeditions were sent to explore Nubia and to find trade routes to the different entrepôts there. The launching point for these expeditions was Elephantine Island at Aswan, and such governors of the area as Sabni, Heqaib, and Harkhuf, who went south from there, can be counted amongst the earliest explorers of sub-Saharan Africa. Indeed, Heqaib achieved the status of a demi-god and was worshipped in his native Elephantine throughout the Middle Kingdom, while Harkhuf's various trips to the south won him the favour of the young king Pepy II, not only in terms of wealth and rank but also in the form of a personal letter from the king. This mark of favour was so rare that Harkhuf had the text of the letter inscribed on an external wall of his tomb. (Fig. 42.) The excited eight- or

Figure 42.   The external inscriptions on Harkhuf's tomb at Kubbet el-Hawa at Aswan include the letter that Pepy wrote to Harkhuf in appreciation for the safe voyage of the pygmy. The interior of the rock-cut tomb, illustrated here, shows Harkhuf holding a staff of office with an inscription including his titles and explaining his responsibilities. Photo Aidan Dodson.

nine-year-old king wrote the letter to thank Harkhuf for the dancing pygmy from the land of Yam that the governor was bringing to him, and to ensure that the pygmy would arrive safely. Loosely translated the letter reads:

> You said in your report that you have brought a pygmy of the god's dances from the land of the horizon-dwellers… You have said to my majesty that his like has never been brought by anyone who went to Yam before. Truly you know how to do what your lord loves and praises… His majesty will give you many noble honours for the benefit of your son's son for all time, so that all people will say, when they hear what my majesty did for you: 'Does anything equal what was done for the sole companion Harkhuf when he returned from Yam, because of the vigilance he showed in doing what his lord loved, praised, and commanded?' Come north to the palace at once! Hurry and bring with you this dancing pygmy… live, hale, and healthy, for the dances of the god, to gladden the heart, to delight the heart of King Neferkare [Pepy II] who lives forever! When he goes down with you into the ship, get stalwart men to be around him on deck, lest he fall into the water! When he lies down at night, get good men to lie around him in his tent. Inspect [him] ten times at night! My majesty desires to see this pygmy more than the gifts of the mine-land and of Punt! When you arrive at the residence and this pygmy is with you live, hale, and healthy, my majesty will do great things for you![2]

It is this same enthusiastic young king Pepy II who may unwittingly have contributed to the demise of the Old Kingdom. One reason for this was that the king simply ruled and lived too long – he died when he was approximately ninety-four after a rule of eighty or so years. He was probably a weak and ineffectual ruler at the end of his life, and power was dissipated into too many other hands. His father, Pepy I, had also enjoyed an overly long reign, possibly setting into motion this process of decentralization. Conversely, the rulers of Dynasties 7 and 8 were very short lived – indeed, for dramatic emphasis Manetho states that the 7th Dynasty consisted of seventy kings who ruled for seventy days. None of these kings seems to have been able to maintain control of the country or its resources, as can be inferred from the tiny, rubble-filled pyramids that were constructed for some kings of this era. In the past, scholars tended to place Dynasties 7 and 8 in the First Intermediate period. Indeed, it is quite possible that Dynasty 8 continued only in Memphis during the First Intermediate period. This division has now been revised, although perhaps only temporarily, as new evidence might alter our understanding of this period. These dynasties were related by blood to Pepy but held only tenuous control of the Memphite area, and it is possible that Dynasty 8 existed concurrently with power-bases in other parts of the country.

Prior to and during the rulership of the Pepys, power was slipping away from the king and his immediate courtiers and into the hands of provincial noblemen. Because many of their positions were hereditary, the nobles' power was consolidated and their wealth increased. Opportunities for social mobility increased, resulting in the beginnings of a 'middle class' and a general rise in prosperity for the non-royal components of the population. Royal power was further dissipated by the marriage of princesses to provincial nobles and by the kings' taking wives from the nomarchy.

The shift in power from the king to provincial nobles is graphically manifested in the location, architecture, and decoration of tombs. Instead of nobles' clamouring to be buried near the king in the capital as a mark of loyalty and royal favour, an increasing number chose to be interred in their own cities. Their tombs were large, and some nobles tried to emulate the layout of a royal sepulchre by building temples and causeways that connected to their tombs (see Chapter 8 for details). The tombs themselves were lavishly decorated, and the nobility usurped the iconography that had been reserved for royalty, such as the wearing of a false beard or a *shendyt* kilt, or hunting with a bow and arrows. Images of divinities and of religious texts that had previously been limited to royal sepulchres started to appear in the tombs of elites. The positioning of powerful people in the provinces may have started as a bid to extend and consolidate royal control, but if this was the case, the plan backfired, giving provincial nobility control over their areas, while royal power ebbed dramatically.

Priests and temples also contributed to the decline of a strong central government. Starting with Dynasty 5, the priesthood of Re dramatically increased in power, eroding royal control. Other temples also enjoyed privileges, such as exemption decrees, that ultimately detracted from royal power. Exemption decrees excused temples from paying tax and thus gave the temples more wealth and control. Royal mortuary temples also fell into this category, and by the end of the Old Kingdom the king must have felt a dramatic decline in the amount of land and resulting income at his disposal.

Some scholars posit that climatological change was a further cause of the stress that was a factor in the collapse of the Old Kingdom. A series of low Niles and the continued gradual desiccation of the Sahara would certainly have contributed to a general lack of food. This food shortage would have been aggravated by an increase in population as nomads sought the relative security of the Nile Valley. No doubt the new arrivals were unwelcome and minor skirmishes resulted; this civil unrest likely contributed to the general dissatisfaction of the populace and to the end of the stability of the Old Kingdom.

> ### The Last Queen of the Old Kingdom
> According to Manetho, one of the first female rulers of Egypt was the beautiful Nitokris, who reigned during the declining years of the Old Kingdom, allegedly for twelve years. Herodotus relates a strange tale concerning her. He writes that she succeeded her murdered brother as king. To avenge his death she conceived of a cunning plan: she had a large subterranean hall constructed and held a great feast for its inauguration. She invited her brother's murderers to the banquet and, while they were feasting, flooded the chamber so that they all drowned. Then she flung herself into a chamber filled with ashes to escape retribution for her deed. Presumably she escaped safely from this chamber and continued her rule.

First Intermediate Period (2160–2066 BC)

The First Intermediate Period as defined now, consists of Dynasties 9, 10, and the first part of 11 (the balance of Dynasty 11 is regarded as part of

Middle Kingdom history). As far as scholars can determine, because of the erosion of central authority, Egypt broke into a number of smaller political units, many of which were based on nome boundaries. These units periodically engaged in warfare, as each nomarch, who occasionally went as far as dating events by his own 'regnal' years, attempted to extend his dominion. Different nomes throughout Egypt held sway over large tracts of land during this period. Eventually, a strong power emerged in the north, near the Fayyum, at the site of Herakleopolis (modern Ihnasiya el-Medina), with a counterpart in the south at Thebes. The Herakleopolitan kings constituted Dynasties 9 and 10 in Manetho's list and ruled concurrently with the earlier rulers of the Theban 11th Dynasty.

The rulers of Thebes and Herakleopolis areas managed to subdue all others in their vicinity and ultimately fought one another for control over all of Egypt. Recently, excavations at Ihnasiya have shown a stratum of burning, perhaps the remainder of one such struggle. After a series of battles, the southern king, Mentuhotep II, finally vanquished the northern ruler and reunited Egypt under his rule, ushering in the next strongly centralized period of Egyptian history, the Middle Kingdom.

The kings and their courts of the First Intermediate Period had basically followed the traditional model of a strong king with loyal, dependent courtiers who clustered around him in life and in death. Unlike in the majority of the country, art and architecture flourished in these courts. At the same time, there was a marked increase in social mobility and a correspondingly wider access to resources. Iconography and texts that had been been reserved for the royalty and the highest elite were now used by commoners, who experimented further in art and literature, setting the stage for developments in the Middle Kingdom.

Egypt's Economy

The Egyptian economy was based on trade and barter; coinage or currency was not introduced until the Persian period. Basically, Egypt's economy was redistributive: taxes, primarily in the form of grain, were collected by the king and the temples and were used to pay people in their employ, who distributed the grain amongst their dependents. Additionally, small-scale markets occurred regularly in towns and villages; Egyptians also bartered informally amongst themselves, and sometimes with the temples, for additional goods and services.

Middle Kingdom (2066–1650 BC)

Dynasties 11 (mid) through 14 constituted the Middle Kingdom.[3] It was a time of change for Egypt, and the king's position was no longer unassailable. Nonetheless, King Mentuhotep II was hailed as a latter-day Menes and in later King Lists was accorded a special status. He re-unified the country, consolidated its borders, established border guards, and reorganized the bureaucracy by rewarding those who had been loyal to him and divesting any threateningly powerful individuals of their ranks, titles, and wealth. He re-surveyed the nome boundaries and installed people who had been loyal to him as nome heads. (Fig. 43.) The capital seems to have been established at Thebes, although Memphis once again gained some prominence and administrative power. Once he had established domestic peace and control, Mentuhotep set about extending Egyptian control over Lower Nubia, starting a campaign that ultimately culminated in Egypt's annexation of Nubia in the 12th Dynasty. Also under Mentuhotep, royal workshops were re-established and the arts flourished, as is attested to by the architecture and decoration of the king's magnificent tomb in Thebes.

Mentuhotep's successors continued his programme of consolidation and expansion. The kings sent expeditions to the deserts to extract gold and amethyst, and to quarry hard stones, and they constructed richly decorated cult temples and royal tombs and their attendant complexes.

Although the cult of Re remained important, the gods favoured by Mentuhotep II gained ascendancy. Thus, the warlike Theban god Montu was given a prominent position in the pantheon, with the pharaohs of the 11th Dynasty incorporating his name in theirs to show their respect and allegiance. A large temple to Montu was constructed at Karnak, and perhaps the origins of the Amun Temple at Karnak also date to this period.

Choosing a Sarcophagus

King Mentuhotep IV sent an expedition under the direction of his vizier Amenemhat (the future Amenemhat I) to the Wadi Hammamat to quarry a piece of greywacke stone for his sarcophagus. As Amenemhat recorded in a graffito carved into the rocks of the wadi, the stonemasons were trying to decide on which piece to take, when a gazelle suddenly came into the valley, leapt onto a large chunk of stone, and gave birth there. Taking this as a divine sign, the masons chose this block, and the gazelle, the divine messenger, was slaughtered as an offering to the gods.

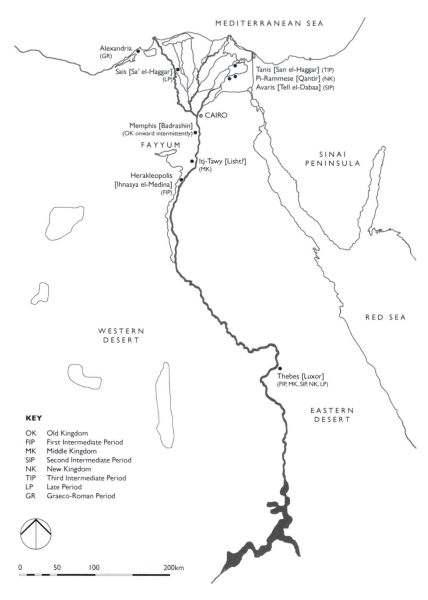

MEDITERRANEAN SEA

Alexandria
(GR)

Sais [Sa' el-Haggar]
(LP)

Tanis [San el-Haggar] (TIP)
Pi-Rammese [Qantir] (NK)
Avaris [Tell el-Dabaa] (SIP)

○ CAIRO

Memphis [Badrashin]
(OK onward intermittently)

FAYYUM

Itj-Tawy [Lisht?]
(MK)

Herakleopolis
[Ihnasya el-Medina]
(FIP)

SINAI
PENINSULA

WESTERN
DESERT

RED SEA

Thebes [Luxor]
(FIP, MK, SIP, NK, LP)

EASTERN
DESERT

KEY

OK   Old Kingdom
FIP   First Intermediate Period
MK   Middle Kingdom
SIP   Second Intermediate Period
NK   New Kingdom
TIP   Third Intermediate Period
LP   Late Period
GR   Graeco-Roman Period

0   50   100   200km

Figure 43. Map showing the capitals of Egypt at different periods. Drawing Nicholas Warner.

Dynasty 11 may have ended somewhat ignominiously, with Amenemhat I, the vizier of the last king of the dynasty, Mentuhotep IV, usurping the throne, perhaps in a military coup. Amenemhat I and his successors subsequently ruled effectively for some two centuries. Upon his accession, Amenemhat gained loyalty and control by making a royal progress through the country, no doubt rewarding those who swore an oath of loyalty to

Figure 44. The barque shrine of Senusert I was, if not the earliest, then one of the first buildings erected at Karnak. It was built to celebrate the king's heb-sed *and then became a barque shrine on a processional route. Dismantled in the New Kingdom and used in the building of the third pylon, it has been resurrected in Karnak Temple's Open Air Museum. Photo Salima Ikram.*

him. He replaced officials loyal to the 11th Dynasty with his own men, re-surveyed nome boundaries, and reassigned nomarchs. Thebes remained an important city, dedicated to the particular god of the 12th Dynasty, Amun, whose temple at Karnak over time became the largest stone construction to be dedicated to a deity. (Fig. 44.) Amun rapidly became syncretised with Re, and, save for a brief hiatus in the 18th Dynasty, Amun-Re remained the chief god of Egypt until the country's conversion to Christianity some two thousand years later. The administrative capital, however, was moved north to the newly founded town of Itj-Tawy ('Seizer of Two Lands' in Egyptian), near modern-day Lisht, south of Memphis. The pyramid complexes of the kings were located in sight of the new capital.

No doubt owing to the irregular manner in which they first came to the throne, the kings of Dynasty 12 were careful to maintain political control and to ensure smooth successions throughout the dynasty. A possible inno-vation that guaranteed the succession was the establishment of co-regencies. An ageing king took a co-regent during his declining years, thus training him as well as publicly acknowledging and establishing him as his successor.

The 12th Dynasty rulers also modified the position of vizier; instead of one very powerful vizier for the whole country, there were now two, one each for Upper and Lower Egypt. Later, when Nubia was added to Egypt's domains, a post for its governor was established that further balanced the power of the vizierate. King Senusert III (c. 1881–1840 BC) apparently believed that such measures were insufficient, however, and that the nomarchs were again gaining too much power, so he reorganized the bureaucratic structure of the country, greatly diminishing the status of the nomes and splitting Egypt into three *warets*, or divisions. Thus Upper and Lower Egypt and Nubia were all under direct royal control, with ministries attached to each. An official headed each ministry, but he could not act with total independence: checks and balances appear in the form of an assistant and a *djadjat*, or council of advisors. This limited the power of the elites and increased the number and strength of what might be termed a middle class, a growing portion of the population with increasing access to commodities and symbolic resources.

Within Egypt, the 12th Dynasty government exploited and developed the Fayyum Oasis. Drainage systems, dykes, barrages, and canals were dug and constructed, and the area became a rich source of agricultural wealth. This favoured area also became the burial place for some of the Dynasty 12 kings and their courtiers, as well as a location for several cult temples. Expeditions to the deserts to mine gold, amethyst, quartzite, turquoise, copper, and malachite flourished.

The Labyrinth of Hawara

One of the wonders of Egypt particularly noted by the Greeks and Romans was the mortuary temple of King Amenemhat III's pyramid at Hawara, dubbed 'The Labyrinth' by classical writers. This semi-subterranean building was built out of sparkling white limestone and featured a complicated series of courts, colonnades, passages, rooms, and crypts that reflected the geography of Egypt. Herodotus reports that it had at least three thousand rooms, although this is doubtful. Here the king was worshipped as a god. Monolithic stones were used to roof it, and it was exquisitely carved and painted and was filled with statues of the king and many gods of the Egyptian pantheon. Unfortunately, by the time the archaeologist William Matthews Flinders Petrie came to excavate it (1888), little was left but some scattered remains, as the stone had been taken for buildings in the Fayyum. Perhaps further work in the area can reveal vestiges of this grand monument. (Fig. 45.)

During the 12th Dynasty trade and foreign relations flourished with cities in Syria, Palestine, Lebanon, and Punt, as well as in Nubia. Occasional

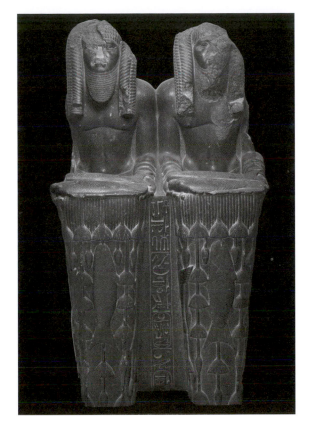

Figure 45. King Amenembet III showed himself in what appear to be non-canonical ways, such as in this pair statue depicting the king twice as a deity associated with the fecundity of the Nile. He is wearing an unusual wig and beard and is carrying fish, ducks, geese, and water-plants. Some scholars suggest that the style evokes Mesopotamia, while others believe that it alludes to Nubia; both interpretations are possible. This type of image was adapted and used by subsequent rulers, particularly in the New Kingdom. Photo courtesy Sandro Vannini and the Egyptian Museum, Cairo.

skirmishes and a few battles with Egypt's northern neighbours did mar smooth trade relationships amongst these countries, but for the most part interactions remained cordial and the boundaries between the different areas were respected. Indeed, toward the end of the 12th Dynasty, a large influx of southwest Asian peoples immigrated to Egypt and established themselves there, mingling, to some extent, with local populations. It was in fact these settlements that were the basis of a later Hyksos domination of northern Egypt.

However, the situation was different on the southern border where a significant amount of military activity occurred. After establishing good trade relations with, and outposts in, Nubia, the Egyptians turned to more aggressive ways to seize control of what was seen as the gateway to all the riches of Africa. A series of campaigns led the Egyptians to establish a series of at least eight enormous mud-brick forts at the Nile's Second Cataract between Semna and Buhen. (Fig. 46.) Erected on high ground with a good water supply, forts were generally protected by a dry moat, thick crenellated walls, and a glacis that made access difficult. Only one gateway with a double set of doors would give access to the fort; drawbridges further protected these solid gates, as well as, possibly, portcullises. Within the walls, forts were well organized and respected the rules of orthogonal (gridded) town planning, complete with drains that ran down the main streets. They contained barracks, residences for officers, temples, offices, and, of course, vast storage rooms or magazines for the goods that had been taken from or traded with the Nubians, as well as for wheat and other staples. The traded goods included gold, ivory, ebony, spices, animal skins and tails, live animals, and in times of war, slaves. Trade in these items remained a key element in the relationship between Egypt and Nubia.

The Middle Kingdom was also the golden age of Egyptian literature, expressed in language now categorized as 'Classic' or 'Middle' Egyptian. This perception of a 'classical' phase of language and literature is not just a modern construct; the ancient Egyptians themselves seem to have held this view, based on the number of New Kingdom and later copies of Middle Kingdom texts. Many new texts were composed during this time, while other, earlier ones, had their compositions finalized. Stories such as the delightful 'Shipwrecked Sailor'; the moral, ponderous but well-composed 'Eloquent Peasant'; and the pseudo-historical tales 'Sinuhe' all date to this period, as does the rare pessimistic text such as 'A Dispute Between a Man and His Ba', which is unique as it touches on the very un-Egyptian idea of suicide. Many exquisite love poems were also written during the Middle Kingdom. Instructional texts, known generically as Wisdom Literature, first encountered in the Old Kingdom, abound, but they struck a different tone. Instead of being outlines for the good behaviour that leads to social acceptance, advancement, and the living of a *maat*-filled life, some of these Middle Kingdom texts, such as 'The Instructions of King Amenemhat I to His Son Senusert I', consisted of instructions from a king to his son for a successful rule. The advice includes being wary of the vizier (not surprising, considering how Amenemhat became king), distrusting most men, being strong, and invoking the gods in everything. Other texts from this

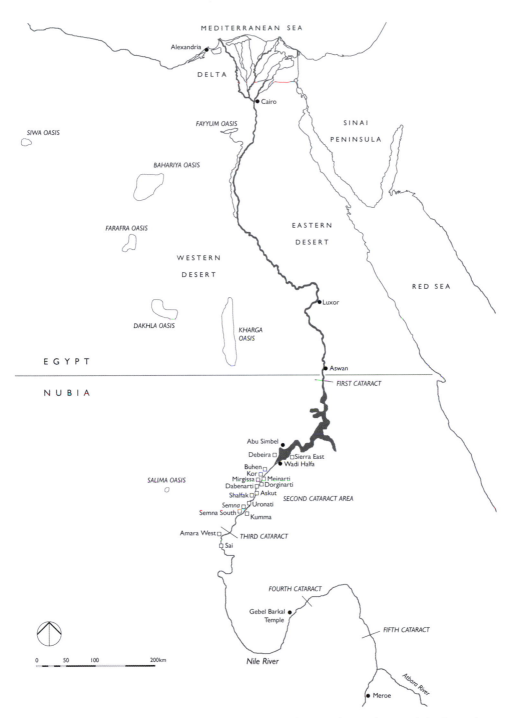

Figure 46. The majority of Egyptian forts in Nubia are clustered around the Second Cataract. Drawing Nicholas Warner.

period deal with mathematics, medicine (veterinary and gynaecological), and religion.

The Middle Kingdom also saw changes in Egyptian religion. The cult of the god Amun became increasingly important, and was syncretised with that of Re, creating the new state deity, Amun-Re. In addition to Amun's cult, the cult of Osiris (see Chapter 5) rose to prominence, with people from all over Egypt flocking to make pilgrimages to Osiris's sacred site at Abydos. Visitors made offerings of food, drink, and prayers here and erected statues and stelae of themselves praising the god. Some images show worshippers in prayerful positions, their hands turned palm up, importuning different gods. Funerary texts based on those used for royalty started to appear at the end of the Old Kingdom, took hold in the First Intermediate period, and flourished during the Middle Kingdom. Although the Middle Kingdom is generally held to continue through at least the first half of Dynasty 13, its heyday remained Dynasties 11 and 12. The last ruler of the Dynasty 12 was Queen Sobekneferu, who was the first woman to take on the whole royal titulary and to appear in a King List (that of Saqqara). She was apparently a daughter of Amenemhat III and was possibly unrelated to her immediate predecessor, King Amenemhat IV, who seems to have been of non-royal birth. Nothing is known of her death or burial place.

The first kings of Dynasty 13 might have been descendants of Amenemhat IV, but it is clear that a number of that dynasty's kings were commoners by birth and that the throne often remained within a family group for only a generation or two. Most of the reigns were short, and the succession of rulers is, on occasion, unclear. Needless to say, this rapid succession of short-lived rulers was either a cause or an effect of the disorganization and economic decline characteristic of the country at this time. At least one part of Egypt, the north-east Delta, seceded under rulers of Canaanite origin (Dynasty 14), but the rest of the kingdom seems to have held together until around 1650, when a new wave of Canaanites, the so-called Hyksos, succeeded in driving the native kings out of Lower Egypt altogether. In southern Upper Egypt a small indigenous line – Dynasty 16/17 – continued to rule.

Second Intermediate Period (1650–1549 BC)

The term 'Hyksos' is derived from the Egyptian phrase, *beqa khasut*, or 'Chiefs of Foreign Lands'. The Hyksos seem to have originated in Syria/Palestine; their pottery, houses, and material culture attest to this. The Egyptians add support to this premise by also calling the Hyksos *Aamu*, or speakers of a Western Asiatic tongue. According to earlier scholarship, as well as ancient Egyptian rhetoric, these bellicose people invaded from the Near East and established an independent kingdom in the Delta, making forays into the more southern parts of Egypt. This depiction mainly follows New Kingdom royal propagandistic texts that reviled the Hyksos and stressed the greatness of the Egyptians themselves. New evidence of earlier settlements of these people and their consolidation of power indicates a less violent takeover than that implied by the later Egyptian texts.

The Hyksos owed their military success in part to their mastery of the horse and chariot (both unknown in Egypt until that time), and their superior weapons, such as the double bow, sharp axes, and scimitar-like swords. They established their capital in the eastern Delta at the site of Avaris, or modern Tell el-Dab'a. It is possible that the later Egyptian texts exaggerated the belligerence and tyranny of the Hyksos for dramatic effect, but evidence from Tell el-Dab'a does suggest a violent overthrow of Dynasty 14 by the Hyksos, and soon afterwards a rapid expansion out of their core territory.

The Hyksos adopted various aspects of Egyptian royal identity, and several Egyptians held significant posts in their administration. In other matters they retained their Syro-Palestinian traditions, or versions of these that they merged with Egyptian ones. Their names invoke their particular deities, such as Baal and Anat, who shortly entered the Egyptian pantheon, with Baal becoming incorporated with Seth. Their gods also had Egyptian names in addition to their Asiatic ones. Hyksos burial customs show a mixture of Egyptian and Near Eastern traditions: their brick-lined tombs are typical of the Near East, as are the donkey burials outside the tombs. However, the pairs of trees that mark the entrance to many Hyksos tombs suggest the influence of Egyptian rituals related to the sites of Pe (Buto) and Nekhen (Hierakonpolis/el-Kab).

It is unclear how far south the Hyksos penetrated, although there is evidence for a presumably brief occupation of much of Upper Egypt. As recorded in a stela erected by the warrior, King Kamose of the 17th Dynasty (1553–1549 BC), the Hyksos appear to have been closely aligned with the Kushites, the Nubian rulers at Kerma. They used the oases routes for safe communication, circumventing the Nile and Thebes, in order to plan a two-pronged attack on the Thebans. Kamose captured one of their spy-messengers and managed to thwart the Hyksos-Kushite plan. A recently discovered text at el-Kab tells of a Nubian invasion of southern Egypt. However, by the mid-sixteenth century BC, the Theban-based Dynasty 17 seems to have been secure in the south, and its temple-building programme included the area from Elephantine to Abydos, and perhaps even further north. Ultimately, civil war broke out again and the Thebans progressively drove the Hyksos out of Egypt, culminating in their definitive defeat at Sharuhen in Palestine by King Ahmose I, founder of Dynasty 18.

The Hippopotami and the Hyksos

As the Hyksos wished to rule all of Egypt instead of just the north, one of the most famous Hyksos rulers, Apopi (Apophis in the Greek transliteration), trumped up an excuse to challenge an equally notable Theban ruler, Seqenenre, to do battle. Apopi sent a messenger with a letter to Seqenenre complaining that the canal to the east of Thebes was overfull of hippopotami whose noisiness kept Apophi from sleeping. Seqenenre was understandably dumbfounded, as Avaris and Thebes are several hundred kilometres apart, and he asked what he was supposed to do about it. Alas, the story breaks off here, so we do not know the end. However, the mummy of King Seqenenre Taa II shows that he engaged in several battles, was injured, and then was brutally murdered whilst recuperating. Obviously, he took up the challenge and paid a high price for it. (Fig. 47.)

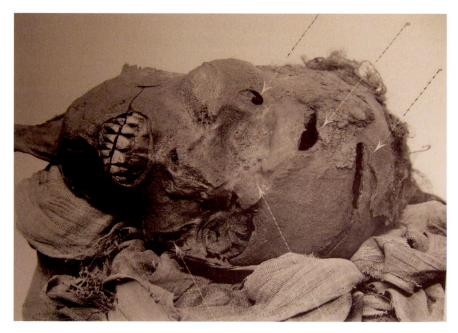

Figure 47. The mummy of Seqenenre Taa shows evidence of a brutal attack upon the king with knives and axes that resulted in his death. Photo Emile Brugsch.

New Kingdom (1549–1069 BC)

The New Kingdom, comprising Dynasties 18 through 20, was a period in Egyptian history during which the country not only prospered internally but also flourished internationally. During this time, Egypt expanded its borders again into Nubia and annexed significant parts of the Near East. Art, architecture, literature, music, and dance thrived, and many of Egypt's greatest rulers made their indelible mark upon history through their conquests and innovations.

King Ahmose I, the first king of the New Kingdom era, was quite young when he ascended the throne, and thus his mother, Queen Ahhotep, apparently acted as regent during the early part of his reign. It was quite usual in Egypt for the mother of a young king to act as regent when her son was young. Ahhotep may even have led the army after the death in battle of Seqenenre. Ahmose, once he had gained control of the country, embarked on an extensive building programme, constructing temples as well as adding to already existing temples throughout Egypt, a custom that was continued by his immediate successors. (Fig. 48.)

Figure 48. Ahmose awarded Ahhotep with the 'Gold of Valour', a necklace of three large gold flies, alluding to tenacity and bravery on the battlefield. Photo courtesy Sandro Vannini and the Egyptian Museum, Cairo.

Subsequent rulers continued to strengthen Egypt's borders, build cult and funerary temples, and re-establish their power in Nubia. Campaigns were also launched in the Near East, and parts of Syria were annexed by Egypt, first by Thutmose I and then particularly by his grandson, Thutmose III, proving that Egypt was becoming as an international power.

The Elephants of Ni

Throughout their history, Egyptian kings used images of hunting to demonstrate their power to conquer chaos, establish *maat*, and rule over the natural world. Elephant hunts became popular in the New Kingdom, as kings such as Thutmose I and his grandson, Thutmose III, hunted Syrian elephants (a sub-species of the Asian elephant) in Syria, particularly in the area of modern Apamea (ancient Ni). Vanquishing these large, threatening-looking beasts added lustre to tales of royal bravery and derring-do. However, according to the tomb biography of Amenemhab, a courtier of Thutmose III, the king was almost killed by a rampaging elephant in Ni and survived only because Amenemhab managed to slice off the elephant's trunk , thereby saving the king's life.

Perhaps the greatest of Egypt's female pharaohs came to the throne during Dynasty 18: Queen Hatshepsut. She initially took power as regent for her nephew and stepson, Thutmose III, but later assumed the full titulary of a king and was depicted dressed in male kingly garb. She legitimised her right to the throne not only on grounds of her bloodlines and marriage but also because, she claimed, as would a number of later New Kingdom monarchs, that she was the physical daughter of the god Amun-Re; thus she had texts and scenes to this effect carved in her funeral temple at Deir el-Bahari.

Archaeological and textual evidence indicate that to some extent Thutmose and Hatshepsut shared a sort of co-regency. They divided the labour, with Thutmose occupying himself more with military activity outside of Egypt and Hatshepsut dealing with more domestic or purely diplomatic and economic matters. For example, Hatshepsut organized an expedition to the land of Punt, probably located on the coast of East Africa, to bring back, amongst other things, incense trees. Sometime in the twentieth or twenty-first year of her rule Hatshepsut vanished from the historical record (Fig. 49), and Thutmose III took sole command of Egypt. His rule was extremely successful, extending Egypt's borders to their most northern and southern extents. His son and successor, Amenhotep II, maintained his

Figure 49. Images of Hatshepsut were erased from every monument that she built, possibly by Thutmose III. In this scene from Karnak Temple Hatshepsut is being purified by Horus and Thoth; her names and the outline of her figure have clearly been chipped out. Photo Salima Ikram.

father's expansionist policies. He also engaged in sporting activities and was famous for his prowess at archery, taming wild steeds, rowing, and wielding a lance – he was truly an atheletic pharaoh. (Fig. 50.)

The reign of Thutmose IV, Amenhotep II's son, marked a shift in some of Egypt's internal and religious policies. Thus, Thutmose IV started to enhance the status of the cults of other gods, particularly the sun god Re, and Aten, a form of Re ignored since the Old Kingdom. One theory is that this was a conscious strategy of the king to limit the power of the priesthood of Amun, but there is no ancient evidence for such a view. (Fig. 51.) The process was intensified by his son, Amenhotep III, who set about modifying not only Egyptian religious beliefs but also the art and architecture of the period (see Chapter 8). In addition to his many building projects and his elevation of

Figure 50.   Amenhotep II erected several monuments commemorating his atheletic prowess. Here he pierces a metal target with arrows he has fired while driving his chariot. Photo Salima Ikram.

Figure 51.   The Great Sphinx at Giza was carved from the bedrock by King Khafre as a guardian for the necropolis and a tribute to the sun god. It was subsequently restored by many rulers. The stela between its paws was erected by Thutmose IV. According to the text, Thutmose, who was then a prince, fell asleep near the monument after hunting and dreamt that the Sphinx promised him the crown if he freed the statue from the sand. He did this, and became king after the unexpected death of his elder brother. Photo Marjorie Fisher.

the stature of the god Aten, he also continued to ensure Egypt's international position through marriage, diplomacy, and warfare. He took a Near Eastern princess as a bride to cement relationships in the north, and fought against the Nubians, as well as built temples to Egyptian deities in Nubia to maintain Egypt's possessions in the south. He also deified himself to a greater degree than had his predecessors, going as far as to be shown in Nubian temples worshipping himself.

It is Amenhotep III's son, Amenhotep IV, who later took the name Akhenaten, who stands out as an anomaly in Egyptian history. His reign is known as the Amarna period, after the modern name of his capital city – Tell el-Amarna. During his seventeen-year reign, Akhenaten took the cult of Aten to new heights by virtually abolishing the cult of Amun and closing down Amun's temples throughout Egypt. He also built, as a direct challenge to Amun, a large temple dedicated to Aten to the east of Amun's great temple at Karnak. Akhenaten managed to build several more temples to the Aten in Egypt. Various factors contributed to this accomplishment. First, these temples needed less actual construction as they were dedicated to the sun god and thus were open to the sky. Second, rather than use limestone, Akhenaten had the temples built, and the statues in them sculpted, from sandstone, which is easier to shape and carve. Finally, Akhenaten utilized a smaller-size block called a *talatat* (from the Arabic word for three, *talata*, as it measures three handbreadths) in constructing the temples, which was quicker to cut and easier to manoeuvre into place.

Initially during Akhenaten's reign other gods besides Aten continued to be revered, albeit to a lesser degree than they had been before the Aten achieved the status of supreme god. The king changed his name from Amenhotep, which translates as 'Amun is Satisfied/Peaceful', to Akhenaten, the 'Soul/Manifestation of the Aten', to reflect his new allegiance, as well as his own emphatically divine status as Aten's representative on earth. The king also moved the capital and court to a new site, founded on relatively virgin soil in Middle Egypt, and named it Akhetaten ('the Horizon of the Aten'). Fifteen large boundary stelae, some of which still stand today, delineated the new capital, which was designed to function both as a microcosm in which the movements of the king reflected those of the sun and as a vast stage for ceremonial and political display. During his reign, much of Akhenaten's attention was focussed on religious affairs and the construction of his new capital rather than on matters of state. Thebes lost its religious and civil authority, although Memphis maintained some of its administrative status. The

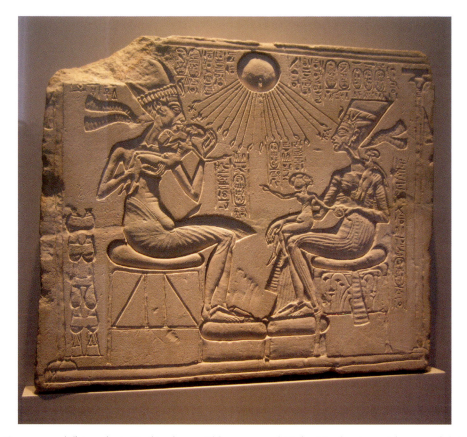

Figure 52. This stela in Berlin shows Akhenaten and Nefertiti relaxing with some of their children. The Aten shines above them, holding ankh *signs towards the royal pair, giving them life. The body proportions of the royal family are odd, with elongated heads, long thin limbs, and distended bellies and buttocks. The intimacy of this family scene was unprecedented in Egyptian formal art. Photo Nicholas Warner.*

Egyptian population was encouraged to worship the king and his family, and through them, Aten. (Fig. 52.)

Akhenaten also pushed to new limits his father's artistic style of showing himself with slanted eyes and exaggerated, well-modelled lips. These depictions, which differed dramatically from the established canon of Egyptian art (see Chapter 8), must have made their viewers uncomfortable. In reliefs, sculpture, and painting, the king and his family are characterised by elongated heads and eyes, attenuated limbs, and large bellies and buttocks; naturally, loyal courtiers followed suit in the artwork that they commissioned, for to emulate the king was the highest form of both loyalty and flattery. Some scholars have suggested that these depictions actually reflect a disease from which Akhenaten suffered; however, if this is the case, the disease has yet to be identified, because although Marfan's and Frölich/Froelich's syndromes have been suggested, neither completely fits what is known about Akhenaten. Unfortunately, we do not have Akhenaten's body, so none of these diagnoses can be checked. Uniquely, naked images of the king show him as a sexless being. Perhaps such a depiction was meant to identify Akhenaten with the sun-disk, a similarly sexless but potent and life-giving entity.

Historians ascribe Akhenaten's actions variously to genuine religious belief, perhaps as a result of a disordered mind; to astute political manoeuvring designed to reassert the authority of the king over the priests of Amun; or to a combination of these factors. These options are still hotly debated. Regardless of the reasons for Akhenaten's behaviour, its results were ultimately disastrous for the country. The people became alienated from their king and their gods, and Egypt's internal and external affairs suffered dramatically. After Akhenaten's death – whether from natural causes or not – his successors moved the religious capital back to Thebes, with Memphis remaining as a strong administrative centre; restored the worship of Amun; relegated the Aten cult to its previous status; and deliberately erased the intervening years from the historical record by effacing Akhenaten's name wherever it occurred and demolishing his monuments.

Queen Nefertiti

Queen Nefertiti, Akhenaten's wife, is a curious figure in Egyptian history. She ruled side by side with Akhenaten and seems to have wielded almost as much power as he did. In Karnak she is shown smiting the enemies of Egypt, just as kings do, and together with her husband, she was revered by the populace. In the past, some scholars have suggested that she even ruled briefly, albeit in male guise, and they identify the enigmatic ruler Smenkhkare as Nefertiti in male garb. Now it seems clear that she became her husband's co-ruler under the name Neferneferuaten, succeeding a shadowy male monarch, Smenkhkare, in that role. The most famous image of her is a bust excavated from a sculptor's studio at Akhetaten; it is now in the Staatliche Museum in Berlin.

The return to status quo, carried out under the auspices of Akhenaten's young son Tutankhaten (soon to be Tutankhamun) was maintained by

Figure 53. Tutankhamun is shown here as the creator god, Nefertum, emerging from a lotus/lily. The young king's head is shaved, and the artist has rendered the small dots of newly emerging hair. The statue was originally adorned with gold earrings, now lost. Photo courtesy Sandro Vannini and the Egyptian Museum, Cairo.

his immediate successors and by the early rulers of the following dynasty. (Fig. 53.) The early kings of the 19th Dynasty matched, if not exceeded, the acts of their 18th Dynasty predecessors in terms of consolidating the country, promoting the arts, building temples and palaces, fostering trade, and expanding Egypt's empire both in the north and in the south, regaining and extending the areas lost during Akhenaten's reign. King Ramesses II moved the royal residence to a new site, Pi-Ramesse (modern Qantir), in the eastern Delta. It was apparently the area from which the Ramesside royal family originated. Located astride a branch of the Nile, the site was well placed for communications with countries to the east of Egypt.

Figure 54. Ramesses II's mummy when it was first unwrapped in the nineteenth century. Photo Emile Brugsch, private collection.

The Pharaoh with a Passport

The mummy of Ramesses II is the only royal mummy to have travelled to France with an Egyptian passport. The mummy, which was deteriorating, was sent to Paris for special treatment at the Musée de l'Homme. The passport listed its occupation as 'pharaoh', and the mummy was greeted with a red carpet and all the honour due a living head of state. In Paris, scholars used, amongst other tools, UV light to treat the deteriorating mummy. Their thorough examination of the remains, including X-raying the mummy, revealed the king's poor dental health and the unusual mummification techniques the Egyptians used in fleshing out his nose with coriander seeds. The stuffing of the nose suggests that the king wanted his beaky profile, seen on so many monuments, to be perpetuated through eternity. (Fig. 54.)

The rulers of the second half of the 19th Dynasty and most of the 20th Dynasty, save for Ramesses III, failed to distinguish themselves in any way. Many had short reigns during which little could be achieved, while others were beset by ill health or internecine violence. Additional complications resulted from a group of marauding invaders, called the Sea Peoples. Their origins are obscure, but they seem to have been a loose federation of pirate-like folk from areas as far away as Sardinia, who terrorized and destroyed the states bordering the Eastern Mediterranean before being stopped at Egypt's borders by Ramesses III. (Fig. 55.) After Ramesses III's reign was ended by a palace conspiracy, his successors presided over a steady economic and political decline, including violent struggles in Upper Egypt, and the loss of Egypt's control over Nubia. By the time of the death of Ramesses XI, Upper Egypt was essentially an independent entity, a situation that was to persist for much of the succeeding Third Intermediate Period.

Figure 55. Ramesses III's funerary temple is unusual in its architecture. A unique feature of the entrance is the migdol gate, thus named because it is in the style of a fortress type commonly encountered in the Levant. Photo Salima Ikram.

Third Intermediate Period (1064–656 BC)

The uneasy Third Intermediate period in Egyptian history covered Dynasties 21 to 25. During the first of these dynasties, the pharaoh ruled from Tanis, in the Delta, while a series of military high priests from the same family ruled south of Beni Suef/el-Hibeh. Dynasty 22, consisting of kings of Libyan ancestry, initially reasserted strong central rule from the north, but, under Osorkon II, Thebes acquired its own king (Dynasty 23), and the succeeding decades saw many local rulers rising in the north, some of whom ultimately claimed royal status.

Heroes or Thieves? Protecting the Burials in the Valley of the Kings

During the 21st Dynasty, when policing the Theban necropoleis was difficult, the priests of Amun decided to protect the royal burials in the Valley of the Kings from further violation and vandalism. They gathered together the mummies of over thirty royal individuals and reburied them with some of their grave goods in the hidden cliff tomb of Pinudjem II, the High Priest of Amun. Most of the kings that were rewrapped have been found devoid of amulets and jewels, and quite possibly their rich adornments were taken to be used in the burials of the kings and high priests of the 21st Dynasty, making this supposedly pious act of reburial actually a way of concealing the theft. Luckily for us, this hidden tomb in Deir el-Bahari was discovered in 1881 by a group of well-known thieves from the Abd el-Rassul family. After they had a falling out, one of the thieves informed the Antiquities Service of the tomb's location. Working day and night over a period of four days in the searing heat of July, the antiquities officials removed the mummies and their belongings from the tomb and loaded them onto a steamer. As the boat made its way down the Nile to Cairo, villagers lined its banks. The women wailed and ululated and the men fired their shotguns as a way of saluting the pharaohs on their last royal progress down the Nile. When the steamer reached the port of Bulaq in Cairo, its cargo was received by museum officials and taken to the institution. Other royal mummies were not as well received in Bulaq – upon arriving in the city of Cairo in the 1880s, the mummy of King Merenre was ignominiously taxed as salted fish!

Following Nubia's reassertion of independence during the Third Intermediate period, a new kingdom of Kush grew up in Nubia, based at the city of Napata, and flourished as an independent entity with rulers who adopted and maintained many Egyptian habits and customs, in particular devotion to

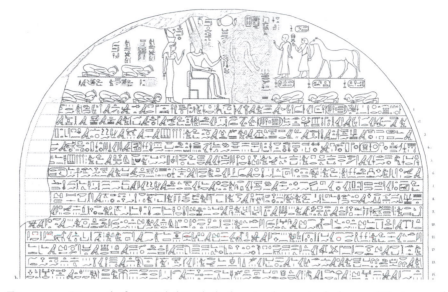

Figure 56. Piye stela from Gebel Barkal, showing horses in the lunette. The image of Piye himself has been scratched out, although his name appears in the cartouche above. Drawing Auguste Mariette.

Amun-Re and identification of Thebes as their spiritual home. Under King Kashta, Kushite control crept northwards, forming a united Nubia. By the time of Kashta's successor Piye (whose name is also rendered as Piankhy), the Nubians were the overlords of Thebes.

In Egypt, seeing a power vacuum in the politically fragmented north of Egypt, Piye took advantage of it by marching northwards and taking over the rest of the country; he faced little substantial resistance save for a long siege at Hermopolis (Ashmunein), after which he marched to Memphis, where he fought a dramatic river battle, and thence on to the Delta. The course of his triumphs is recorded on a stela now in the Egyptian Museum in Cairo. One section depicts a charming side to Piye's character: his love of horses. When he and his troops entered Hermopolis after the siege they found that the horses of King Nimlot, the ruler of the area, had been ill-treated by their owner and were starving. Piye wrote: 'That [the] horses were made hungry pains me more than any other wrongdoing that you committed!' (Fig. 56.) Furious, Piye punished Nimlot for his neglect of the horses and ensured that the animals were well cared for thereafter.

After establishing his hegemony throughout the country, Piye sailed back to Thebes, laden with the spoils of war. He had already established his sister

Figure 57. In her funerary monument at Medinet Habu, Thebes, Shepenwepet (left)*, the reigning God's Wife of Amun, is shown making an offering to Horus, Isis, and her ancestress, Amenirdis, the Divine Adoratrice and former God's Wife. Photo Salima Ikram.*

in Thebes as the heir to the powerful position of God's Wife of Amun, ensuring his continued control over Upper Egypt. (Fig. 57.) Piye then returned to Nubia; he was buried at el-Kurru, in the first pyramid ever to be built in Kush. Northern Egypt, however, remained under local rule, which, under the short-lived Dynasty 24, had revolted against the Kushites.

Piye's successor, Shabaka, promptly returned to Egypt to put down this revolt and establish a unified Nubian-Egyptian state under Dynasty 25. This state of affairs continued for some decades before it was brought to an end by another power that was gaining strength and control in the Near East, Assyria. The Assyrians had successfully conquered most of the Near East and were now casting their eyes towards Egypt. The Assyrian ruler, Assurbanipal, invaded Egypt and triumphed over the Nubians, who retreated southwards. Assurbanipal established an Egyptian, Psamtek, as a puppet ruler in the conquered area, but Assyrian control rapidly collapsed in the wake of unrest in

Assyria itself, leaving Psamtek I as an independent king of Egypt. In the ninth year of his reign, he finally managed to absorb through diplomatic means the city-state of Thebes (which had remained loyal to the Kushites) into the new Dynasty 26.

Late Period (664–332 BC) and the Macedonian Dynasty (332–310 BC)

The last portion of traditional dynastic Egyptian history has been dubbed the Late Period and encompasses Dynasties 26 through 31. Dynasty 26, the strongest dynasty to rule during this era, was based in Psamtek I's native town of Sais in the Delta and is known also as the Saite period, after its capital and its founder's birthplace. During this dynasty, Egypt's defence was bolstered by the fortification of its borders, the maintenance of a strong army that included many Greek mercenaries, and the formation of diplomatic alliances, both within and outside of the country.

Both Dynasties 25 and 26 are typified by the practice of archaism, or the deliberate invocation of Egypt's past. Although they constructed new buildings during this period, Egypt's kings also initiated a large-scale restoration programme of temples and tombs from the 'golden eras' of Egyptian history. The Saite rulers devoted themselves to restoring the Step Pyramid, Menkaure's pyramid, and other ancient monuments. On tomb walls, specific motifs as well as entire scenes were copied and presented as if they dated to the Old or Middle Kingdoms; sculpture followed suit. Clearly, Egypt's glorious ancestors were being invoked to legitimise the ruling pharaohs as well as to remind the populace of their country's past greatness. Changes harkening back to Egypt's past are also evident in religion. There was an upsurge in popular piety and an increase in all types of cults, particularly cults devoted to animal worship (see Chapter 5).

At this point in Egypt's history several powerful states were jockeying for power in Asia and the Eastern Mediterranean. The Assyrians were ultimately replaced by the Persians, who were busy trying to conquer the entire known world from Persia to Greece and beyond. The Persians invaded Egypt and established their rule twice in the succeeding years. In 525 BC, Kambyses defeated the Egyptians at the battle of Pelusium, and he and his successors formed Dynasty 27, which controlled Egypt for over a century. Shortly after Kambyses's death, Egypt made a bid for freedom, but it was swiftly squashed by the next Persian king, Darius.

Figure 58. Hibis Temple in Kharga Oasis is the largest temple to be erected outside the Nile Valley. It is dedicated to the god Amun and is one of the few temples where the name of Darius, the Persian king, appears. Inside is a rare image of the god Seth as an avenger and protector of Re. Photo Salima Ikram.

Although the Persian kings were rarely, if ever, physically present in Egypt, some were represented in Egyptian style, and they both built and added to temples to the Egyptian gods, particularly in the oases of the Western Desert, an area that they developed for its agricultural wealth. A fairly brief revival of native Egyptian rule under Dynasties 28–30 was ended by a final Persian invasion. Persian control continued until the advent of Alexander the Great, who defeated the Persians once and for all in Egypt, as well as in Greece and in Asia. (Fig. 58.)

Alexander invaded Egypt in 332 BC and handled his conquest gracefully and diplomatically by adopting Egyptian ways, including a coronation at the temple of Ptah at Memphis, and thus endearing himself to the Egyptians. He visited the oracle of Amun at the temple of Siwa, where he was greeted as the son of Amun and the rightful pharaoh of Egypt; thereafter, he was depicted wearing the horns of Amun. Alexander was a firm believer in his own divine birth, which fit in very well with Egyptian royal and religious tradition.

Alexander founded a new capital city on the northern margin of the Delta, Alexandria, situated to maximize access to the Mediterranean as well as to the Nile. Under his successors, Alexandria became one of the most important cities of the Eastern Mediterranean, and a centre of learning.

Alexander died in Babylon at the young age of thirty-three in 323 BC. His associates immediately began to squabble over his empire; ultimately, Egypt fell to his general Ptolemy, who founded the last ancient independent ruling house of Egypt.

Ptolemaic Period (310–30 BC)

Ptolemy I had to contend with possible threats to his control of Egypt from other former generals of Alexander and from soldiers who had fought for Alexander. Nonetheless, he managed to establish his control over the country, and he secured his dynasty by making his son and daughter his co-regents. He further bolstered his claim to the throne by hijacking Alexander's grand funerary cortege as it made its way from Babylon to Macedonia, and then burying Alexander's body in Egypt. Classical authors record that Alexander was initially buried in Memphis, and then his body was moved to Alexandria, where he was eventually interred, suspended in honey for preservation, in a rock crystal sarcophagus in the Sema, the future cemetery of all Ptolemaic kings. Neither the Sema nor the bodies of the Ptolemaic rulers have yet been found.

The Ptolemies presented themselves to the population as Egyptians who worshipped Egyptian gods, although in reality they spoke Greek and prob-ably dressed as Greeks most of the time while in their court at Alexandria. They expanded the city of Alexandria, and added temples, parks, and administrative buildings to their capital, as well as to other cities throughout Egypt. At Alexandria, they founded the famous library named after the city and the Mouseion (a temple to the muses and a forerunner of the modern museum). The library housed thousands of volumes, artwork, a school of philosophy, and later schools of music, medicine, and poetry. This institu-tion made the city a magnet for scholars from all around the Mediterranean, who flocked to Alexandria to research, write, learn, and teach. A portion of this library was tragically destroyed by an accidental fire when Caesar was fighting the Ptolemies, but the remainder continued in use for some time. The Ptolemies were also responsible for constructing the famous marble

Figure 59. A rare image of Kleopatra VII from the back wall of the temple at Dendera. The queen is shown with her son by Julius Caesar, Ceasarion, making offerings to the gods. Photo Salima Ikram.

Pharos, or Lighthouse of Alexandria, which was one of the tallest buildings in the world at that time (according to some ancient writers, at least 115–150 metres [377–492 feet] high), and was identified as one of the Seven Wonders of the Ancient World.

Although the early Ptolemies ruled successfully and created a major empire around the eastern Mediterranean, dynastic infighting from the murder of Ptolemy V onward gradually undermined the regime, which became more and more dependent on the favour of Rome. These intrigues culminated in the reign of Kleopatra VII, the last (and perhaps the most famous) of the Ptolemies, and lover successively of Julius Caesar and Mark Antony. (Fig. 59.) After the latter's defeat at the battle of Actium by Octavian (soon to be the Emperor Augustus), Kleopatra committed suicide rather than be taken prisoner. According to some classical sources, she killed herself by forcing a snake (probably a viper) to bite her fatally. Her son and heir was murdered shortly afterwards, and Egypt became a province of the Roman Empire.

Maintaining Egypt

Religion

When one visits Egypt today, manifestations of its ancient religion are visible in many of its monuments, be they temples or tombs. Regardless of this abundant architectual evidence, and the myriad ancient texts relating to the subject, it remains difficult to understand completely the religion of the ancient Egyptians. One reason is that we are seeing only some manifestations of religious practice and reading only a portion of the writings related to it. Our knowledge is the sum of fragments from different periods, and we therefore cannot grasp the totality of Egyptian religion at any one point in time. Instead, we are cobbling together the known evidence from three thousand years of Egyptian history, most of which dates to the New Kingdom or later. Thus we have formed only an imperfect view of the religious beliefs of the ancient Egyptians, which may actually have evolved in ways far different from those that we presume.

State Religion

There is virtually no record of collections of 'national' Egyptian myths written during the Pharaonic period – the majority of such tales come to us from classical Greek and Roman versions. Furthermore, the ancient Egyptians produced no single text such as the Torah, the Bible, or the Quran that explains their religion or serves as a guide to their rituals and beliefs. However, by examining the extant evidence, we can gain some understanding of the Egyptians' basic belief systems, remaining aware that we are handicapped by our limited knowledge and personal biases. In terms of contemporary belief systems, ancient Egyptian religion might best be likened to Hinduism: both are polytheistic; in both, images of gods are worshipped in temples; and in both, each god has its own priesthood to celebrate the divine cult, control the temples and access to the gods, and organize festivals in honor of the god.

Religion permeated every aspect of Egyptian life, which is not surprising given that the Egyptians even considered the head of their state to be a god. Thus, religion played a political and economic role, as well as a spiritual one, in the daily lives of the Egyptians. In ancient Egypt, as is so often the case in other places and at other times, a formal 'state' religious structure existed side by side with vernacular, more informal modes of worship practiced privately by individuals. These two systems were not mutually exclusive, but were complementary, and to some extent they fulfilled different cultural, social, and political functions.

State religion in Egypt can be defined as the celebration of the cult of the chief god of the pantheon, as well as of the king who was the main manifestation of a divinity on earth, and who acted as the physical link between the Egyptians and their gods. Egypt's state religion occupied itself with building the country's major temples, filling them with wealth, and providing them with priests to celebrate the cult of that temple's god as a key component of the maintenance of *maat*. The daily rituals carried out in these temples ensured the continuation of the cosmos and the maintenance of order both in the land of Egypt and in that of the gods. In addition to regular temple rituals that took place several times each day, special festivals for the god or the king were also celebrated. But temples were not just houses for the gods; they played an important economic role by employing people, collecting taxes, and redistributing wealth throughout Egypt.

Throughout the Old Kingdom, Egypt's 'chief' god was the sun god, Re. In the Middle Kingdom, when the 12th Dynasty assumed power, its kings raised their local god, Amun, to the rank of 'chief' god and fairly soon syncretised

Amun with the original head of the pantheon, Re, thereby creating the god Amun-Re. The quintessential creator god, Amun-Re remained the dominant deity throughout the rest of ancient Egyptian history.

As the head of the state and the priesthood, in addition to being a god himself, the king was in charge of maintaining Egypt's good relations with its divinities so that the land and its people would prosper. To achieve this goal, the king (and his priests) symbolically entered a type of contractual agreement with the gods in which they (and the people of Egypt) agreed to live a life filled with balance and rectitude (*maat*), to respect the gods, and to provide prayers and offerings to the gods. In return, the gods would care for Egypt, safeguard its boundaries, ensure the health of its people, and guarantee that its crops and livestock flourished. Such a relationship or contract is commonly found in other religious traditions and writings, including the Old Testament. The people of Egypt revered the chief god and their king, but they did not necessarily focus their private devotions on them. In confronting the challenges of everyday life, they might choose from amongst the myriad gods of the Egyptian pantheon, depending on whose help was needed (see box on gods). This can be considered analogous to asking for help from specific saints or the Virgin Mary in the Catholic or Orthodox churches. In some ways, the Egyptians viewed all the different divinities in their pantheon as different aspects with specific characteristics and functions of a single great force that ruled the universe.

Maat: The Foundation of Religious Belief and the Moral Code

The most important religious concept in ancient Egypt was that of *maat*. The foundation of the state, and indeed of the whole culture, rested upon this idea. *Maat* is difficult to define precisely, but it might be explained as living a life that promotes and supports what is perceived as the divine order of things. It has been translated variously as 'truth', 'order', 'rectitude', or 'balance/equilibrium', and is the opposite of *isfet*, or 'chaos'. The idea of *maat* was also personified as the goddess Maat, a daughter of Re, and depicted as a woman with a feather (the emblem of Maat) in her hair, or just by the feather of truth alone. Ideally, in order to live eternally after death, one's heart had to be equal in weight to *maat* when weighed in a balance, indicating that one had lived a good life. (Fig. 60.)

Figure 60. The king was often shown offering seated images of the goddess Maat to other deities (here, to the god Ptah at Karnak), implying that the king was responsible for maintaining maat in Egypt. Photo Salima Ikram.

The Pantheon

The Egyptian pantheon contained over eighty divinities. These rank from the more important gods who were established at the dawn of Egyptian history and were involved with the creation of the world to minor deities who played a crucial role in different aspects of Egyptian life and death. The Egyptian word for 'god' was *netjer*, which also had the meaning of 'power'. The hieroglyph for this word is surprisingly abstract: a tall pole wrapped with a linen cloth fluttering loose at the pole's top – in essence, a 'cult flag' of the kind that stood before temples.

The major gods controlled specific spheres, although some of these could overlap; many of these gods also were associated with particular geographic areas or natural phenomena. Thus Re, a sun god, was a creator god and ensured that the sun completed its cycle each day so that the world continued to exist, whereas the goddess Hathor presided over the bringing into being, or birth, not only of human beings but also some of the products of the earth, such as turquoise and copper. Some gods were manifestations of a local presiding spirit or feature, such as Meret-Seger, the goddess of the mountain that towered over the Valley of the Kings on the Nile's west bank at Thebes. Others, such as Maat, were the personification of a concept.

In addition to the major gods, each city had its own god (often these divinities were part of the larger pantheon too), who was more important in local worship than the major state deities were. In some cases, a small village or even a city neighbourhood might have its own demi-god, that is, a local person who had become deified and was regarded as being particularly effective in granting people's wishes. One such individual was Heqaib at Elephantine (see Chapter 4). This canonization of local people is still part of heterodox faith in many countries today, although generally frowned on by most religious bureaucracies. Furthermore, the Egyptians were open to accepting and absorbing divinities from different cultures: when foreigners settled in Egypt bringing their own gods with them, the Egyptians readily incorporated these deities into their own pantheon. Sometimes the foreign gods would syncretise with Egyptian ones, so that the Near Eastern Baal became associated with Seth, the Egyptian god of chaos and foreign lands. Otherwise, deities such as Astarte or Anat were simply added to the Egyptian pantheon. Clearly, in terms of religion, the Egyptians were inclusive rather than exclusive.

As a result, the Egyptian pantheon is very large, with festivals and traditions that link it to the peoples of Africa as well as the Mediterranean and Levant. Religious traditions from all the diverse areas of Egypt were incorporated into the fabric of the country's faith. This resulted in several varying, but equally acceptable, myths about creation and the world order, as well as in the presence of different but equally important divinities that shared attributes and were responsible for the same things.

By the New Kingdom, many of the major Egyptian gods had been organized into groups of three (triads, or trinities) made up of two adult deities and a juvenile god. (Fig. 61.) These groups are sometimes referred to as families, with a mother, a father, and a child, but this description does not always hold true. Members of the group sometimes were exchanged, based on local beliefs, or were grouped in threes to represent the idea of a plurality (see box showing major gods). Furthermore, there is often no text that describes a clear family relationship for the three individuals. Nevertheless, part of the strength of these deities came from their being grouped into a triad because

Figure 61. The Theban triad of Amun, Mut, and Khonsu were the primary focus of Karnak Temple. Photo Salima Ikram.

three was considered a magical number and because the triad included representations of both the male and the female force that made possible the mystical and actual act of creation. Triads were often of local importance and their members were worshipped together as well as separately. Some of these groupings are interesting because of the strong contrasts between the characters of the gods in them and the balance that they struck. Thus, in one triad, the male god Ptah, a creator, was paired with the female goddess Sekhmet, who was often seen as a destroyer, with the third member of this triad, Nefertum, also a creator god, regarded as their complementary partner or even as their son. However, not all gods fit into triads, and many were worshipped individually.

Most Egyptian gods were depicted both anthropomorphically and zoomorphically, as they were generally linked to animals in some way. This is probably because early Egyptian religion was inspired by the natural world and natural phenomena, including animals, were associated with the gods. To the Egyptians, animals seemed to be endowed with supernatural powers, which, together with the animals' 'otherness' from humans, suggested a link with the divine. The Egyptians associated specific animals with particular deities that either shared the animal's attributes and strengths or was thought to protect humans against whatever was threatening about that creature. For

Figure 62. Anubis, the god of embalming, was also a god of travel and was in charge of helping people to pass from this world to the next. Images of Anubis, such as this one now in the Hildesheim Museum, were a vital part of funerary equipment and were particularly common in tombs of the later periods of Egyptian history. Photo Nicholas Warner.

example, the goddess Selqet was simultaneously associated with scorpions and thought to be able to prevent or cure their stings.

The Egyptians were keen observers of nature and carefully selected the divine properties they identified with specific creatures. Thus, the sun god Re is often represented as a lion, the king of the beasts and a creature that basks in the sun. Moreover, the lion's mane, which radiates out from its face, resembles a sun-disk. Thoth, the god of wisdom and writing, is most commonly depicted as an ibis or as an ibis-headed man. The beaks of ibises are long and thin, resembling pens, and Egyptians often saw the birds fossicking in the dirt, searching for worms, or, as the Egyptians might have shaped the metaphor, seeking knowledge. Some gods are represented not by just one animal, but by an amalgam of several, creating a 'super' animal. The 'hawk' that represents the god Horus is actually a super-raptor, a combination of the largest, fastest, strongest, and most beautifully marked of these birds. The god Anubis is actually a combination of a dog, a jackal, a fox, a wolf, and a hyaena and is thus a super-canid.[1] (Fig. 62.) All of these creatures could

*Figure 63. Egyptians believed that sacred animals contained part of the spirit of a god.
While the animals lived they were prayed to and cared for, and after their deaths they
were mummified and buried with honour. This ram mummy, sacred to Khnum, comes from
Elephantine, and is now in the Cairo Museum. Photo Anna-Marie Kellen.*

be found in the desert, particularly where the dead were buried. Therefore, Anubis, as god of mummification and defender of the dead, was thought to give protection against any harm that his creatures might wreak upon a dead body. Sometimes the exact combination of animals used in the creation of a composite creature is less clear: we still cannot identify which animals the Egyptians associated with the god Seth, for example. Scholars have suggested a combination of a donkey, an aardvark, and a fox, all creatures of the desert of which Seth was the master, or the oxyrhyncus fish that ate the phallus of Osiris (see 'The Myth of Osiris' section). It is worth noting that the Egyptian pantheon does not include animals such as the horse or the chicken that were introduced into Egypt later and thus did not play a part in Egypt's origins or in the development of its culture.

From the Late Period until the end of polytheistic Pharaonic civilisation, the Egyptians experienced an upsurge of belief in the intimate relationship between animals and gods. Many temples with resident sacred animals were established, and those that already existed enjoyed a renaissance. According to Egyptian belief, a sacred animal was an animal that was an avatar of a particular god (e.g., ibis for Thoth, cat for Bastet, canid for Anubis), and was differentiated from others of its species by special markings known only to the god's priests. Part of the spirit of the god entered the animal for the duration of its life, and the animal became a manifestation of that god on earth. Sacred animals had oracular and healing powers; they were kept in special pens and thus were more accessible to the populace than were the statues of gods held in conventional temples. Upon their deaths sacred animals were mummified and buried in lavish tombs as befitted a god. The Egyptians believed that the animal's divine spirit then migrated to another animal. One such creature was the Apis bull, the avatar of Ptah. A human analogy would be the Dalai Lama of Tibet, whose spirit is reborn into a succession of new bodies. (Fig. 63.)

Temples

The imposing stone temples that the Egyptians built throughout the Nile Valley were often called *hwt-netjer*, literally, 'houses of the gods'. These monuments were generally constructed of stone so that they could last for eternity, as the gods existed forever. Many temples that we see today were not the result of a single ruler's building program, but were instead a combination of buildings and parts of buildings added by successive rulers, each dedicated to the glory of a particular divinity. For instance, the great temple of Amun at Karnak that we visit today is the result of over two thousand years of building. The earliest Egyptian temples were not stone built, but were made of mud brick or reeds or both; later they were rebuilt or enlarged using stone. Throughout Egyptian history, smaller chapels that were not state supported continued to be constructed from these perishable but easily renewable materials.

A Selection of Gods

Amun, Amun-Re: initially a god of the Theban region who syncretised with Re when Amun became the state god of the 12th Dynasty. His name means 'the Hidden One', and he represents the potential of growth and fecundity. Coupled with the god Re, he personalises the life force and creation. His chief temple was at Karnak.

Anubis: the god of embalming who transports the dead to the Judgement Hall of Osiris. Son of Nephthys. He is shown as a man with a canine head.

Anuket: daughter of Satet and Khnum, and goddess of the cataracts in the Aswan region. She is also viewed as a daughter of Re.

Atum: a major creator god, based at Heliopolis, with chthonic and underworld connections. He is shown either as a man wearing the crown of Upper and Lower Egypt or as a serpent.

Bastet: shown often as a cat and associated with love, beauty, music, and self-indulgence.

Hapy: a god symbolising the Nile's inundation. He is called 'the Lord of the Fishes and Birds', and is depicted as a man with pendulous breasts and a pronounced belly and wearing a long wig.

Hathor: one of Egypt's most important goddesses. She was viewed as sponsor and spouse of the king and, as such, the wife of Horus, as well as the god's nurse. Her name means 'house of Horus'. Additionally, she is a mother goddess and related to female sexuality. She is also the goddess of foreign lands and of the goods that come from these lands. In some myths Hathor is described as the daughter of Re. She is shown as a cow or as a woman with a cow's head.

Horus: son of Osiris and Isis and the personification of the living king. His avatar is a raptor.

Isis: the sister-wife of Osiris and the mother of Horus. She was responsible for Osiris's resurrection, and she sustains and protects the deceased, as well as being the quintessential mother goddess. One of her epithets is Isis, Great of Magic. She is depicted as a woman with a throne as her crown.

Khepri: a manifestation of a creator god and the rising sun, shown as a scarab beetle. Scarab beetles push dung balls through the sand; the Egyptians associated these dung balls with the sun and mistakenly believed that baby beetles spontaneously burst forth from them, thus making the beetle a quintessential symbol of solar creation.

Khnum: the god of the First Cataract who oversees the inundation, and a creator god, forming men and gods and their souls, or *ka*, on his potter's wheel. He is shown as a man with a ram's head; he and his triad are based at Elephantine.

Khonsu: a moon god who is often shown as the son of Amun and Mut. He helps determine people's life span. He is depicted as a young man with the side-lock of youth, crowned by a crescent moon.

Min: one of Egypt's first deities. He is the chief god of male virility and is shown as an ithyphallic mummiform man with a crown of two feathers. He was worshipped primarily at Koptos and also at Karnak, where he was joined with Amun.

Mut: frequently the consort of Amun, Mut is shown either as a woman wearing a vulture headdress or as a woman with a lioness's head. She is a goddess of motherhood.

Nefertum: sometimes viewed as the offspring of Ptah and Sekhmet, he is thought to be a birth-god is associated with the blue lotus/lily (*Nymphaea cerulea*). Depicted as emerging from a lotus/lily or as a man with those flowers as his headdress, he is also the god of perfumes.

Neith: one of the earliest and most powerful of Egypt's goddesses. Her primary function is that of a warrior goddess, although she is also known as a creator goddess. Her main cult center was Sais, and she is generally shown in human form.

Nephthys: both sister and wife of Seth, and sister of Osiris and Isis. She is one of Osiris's chief mourners and, consequently, a goddess who protects the dead. She is shown as a woman with a temple sign surmounted by a basket on her head.

Nut: the sky goddess and important in funerary religion.

Osiris: the first mummy and mythical first king of Egypt who, upon his death, became god-king of the Underworld. His consort is Isis, and his son is Horus.

Ptah: a creator god and the great god of Memphis. He is the god of craftsmen and a 'sculptor of the earth'. He is shown as a man, often mummiform, wearing a blue cap and holding a staff.

Re: the sun god and Egypt's most important deity; he is associated with creation and the continuation of the world. He is shown as a raptor or as a man with a raptor's head.

Satet: the guardian of Egypt's southern border, and spouse of Khnum. She is shown as a woman wearing the White Crown flanked by antelope horns.

Sekhmet: goddess of plagues and destruction but also protector of women. Often regarded as the consort of Ptah. She is shown as a woman with a lioness's head.

Seth: brother of Osiris, and ruler of the deserts and storms. His totemic animal is a strange mixture of beasts, including dogs, donkeys, aardvarks, and perhaps even a fish.

Sobek: god of fertility and water, shown as a crocodile or a crocodile-headed man. He was particularly revered in the Fayyum and at Kom Ombo.

Thoth: a lunar god who is associated with literacy and learning. His animals are the baboon and the ibis.

There were two major types of temples built in Egypt: cult temples, where the cult of a god (or of a group of gods) was celebrated, and funerary, or memorial, temples, which were structures dedicated to the cult of the king as a god and as a liaison between Egypt's people and the gods. Each temple type had a slightly different function.

Cult temples tended to be located on the east bank of the Nile, where the majority of the population was settled and where the sun, the herald of life, rose. The Egyptians may have chosen the sites for these temples based on mythic events that they believed had taken place at a particular location (e.g., the birth or burial place of a god, or the location of a battle between divinities) or on the topography of the site, such as the shape of a mountain or the presence of a water-course that held religious symbolism for them. Cult temples were dedicated to a primary deity, and if that god was part of a triad, the other two divinities would also be worshipped there. Additionally, small chapels to other gods, including the deified king, would often be erected within the temple precincts, thus extending the group that was worshipped at the site. Cult temples played a pivotal religious, cultural, political, and economic role in the life of the settlements connected to them and drew worshippers from surrounding rural areas. The temples varied in size and complexity depending on the size of the community they served, but every settlement contained some sort of chapel or temple.

Funerary, or memorial, temples were generally constructed on the west bank of the Nile, where the sun set, or died. Every such temple was associated with the burial place of a particular pharaoh. During the Old and Middle Kingdoms these temples were physically connected to the kings' pyramids, but in the New Kingdom and in later periods they were sited at the desert margins, separate from the royal burial place. These temples celebrated the cult of the dead king who had achieved god-head through dying, as well as the cult of the eternal royal *ka*, or spirit. This spirit incorporated the spirits of all the dead pharaohs and was also identified with Horus, the divine ruler of this world, and his father Osiris, the divine ruler of the Otherworld. In addition to the worship of the dead king in all his manifestations, these temples also involved the cults of other deities. In the Old Kingdom, the focus was on Re as the chief state god, together with other selected divinities who were particularly relevant to divine kingship; by the New Kingdom, Amun-Re was the focus, particularly in conjunction with Mut and Khonsu, but also in the company of other deities. These funerary temples, like their counterpart cult temples, played an important part in the religious and economic life of the area, but just as critically, they were involved directly in the maintenance of the surrounding cemeteries.

Temple Architecture

The architecture of temples evolved over time and was in part dictated by the god(s) that a temple served; for example, sun temples were dominated by courtyards open to the light. The majority of cult temples still standing date from the New Kingdom and later; the extant funerary/memorial temples date from the Old Kingdom on and display much greater architectural variation. A commonality of all temples, however, was that the Egyptians believed temples to be not only the mansions of the gods but also, within their walls, a re-creation of the cosmos: the sacred space within the temple precinct evoked the sacred landscape at the dawn of creation. These ideas are particularly apparent in the architecture of cult temples beginning in the New Kingdom and in the architecture of memorial/funerary temples constructed from the end of the 18th Dynasty until the end of the New Kingdom.

Most temples were oriented east–west, in line with the solar cycle. Sometimes this orientation was off, however, because the Egyptians used the Nile as their north–south indicator instead of taking their direction from true north. Thus, where the river bends, the orientation of local temples is skewed to relate to an axis that depends on the river's course. The iconography used within the temple provides clues as to its intended orientation: what was, or was meant to be, the north shows papyrus plants and images of Wadjet, whereas the lily and Nekhbet indicate the south.

The Architecture of Cult Temples

The earliest Egyptian cult temples were constructed of perishable materials that were easily found in each locality. In Lower Egypt the temples consisted of large rooms with arched roofs made entirely of reeds and mud plaster. In Upper Egypt temples were probably constructed of mud brick, as well as of reeds and mud plaster, perhaps with the addition of stone slabs as thresholds and lintels. Initially, all temples were simply one- or two-room buildings, with fetishes of the god on standards outside the entrance. Images of the god, made of ivory, wood, or stone, would presumably have been kept within the temple proper, and had restricted access. Later, images of gods might be made of either gold or silver and other precious materials. Some cult temples, such as that of Min of Koptos, had several monumental stone statues of the god in the open. For these early temples, the sacred area would

Creation Myths

The ancient Egyptians had several myths dealing with the creation of the cosmos and all that it contained. Probably, many of these myths had local origins, but with the unification of the country, they were gathered together and regarded as equally believable, or, depending on a particular situation, one may have been favoured above the others for a time. From the evidence that remains, it does not seem that the Egyptians had difficulty holding onto fairly contradictory concurrent beliefs.

The Heliopolitan Cosmogony is one of the earliest creation myths and originated at the site of Iwnw (Heliopolis in Greek; biblical On), a major solar centre. In this myth, a group of nine gods (the Ennead) created the world. First, the god Atum ('the complete one', 'the all') masturbated (in some stories, he spat) and from his ejaculation created a pair of gods, the male Shu ('air') and his female counterpart Tefnut ('moisture'). They gave birth to Geb ('earth') and Nut ('sky'). (The Egyptians are almost unique in having a male earth god and a female sky divinity.) In turn, Geb and Nut produced two sons, Osiris and Seth, and two daughters, Isis and Nephthys, who were also their brothers' consorts. Clearly, incest was not taboo for gods in Egyptian religion; it was also acceptable for kings, who were regarded as gods. Incest was a taboo for everyone else, however. The tale of Osiris, Isis, Seth, and Nephthys leads into the Osiris myth cycle. (Fig. 64.)

An equally important myth, the Hermopolitan Cosmogony, originated in the Middle Egyptian city of Khemnw (the Greek Hermopolis), which was sacred to the god Thoth. In this tale, a group of eight gods, an Ogdoad, consisting of four couples of male and female divinities, personified the elements of chaos, or pre-creation. These were 'hiddenness' or 'hidden potential', personified by Amun and Amunet; 'formlessness', represented by Huh and Hauhet; 'darkness', embodied by Kuk and Kauket; and the primeval waters, incarnated in Nun and Naunet. These deities created an egg that contained the god responsible for creating the other gods, the land, animals, plants, and humans. Thoth was probably this god originally, which was particularly appropriate since an ibis is hatched from an egg. However, Atum was inserted in this role in some versions of the myth.

The Memphite Theology is another significant creation myth. This was probably an old tale, but the most complete version known to us was recorded on the Shabaka Stone (c. 710 BC, Dynasty 25), named after the king who had the myth inscribed on this piece of basalt; another version, the Bremner-Rhind Papyrus (4th century BC), was written on papyrus. In this myth, Ptah created the world by conceiving it in his heart (equivalent to our mind) and then giving it life by articulating or naming each element of the world and its denizens. The idea of thinking of something (*Hu*) and then causing it to exist through the act of speech (*Sia*) is close to the later biblical story of God's creating the world through speaking it; this story also has parallels in Australian aboriginal myths and in other concepts of speaking

have been delineated by a reed fence or a wall of some sort, the entrance to which was marked by a large gateway. With increased government centralization and economic wealth, these simple prototypes gave way to building complexes that, to a large extent, imitated the original perishable materials but used a more lasting medium: stone.

No clearly identified complete cult temples have been found that date from the Old Kingdom. The closest are the 5th Dynasty sun temples at Abu Sir, which were dedicated not just to the cult of the sun but also to the cult

Figure 64. The deities Nut, Geb, and Shu described the physical world of the Egyptians and were frequently depicted in funerary art and referred to in religious texts. Here, Nut, the goddess of the sky, stretches over her husband Geb, god of the earth. They are separated by Shu, the air. Drawing Keli Alberts and Nicholas Warner.

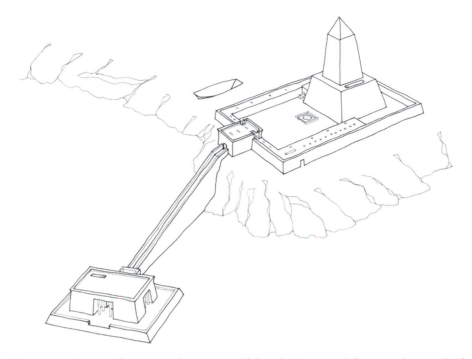

Figure 65. Sun temples were a phenomenon of the 5th Dynasty. These temples were laid out similarly to royal funerary complexes, but instead of the king's burial, the focal point was a squat obelisk atop a pedestal. A Valley temple was connected to the main temple via a causeway. The main temple enclosure consisted of the obelisk, an altar before it, storerooms and smaller rooms on the east, the decorated Room of the Seasons to the west, and a boat pit outside the enclosure, generally on the west. Presumably, boat pits alluded to the voyage of the sun god in the solar barque that he used to cross the heavens. Drawing Nicholas Warner.

of the king. (Fig. 65.) These monuments provided a prototype for temples dedicated to sun gods, and are seen throughout Egyptian history. A wall defines the sacred space, and the major area of worship is open to the sun and to the sky. The main temple furniture consists of a large altar set before a squat obelisk or a pyramidion, where most offerings were given and prayers were recited. Additionally, the Abu Sir temples include small roofed and decorated chambers, but such rooms are not always found in other temples dedicated to solar deities.

Complete Middle Kingdom cult temples are also rare, with the best examples being those at Qasr el-Sagha (unfinished) and Medinet Maadi in the Fayyum, the Horus temple at Thoth Hill in Western Thebes, the temple of Montu at Tod, and portions of the Serabit el-Khadem in the Sinai. (Fig. 66.)

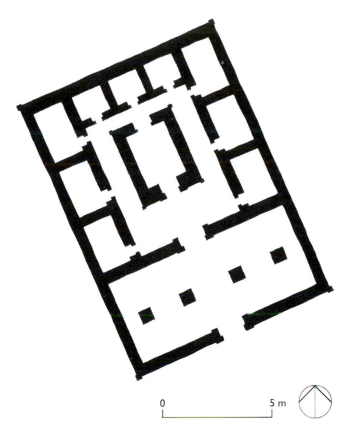

0   5 m

Figure 66. This plan of the Middle Kingdom temple at Tod shows the typical tripartite sacred area preceded by an antechamber, or pronaos. Drawing Nicholas Warner.

The architecture of these temples varies somewhat. The temples of the Fayyum and Thoth Hill perhaps demonstrate the 'norm' for the period. In this architectural version, the main temple building is either one large narrow room or a columned portico that constitutes the antechamber/portico leading to smaller rooms (seven at Qasr el-Sagha and three at both Thoth Hill and Medinet Maadi), with each one of these rooms being dedicated to a separate god. An enclosure wall delineates the sacred precincts, and a set of gates or pylons marks the temple's entrance.

The temple at Tod is a more complicated example and is a precursor of the architectural traditions of the New Kingdom. This temple has an open courtyard leading to a pillared antechamber that opens into a free-standing chamber flanked by three rooms, one on either side, and one at the back. The emphasis here is on symmetry and on situating the image of the god in a separate enclosed space. At Tod, as at most extant Middle Kingdom

Figure 67. Luxor Temple's entrance is marked by its commanding pylons, which are fronted by seated statues of Ramesses II and by obelisks. Photo George Gaddis, private collection.

temples, the decorative programme is not complete, so one must look to New Kingdom temples for a sense of what might have been found on the walls of these earlier examples.

New Kingdom temples provide us with the most complete view of Egyptian temple architecture and the beliefs that formed it. The emphasis on symmetry and balance is seen in the typical ground plan, which incorporates a straight line of access from front to back. The land enclosed by the temple was thought to be a microcosm of the moment of the creation of the world, with the different architectural features reflecting elements of the mythic environment. The temple enclosure wall became an increasingly important feature, for it not only marked the limits of divine space, but it also, in its undulations, evoked the primeval ocean, Nun, from which all life sprang (see box on creation myths). Entrances through the enclosure wall were identified by large gateways called pylons. The form of the pylon resembled the hieroglyph for horizon, *akhet*, indicating where the sun rises and sets, and where each day begins and ends. The pylons were massive trapezoidal structures that contained stairs and a few internal chambers that also gave access to exterior spaces. Here heralds or priests could summon the townspeople and make announcements or lead prayers and rituals. When the king was present he perhaps appeared before the people here. The outward-facing surfaces of the pylons incorporated slots that, according to ancient images of temples, held poles with pennants flying from them, evocative of the hieroglyph *netjer*, or 'god'. Obelisks fronted the pylons; these reified concrete images of the sun's rays and symbols of the power of the sun god, capped with gold or electrum, stood together with colossal statues of the king. Sometimes, a series of small sphinxes that acted as markers and guardians of the temple lined the central axis leading to the pylon. (Fig. 67.)

The internal spaces of the temple were arranged hierarchically, from larger areas to smaller ones, and moving from open, light spaces to darker ones. As one progressed through the temple to the most sacred space, the ground became higher and the ceiling level dropped, so that the naos, or holy of holies, was built at the highest point in the temple grounds, on the equivalent of the primeval mound of creation, and was also the smallest, darkest, and most secret of the chambers. (Fig. 68.)

The standard progression of spaces behind the pylon began with an open courtyard that could be used for sun worship. This space led to another courtyard that was surrounded by columns (a peristyle courtyard) giving way, in turn, to a hall with an equal number of pillars on either side of a broad central passage, similar to a nave. This was known as a hypostyle hall. Column capitals in this hall took the form of lotuses and papyri, the tutelary plants of Upper and Lower Egypt, arranged to the north and south of the axis. Their dense arrangement evoked the scenery of the marshes that emerged from the primeval ocean, Nun, and encircled the primeval hill, the hill of creation. The grandest of all hypostyle halls, in Karnak Temple, was constructed so that the columns flanking the central axis were higher than the others, thus giving a space for clerestory lighting. The remaining spaces were lit through holes in ceiling slabs that permitted shafts of light to illuminate the temple's dim interior. Sometimes Egyptian architects used light to help them 'activate' a temple. Shafts of light, dramatically visible in dim interiors, acted as light-columns, and windows were strategically placed so that the light that shone through them illuminated certain images and texts at specific times, thereby making those objects potent and effective. Small holes have been found at the edges of doorways, indicating that these areas were further illuminated by the addition of plates made of beaten gold or copper that reflected the light as people carrying lamps passed through the opening. (Fig. 69.)

After a temple's hypostyle hall one entered the surround for the holy of holies, the naos or sanctuary where the image of the god was kept on a

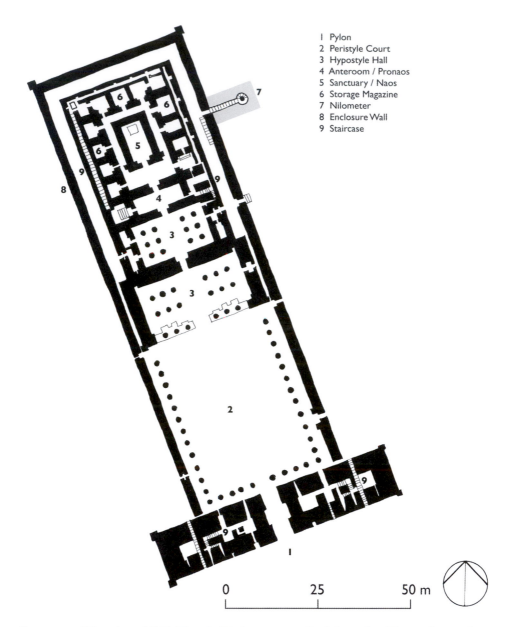

1 Pylon
2 Peristyle Court
3 Hypostyle Hall
4 Anteroom / Pronaos
5 Sanctuary / Naos
6 Storage Magazine
7 Nilometer
8 Enclosure Wall
9 Staircase

0   25   50 m

Figure 68. This plan of Edfu Temple (Ptolemaic period), dedicated to Horus, shows what an ideal temple might look like: entrance pylons, an open courtyard, a hypostyle hall, a pronaos or ante-room, the naos, places to store ritual equipment, areas for robing, ways to access the roof for special rituals, and a Nilometer – all enclosed by a wall. One feature not seen here is a sacred lake. Drawing Nicholas Warner.

Figure 69. The hypostyle hall at Karnak Temple, which Seti I started building and his son, Ramesses II, completed. This many-columned hall with clerestory lighting is a masterpiece of Egyptian architecture and central to Karnak Temple (19th Dynasty). Photo George Gaddis, private collection.

plinth, often fronted by an altar. This was the highest and darkest part of the building and represented the primeval hill where the first god lived. The god of the temple assumed the identity of the first god by being placed in the naos, generally a free-standing chamber set within the larger structure, with an ambulatory or walkway surrounding it. This ambulatory led to rooms at the sides and back of the naos that were used to store temple furniture and offerings, and sometimes for libraries. Some temples contained crypts beneath their floors for additional storage and to protect the most important and valuable temple furnishings; some of these spaces might also have served a ritual purpose. Additionally, some temples, particularly those dating to the Late and Graeco-Roman periods, had hollow spaces in their walls where priests could move unseen from room to room and perhaps even act as the god's voice delivering oracles. Often, stairways led from the precinct of the naos to the roof, where there might be more chapels, but which was also the site for rituals associated with the New Year, as well as for any other rites that involved the heavens. Beyond the naos, additional courtyards and rooms could be and often were constructed. Such chambers, however, were only of secondary importance.

Frequently the temple enclosure included a sacred lake within its boundaries that was a physical manifestation of Nun and consisted of a small stone-lined lake or pond that could be entered by steps. Its water could be used for ritual purification, and the god's barque, which held his wooden naos containing his statue, could be taken to sail upon it. Many temples also contained a Nilometer, which was connected to the river by steps or a tunnel. This device permitted the temple's priests to measure the rise in the Nile's level, and it was used mainly to monitor the river's height at inundation, so that the flood level could be predicted. The king and the temple used this information and its likely consequences for annual crop yields in estimating the taxes that they would levy (see Chapter 7).

In temples of the Graeco-Roman period, small buildings, called *mammisi* or birth-houses, started to be erected within the enclosure wall and near the entrance to the main temple. These small temples illustrated the divine birth of a god. They were often dedicated to the youthful form of Horus (Harpocrates, or Horus the Younger), and thus to the royal cult as a manifestation of Horus on earth. Presumably, these buildings were a focus for worship not only for the young god pictured on its walls but also for the cult of the king (Horus on earth), and possibly also for people concerned with their own fertility or that of the land and livestock.

Within a temple enclosure wall was not just the temple proper (and later the *mammisi*); it also encompassed all of the support services that allowed the temple to function effectively. These included houses for the temple's priests; a temple garden where medicinal and ritual plants and herbs, as well as basic food crops, could be grown; poultry yards; and pens for animals to be used sacrificially or to feed temple personnel. Workshops for temple butchers, bakers, brewers, vintners, carpenters, metalworkers, weavers, and potters were also integral elements of a temple enclosure but were located slightly apart from the temple proper. Secondary buildings such as the *per-ankh*, or 'House of Life', a scholarly institution where scientists studied and worked and that also served as a library and scriptorium; temple administration offices and archives; scribal and priestly schools; and healing institutions were also found on the temple grounds, as were vast granaries and storerooms that contained the temple's wealth. Thus, temple enclosures can be taken as a microcosm of the larger settlements found throughout the country. (Fig. 70.)

The Decoration of Cult Temples

The basic decorative scheme for cult temples was fairly straightforward. The chief function of temple decoration was to reproduce, in perpetuity, an ideal balanced relationship between the king and the gods that ensured the survival of *maat* and Egypt. Exterior walls were carved with images of the king's exploits, especially of his deeds associated with warfare. The pylons featured stock images of the king smiting the enemies of Egypt; it did not matter if a particular king had ever fought against any of these peoples, he just had to be represented doing so. (Fig. 71.) These images acted as an apotropaic device that protected the temple from evil and at the same time perpetuated the role of divine kingship as it related to the conquest of chaos, manifested by Egypt's enemies. In addition, temple doorways were marked with winged sun-disks, images of strength and protection. Interior walls tended to bear scenes of the king's making different offerings to the main gods of the temple, as well as to other appropriate divinities; these images illustrated another aspect of his royal role – as an intermediary with and a pacifier of the gods. In return, the gods were shown rewarding the king with a long and stable reign, indicating that they would ensure the well-being of Egypt and its inhabitants. (Fig. 72.) The majority of the texts carved on temple walls offered formulae and phrases of praise, and most ceilings were decorated with five-pointed stars, evoking the sky goddess, Nut, and placing the temple within a divine landscape.

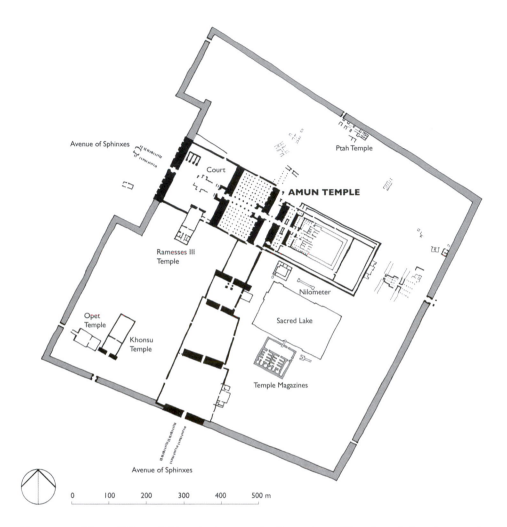

Figure 70. *Plan of Karnak Temple showing the Great Amun Temple and the other temples that formed part of this great religious complex. Drawing Nicholas Warner.*

Additions to and variations in the basic schema of decoration existed, and made each temple unique. (Fig. 73.) In some instances, a particular religious tale was illustrated on the temple wall, together with its text. One example can be seen at Edfu Temple and features the myth 'The Contendings of Horus and Seth', in which the two gods battle for dominion over Egypt. At Luxor Temple, a frontal view of the temple itself is shown, as are the procession and rituals associated with that temple's major cultic event, the Opet Festival. Esna Temple is adorned with special cryptographic hymns to the god Khnum that are written almost entirely

Figure 71. On this pylon at the temple at Medinet Habu, Ramesses III is smiting his enemies while Amun looks on and offers victory. This motif first appears in the Narmer Palette (Dynasty 0/1; Fig. 125) and becomes a standard iconographic symbol of the king's strength & protection of Egypt. Photo Salima Ikram.

using different hieroglyphs for 'ram', and Kom Ombo Temple shows a set of medical tools.

The Architecture of Funerary/Memorial Temples

Far more examples survive of funerary temples than of cult temples. Those from the Old and Middle Kingdom are associated with pyramids, and vary considerably in form prior to the 5th Dynasty. In the Archaic period funerary (also called mortuary) temples were actually separated from the burial place and were located near the cultivation. In the pyramids of the 3rd Dynasty they took a variety of forms and were often located on the pyramid's north side, aligned with the North Star; at the end of the dynasty, however, the focus shifted to the east and the sun. From the early 4th Dynasty onward, each king's pyramid had two temples attached to it: a Valley temple and a funerary/mortuary/memorial temple. Both were located on the east side of the pyramid so that they could face the rising sun, symbol of the promise of solar resurrection that emphasized

Figure 72. King Thutmose III offering nw *pots filled with wine to the god Horus who in turn promises many* heb-sed *festivals to the king at the 18th-Dynasty Anubis Chapel in the mortuary temple of Hatshepsut at Deir el-Bahari. Photo Salima Ikram.*

the king's identification with a sun god. The Valley temple was closer to the Nile Valley: it received the body of the deceased king, and its priests were probably involved in the king's mummification, as well as in funerary rituals. This building was connected via a causeway, a long covered corridor, to the funerary temple, and it acted almost as an antechamber to the main upper temple. The larger, Funerary, Temple, also called a Mortuary or Memorial temple, was constructed adjoining the east face of the pyramid. Until the 5th Dynasty there was little standardisation in temple plans, although often both Valley and Funerary temples shared certain elements, such as an open court for solar worship, chambers for images of the king and the gods, and storage rooms.

The 5th Dynasty saw a certain amount of standardisation in both types of temples. Valley temples featured quays to permit boats to dock and were fronted by columned porticoes that led to a T-shaped hall, often with a side room to the south. As before, a causeway connected the Valley temple to the Mortuary temple. The latter was accessed through a narrow entrance hall that led to an open, colonnaded court. This court opened into a transverse corridor that led to a series of smaller rooms, including small chambers that

Figure 73. In some instances, special divinities have columns that evoke them, such as the Hathor-headed columns found in temples and shrines to Hathor, including this example at Dendera. Photo Antonio Beato, private collection.

were meant to display statues of the king and the gods, as well as an offering hall. Magazines (storage rooms) were located on the side of the building. This basic template persisted to the end of the Old Kingdom. (Fig. 74.)

The Middle Kingdom saw great variations in the design of temples attached to royal burials. (Fig. 75 a and b.) Temples ranged from simple building complexes, such as had been common previously, to elaborate maze-like constructions, such as that favoured by Amenemhat III that earned it the sobriquet 'The Labyrinth' in Late Antiquity. Some of these variants persisted into the early part of the New Kingdom, although they maintained the

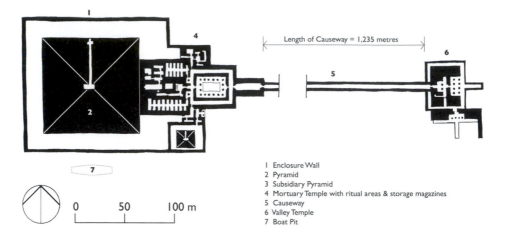

Length of Causeway = 1,235 metres

1. Enclosure Wall
2. Pyramid
3. Subsidiary Pyramid
4. Mortuary Temple with ritual areas & storage magazines
5. Causeway
6. Valley Temple
7. Boat Pit

Figure 74. Pyramid complexes of the 5th Dynasty, such as this one belonging to Sahure, showed a degree of standardisation not seen in earlier times, although the main elements of a pyramid complex had been established by the 4th Dynasty. This complex does not actually have a boat pit (7), but these pits have been found with many other royal burials of the Old Kingdom. Some other complexes have additional satellite pyramids belonging to queens and princesses. Drawing Nicholas Warner.

essential elements established in the Old Kingdom. (Fig. 76.) By the middle of the 18th Dynasty, however, funerary temples had adopted the same basic plan as that for cult temples. (Fig. 77.)

The Decoration of Funerary/Memorial Temples

The earliest funerary temples until those of the 3rd Dynasty were built mainly of mud brick, and virtually nothing is known of their decoration. Those of the 4th Dynasty were fairly plain, their chief enhancement provided through the different colours of the stone used in their construction. The stones included

Figure 75. Mentuhotep II's mortuary complex at Deir el-Bahari was unusual in that it combined the funerary temple with the tomb. The building was nestled in the Theban hills, fronted by trees. A small subterranean chamber, reached by a passage (the Bab el-Hosan), was located at the front edge of the enclosure and perhaps acted as a cenotaph, as it contained an empty sarcophagus and a statue of the king. Archaeologists are not sure whether the main structure was crowned by a mastaba (top) or by a pyramid (bottom); both reconstructions are shown here. Drawings Nicholas Warner.

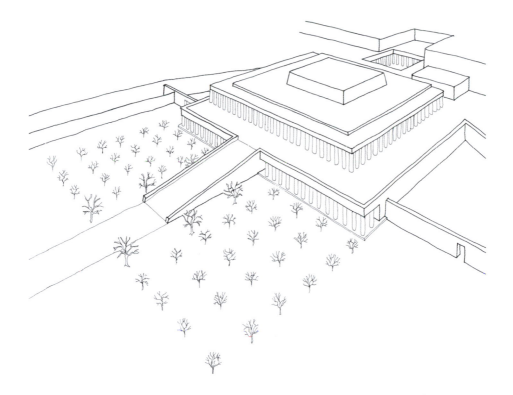

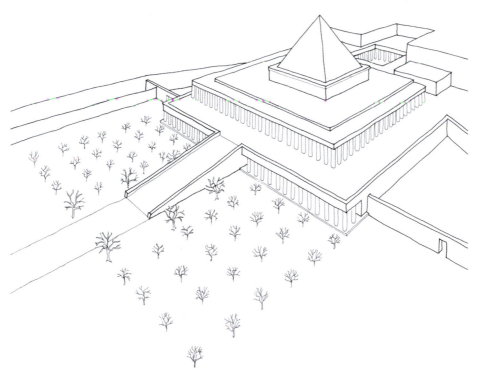

Maintaining Egypt: Religion

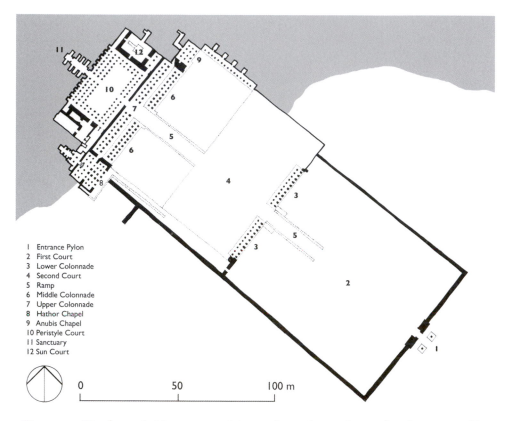

1 Entrance Pylon
2 First Court
3 Lower Colonnade
4 Second Court
5 Ramp
6 Middle Colonnade
7 Upper Colonnade
8 Hathor Chapel
9 Anubis Chapel
10 Peristyle Court
11 Sanctuary
12 Sun Court

0   50   100 m

Figure 76. Hatshepsut's Mortuary, or Memorial, temple was designed and constructed by Senenmut, her master of works and a favoured courtier. Called Djeser-Djeseru (Holy of Holies) in Egyptian, it is an unusual building consisting of open courtyards and ascending podia enhanced by colonnades and is set into the natural bay of the cliffs of western Thebes. It contains not only areas for the worship of Hatshepsut and members of the royal family but also sanctuaries dedicated to different gods, with the most important reserved for Amun, Re, Horus, and Anubis. Hatshepsut's kingly tomb, which is accessed from the Valley of the Kings, is almost beneath her temple at Deir el-Bahari. Drawing by Nicholas Warner.

red granite, which symbolised solar energy and blood; white calcite, which indicated light and purity; and black basalt, which represented the black soil of Egypt. The king's name was inscribed in several places, particularly on the causeway. (Fig. 78.)

From the 5th Dynasty onward, this form of simple decoration, which was inherent in the materials used, changed, and Egyptians began to carve the interiors of Valley and mortuary temples with scenes associated with royal rebirth and the maintenance of *maat* and divine kingship. These images

Figure 77. The enclosure wall of the Temple of Millions of Years of Ramesses III at Medinet Habu encompasses not only the temple but also subsequent edifices, both sacred and secular. The temple is a Memorial temple, and although it contains Osirid columns most of its other architectural features are identical to those of cult temples. Photo Marjorie Fisher.

Figure 78. The design of Hatshepsut's Funerary temple (on the right) was partially inspired by the earlier temple of Mentuhotep II (left). Hatshepsut's temple fits elegantly into the landscape. This spot was important as it was probably associated with a shrine of Hathor, a goddess of kingship, and was also roughly aligned with Karnak Temple to the east. Photo Aidan Dodson.

Figure 79. When being invoked in a deceased or divine state, the king (Ramesses III at Karnak, in this instance) was often shown on pillars as Osiris. Photo Salima Ikram.

included the king's making offerings to different gods, being suckled by goddesses, maintaining *maat* in the guise of a sphinx trampling Egypt's enemies, hunting wild creatures that represented *isfet* (chaos), and slaying a white hippopotamus (also a symbol of chaos). The causeways were decorated with scenes showing phases in the construction of the royal tomb, as well as with scenes from the daily life of the ancient Egyptians. By the New Kingdom, these temples also included scenes depicting specific events from the king's rule, including expeditions to foreign countries, successful hunts, and victories in battle. (Fig. 79.)

Temple Rituals and Prayers

The temple was the centre for cultic activity in Egypt. Here the daily cult and special festivals associated with the temple's god were celebrated, helping to create *maat* on a daily basis and thus ensuring the country's continued safe existence. The recitation of prayers and enactment of appropriate rituals activated the cosmic power of the temple and its god, and preserved *maat* in this world and in that of the gods. Although we do not know all the details of the daily temple ritual, we do have some idea of what occurred based on certain papyrus documents and on the scenes and texts engraved on temple walls.

A temple's god was treated as a living being and had to be awakened, have incense burned before the statue to 'open' its nostrils, and be bathed, clothed, fed, and worshipped three times a day, at sunrise, noon, and sunset. Ideally, the king officiated on these occasions in every Egyptian temple. In practice this was not feasible, and high priests replaced the king in all temples, save for the one in which he was physically present.

While reciting appropriate prayers, the high priest would approach the naos and unseal the door. Incense would be burned because gods breathed only sacred, censed air. The priest would then open a smaller naos that held the god's image. This naos was also censed, prayers were recited, and hymns were sung. Then the statue would be purified with water and natron (a cleansing agent associated with purification and divinity), anointed with sweet-smelling oils and perfumes, and dressed in fine new linen. Throughout the process, the high priest and his attendants rendered suitable prayers, hymns, and ritual gestures. Once the god was dressed, offerings of foodstuffs such as wine, milk, beer, oil, meat, and bread would be made, as well as other offerings of garlands, bouquets, incense, and linen, and more prayers recited, before the priests returned the statue to the naos, which they resealed. Then the priests would exit the chamber, brushing away their footsteps and sealing the door behind them. In return, the god was expected to continue to bless Egypt and to help the pharaoh to control nature and to keep Egypt's enemies at bay.

Once the offerings had been consecrated to the deity and then magically accepted or consumed by the god, they were removed and probably reverted to the priests. Presumably, the priests lived off these offerings once they had been consecrated to the god. Any surfeit from sacrifices was sold off, as is attested to by documents, such as Papyrus Bulaq 18, which includes, amongst other items, details about the sale of an excess of sacrificial beef by a temple. One type of offering, however, that was consumed exclusively by the deity was a burnt offering. Burnt offerings were foodstuffs that were doused in oil and set aflame so that their smoke could rise up to sustain the god.

Accessing the Gods and Their Temples

Unlike certain modern religious traditions, ancient Egyptian temples were not congregational in nature except perhaps during festivals and then only in certain localities. Temples were not accessible to everyone. Direct contact with a god's image was limited to the king, the high priest, and a handful

Figure 80. Priests carrying the sacred barque of Amun at Karnak Temple. The barque is decorated with ram-heads, and the naos is covered, rendering the god invisible.
Photo Salima Ikram.

of other high-ranking, initiated prelates. Most priests, and most private individuals, had no direct dealings with the figure of the god. In fact, access to different parts of the temple depended on a person's rank, education, and level of initiation within the priesthood. The area within the larger enclosure walls, just outside the pylon, and the first courtyard were accessible to most people, particularly when the festivals of the god were being celebrated. The remaining areas of the temple were restricted to initiates.

When the god's image appeared in public (within a small shrine covered with a shroud and situated on a model boat or sacred barque) for festivals and in processions, it could be approached by the populace, who could then directly address the god. (Fig. 80.) Processional routes were punctuated by barque shrines where the god's boat could pause and be seen, and perhaps the god could give oracular advice (see Fig. 44). Otherwise, people could come to the temple's outermost courtyard and direct their prayers to an engraved image of the god there, or could address their concerns to images of the king as god. Sometimes special chapels for people in need of spiritual succour, such as the 'Chapels of the Hearing Ear', were erected in an accessible area. These were situated at the back of temples, behind the sanctuary and in the outer wall, and thus were open to the populace. These chapels were particularly popular as healing centres. Other healing centres, featuring ritual bathing or dream therapy, were also constructed within the temple enceinte or enclosure, particularly during the Late period and thereafter. However, the majority of Egyptians carried out their daily worship either at home or in small shrines rather than in the state-built temples.

Festivals

Festivals played an extremely important role in the life of the temple. The major festivals for any temple were associated with its chief divinity. Thus, the creation or the birth of the god and the major events in his or her career were the main focus of celebrations and were unique to each temple. Other festivals were more general, occurring simultaneously in temples all over Egypt and unifying the country on a grand scale. These would occur in conjunction with cyclical events, such as the rising of the star Sothis that signalled the advent of the New Year, or the different stages of the Nile flood. Smaller celebrations would mark the phases of the moon and other notable astronomical and natural phenomena. Significant events such as royal coronations, the *heb-sed* race that celebrated the 30th anniversary of a king's reign, or the birth of a royal child would also precipitate festivities in temples throughout the land.

Some areas of Egypt had special festivals associated with them, such as the Theban Festival of the Valley. In this celebration the statue of Amun-Re of Karnak sailed across the Nile to the west, visiting the memorial temples of the kings as well as barque shrines that had been erected in major cemeteries. This ritual served to unite the dead with the living and was a kind of large-scale family reunion for divinities, royalty, the elite, and commoners.

In addition to featuring special rituals with accompanying music and dances and the recitation of specific hymns and prayers, festivals were also large-scale celebrations that offered the entire population, not just the priests, a spiritual encounter. The god would appear in a procession and be available to the populace for consultation and praise. Food would be distributed to the people from the offerings and sacrifices made to the god. Outside the temple, pilgrims from surrounding areas would gather and perhaps stay for several days. Festivals also attracted itinerant merchants and travelling entertainers, much as religious festivals do today.

Priests

Until the New Kingdom there was no completely separate priestly class in ancient Egypt; almost anyone could become a priest of some sort. Often, individuals who were priests also had other duties within the state or temple administration, and one person could hold several priestly titles. Both men and women served the gods, although it was more common to have groups of priestesses in the temples of goddesses, particularly in the Old Kingdom. Thereafter, it seems that men came to dominate the priesthood, although priestesses still existed in less significant positions. Priests were known as servants of the god, or *hemw-netjer*, and were supervised by an overseer called the *imi-ra hemw-netjer*. The chief priest of every temple was in theory the king, but in actuality the king delegated his role to the high priest of a specific temple. Each high priest had a special title depending on which temple he served. For example, the High Priest of Ptah at Memphis was known as *wr kherep hemout*, or Great Director of Artisans, and the High Priest of Re at Heliopolis was known as *wr maa iunu*, or The Greatest of Seers in Iunu (Heliopolis).

A special type of priestess was known as the God's Wife; she might be classed as the female equivalent of the high priest, although her duties were different. Furthermore, in the 18th Dynasty her role was solely religious; however, in the 25th Dynasty the God's Wife had political as well as religious authority.

Many other priests serving in a temple had specialized jobs: the main duty of the *khery-heb*, or lector priest, was to recite the prayers that accompanied specific rites; the *sem*-priest officiated at funerals and was responsible for many of the objects, such as cloth, oils, and perfumes, that were used in the daily liturgy; and special priestly prophets, scribes, butchers, and land stewards could also be found. Temple musicians, singers, and dancers, of both sexes, also held significant positions in the various temples, as they all had vital roles to play in temple rituals and during festivals.

Many Egyptians served in the lowest rank of priest, a *waab* (pure one), for three months of a year on a rota system. This allowed a large percentage of the Egyptian population to have some sort of contact with the gods, and to be a part of the Egyptian religious establishment, as well as to enjoy the material benefits of payment in kind for such work. Priests were paid through the temple's offerings: the goods were consecrated to the gods and then were divided amongst the priesthood and temple staff according to their rank. Excess could be sold or gifted. Sadly, there is evidence of corruption amongst priestly staffs: a 20th Dynasty text relates how some priests sold sacred animals for personal benefit, and another, dating to the 26th Dynasty, describes how a struggle for priestly income led to murder.

Cult and mortuary temple priesthoods might have had slightly different organizational structures, particularly in the Old Kingdom. Funerary priests were divided into groups, or *phyles*, that rotated in their service to the deceased, whereas priests who served the cult of a god tended to hold, save for the *waab* priests, permanent positions. Sacerdotal positions were often hereditary, and a title could remain in a family for several generations.

Priests (and priestesses) were presumably trained within the temple during their youth, particularly if they were holding an inherited post. For the most part, they were literate, and the higher-ranking ones tended to be nobles rather than commoners. When serving in the temple, they had to maintain certain levels of purity, which included washing regularly, shaving their bodily hair, chewing natron and spices to keep their breath fresh, and keeping their nails trimmed, as well as abstaining from certain foods at specific times.

Private Religion and Personal Piety

Priests officiated at all the daily rituals in major temples, occasionally with members of the elite participating. During festivals, the common people were also included in rituals and prayers, especially when the god went in procession. Otherwise ordinary Egyptians had to content themselves with passing their prayers to the gods via the priests or with addressing their prayers to the external temple images of divinities. Within the temples, priests could convey prayers and offerings to the gods into the sacred areas, and offerings in the form of votive statues and stelae of all shapes and sizes crowded the courtyards, halls, and chambers of the temple. In fact, these areas could become so crowded that they had to be periodically cleared to make way for new votive offerings: all the old statues and stelae were tossed into a large pit within the temple precinct so that they could still carry out their job of sending prayers to the god. Examples of these statue-filled pits have been found by archaeologists and are called 'caches' or 'cachettes', places filled with hidden items. Because temples as they appear today are largely bereft of their statuary and votive offerings, these finds have been especially useful in allowing us to visualise the temple interiors as spaces that were once densely packed with such dedications.

Gods also provided oracular advice to the Egyptian people, often through the medium of the priests. If familial or legal issues could not be resolved by civic means, the god would be approached on a specific day devoted to oracular activity, and the divinity would be asked to decide the issue. An individual could address questions phrased in a certain way, and the sacred barque containing the divine image might move to indicate a 'yes' or 'no' answer. If the deity in question was manifested as an animal, either sounds or movements would indicate the god's decision. Doubtless some corrupt priests benefited from this practice, as they were the ones who interpreted the god's response.

In general, though, commoners (as well as nobles) worshipped the gods in domestic shrines; in small chapels, including wayside shrines; or in special temples that might answer their specific needs of the moment, such as the Chapels of the Hearing Ear described earlier. Depending on what was desired, one would visit the appropriate deity in such a venue. Thus, students who wished to succeed in their examinations would pray to Thoth, while people whose love lives needed help would pray to Hathor or Bastet. At harvest time farmers would offer to Renenutet, the goddess of harvests and plenty, and people about to embark on journeys would invoke Anubis.

In wealthier homes, domestic shrines were set up in the garden or within the house; possibly such estates contained more than one shrine. In homes owned by less wealthy families, shrines were set up within the house. A house shrine consisted of the image (or images) of a god (or gods), often set within a niche, and a place for offerings before it. The size of such a shrine varied depending on the size of the house and on the level of piety of the homeowner, and probably also the degree to which the homeowner wished to display his piety. These shrines were the site of daily devotions that might occur as often as three times a day, as in the temples, as well as whenever the residents wished for spiritual succour. Examples of such shrines have been excavated at the sites of Deir el-Medina, Abydos South, and Tell el-Amarna. The main function of these house shrines was to protect the family by providing them with a place to venerate the gods, who, in return, would watch over the family both in this world and in the divine and eternal sphere. (Fig. 81.)

The gods who graced domestic shrines were rarely the gods of the state religion; instead, they tended to be gods with whom the person establishing the shrine felt a rapport or who was a patron for that person's particular metier. Thus, scribes would revere images of Thoth, while musicians, singers, and dancers would favour Hathor and Bastet. Magicians might erect a shrine to Isis or Heka (another deity concerned with magic), while craftsmen would worship Ptah, and embalmers Anubis. In addition to the main gods, minor protective divinities such as Bes and Taweret were a part of every household. Bes was depicted as a leonine dwarf, brandishing knives or percussion instruments, while Taweret's image showed the deity with the head and body of a hippopotamus that had pendulous breasts and a pregnant belly, a lioness's paws for hands and feet, and, often, was wearing a woman's tripartite wig

Figure 81. Statuettes and stelae depicting favoured gods were the focus of household shrines. Favourite domestic deities were the goddess Tawesret and the dwarf god Bes. Tawesret, shown as a hippopotamus with some leonine features, often had her mouth parted threateningly to scare away demons. Now in the Metropolitan Museum of Art in New York, these figurines of Tawesret, who protected homes, women, and children in particular, might have been kept in house shrines. Photo Salima Ikram.

that extended into a crocodile tail down the back. Bes and Taweret were frequently painted on the walls of rooms where people slept or where childbirth took place. Their fearsome aspects were thought to scare away demons and evil spirits and to protect the home's inhabitants. Their images were also carved on beds in order to safeguard a body when it is at its most vulnerable and to protect the sleeper's dream life (as well as his or her physical body) from attack by demons. These two divinities, sometimes paired as husband and wife, also appeared in temples, particularly in the *mammisi*, and images of them were often worn as amulets.

Local gods were extremely popular, as they were seen as successful intercessors between local people and the major gods. Sometimes the Egyptians just referred to a deity as the 'city god', using the word that denotes city without providing a specific name. In other instances, a local god might be likened to a modern saint: a native of the area who had lived an extraordinary life and upon death had been elevated to a semi-divine state. Such individuals included the famous Imhotep, the architect of King Djoser's Step Pyramid and a renowned physician; Hekaib, a governor of Elephantine Island; and Amenhotep, son of Hapu, who was architect to King Amenhotep III. Such gods were generally worshipped only locally, save for Imhotep, whose cult spread throughout Egypt during the Ptolemaic and Roman periods. There are several other less famous examples of this type of cult (see Chapter 4).

Certain kings and queens who had been venerated as full gods during their lifetimes, and even more so after their deaths, also acted as patrons for specific localities. The most notable of such patrons was manifest in the joint cult of Amenhotep I and his mother, Ahmose-Nefertari, that was particularly popular amongst the workmen of Deir el-Medina, as well as throughout Thebes. Images of the king and his mother abounded in tombs of the New Kingdom, and stelae dedicated to the royal pair have been found in temples throughout the area.

Ultimately, Egyptians used a variety of means to connect with the gods, whether for spiritual strength or to achieve certain goals. Commoners, like royalty, would make offerings and praise the gods in order to attain their ambitions. Individuals would dedicate special offerings of food and drink or votive statues (of stone, faience, or hand-crafted out of mud), bits of linen, jewellery, stelae, and vessels, or they would offer up special prayers so that the gods would be appeased and would answer their wishes.

Funerary Beliefs

The Egyptians believed that after they died, if they had lived in accordance with *maat*, they had the potential to be resurrected and to live eternally, with both their bodies and their souls participating in the process. Thus, mummification was important because it preserved the body and was a vehicle for the soul (see Chapter 9). According to Egyptian belief, once they died and were mummified, their souls underwent a series of tests before different gods and, if they passed, finally came before the god Osiris, who was enthroned in the Hall of Judgement. If he judged them to have lived a just life, they would

Atenism

During the reign of King Amenhotep IV, the cult of the sun god Aten rose to supremacy. This god, whose name is known to have occurred as far back as the Old Kingdom, was given prominence from the reign of Thutmose IV, Amenhotep IV's grandfather, onward. This focus on Aten was at least in part a political ploy; the king intended the cult of Aten to balance the influential priests and cult of the state god, Amun. The Amun priests had become so wealthy and powerful that they were challenging royal authority. Aten is a version of the sun god shown as a sun-disk whose rays end in hands. The god indicated his approbation and blessing of the royal family by holding *ankh* (life) signs in his hands to their noses, imparting eternal life. Whether out of religious conviction or political manoeuvring, Akhenaten replaced Amun with Aten as the principal state deity and disbanded the priesthood of Amun. Any images or mention of Amun (including pictures of ducks and rams, animals associated with Amun) were eradicated during this process, and Amenhotep IV changed his name to Akhenaten ('Soul/Manifestation of the Aten'), very obviously shifting his allegiance to the new god whose priests would support him.

During the Amarna period, the Aten reigned supreme, although other deities were still worshipped, albeit with much less devotion. Household divinities, such as Bes and Tawesret in particular, remained popular, and amulets of these gods have been found at Amarna. Akhenaten abandoned Thebes, the city of Amun, as a capital, and moved his court to Akhetaten ('the Horizon of the Aten'), a new city, situated in Middle Egypt, that he dedicated to his favourite god. However, after Akehnaten's death, his successor Tutankhamun restored the old order and Amun reigned supreme in Egypt once again.

pass into the Afterlife (also known as the 'Fields of Iaru', or *Imenti*, 'the West'), where they would enjoy an eternal existence.

This belief in rebirth and resurrection was tied closely to the solar cycle in which the sun sets (dies) in the evening and is reborn the next day, as well as tied to the rise and fall of the Nile. Natural cycles were critical for the ancient Egyptians, not just in their funerary beliefs but also in their daily lives, where cultic ritual ensured continuation of the cycles that made all life possible.

The concept of the soul in ancient Egypt is complex, and tripartite, consisting of the *ka*, the *ba*, and the *akh*. The *ka* was shown as a pair of upraised arms and was one's double, created at the same time as the body and identical to it in every way. Once a person died, the *ka* continued to require nourishment; it could move around the tomb, benefiting from the offerings left there. The *ba* was depicted as a human-headed bird and was the part of the soul that could take flight and be separated from the body. After one's death, this aspect of

Figure 82.   The ba *of the deceased hovers beside the corpse in this picture from a funerary papyrus in Berlin. Photo Nicholas Warner.*

the soul could range where it pleased, both in this world and the next. The *akh* might be likened to the 'divine spark', and its role in the afterlife of non-royal people is obscure. For kings, the *akh* joined with the gods and the eternal stars, keeping watch over Egypt throughout eternity. (Fig. 82.)

The Egyptians' belief in resurrection was inspired by the myth of Osiris (see the next section), who was the quintessential god of renewal and rebirth. Quite possibly the Osiris myth reflected actual events in the distant historical past, events that had happened so long ago that they had become clouded by myth over time. Typically, Osiris was shown as a man wrapped in white mummy bandages, his arms crossed over his chest, and his hands clasping the royal crook and a flail. He wore the *atef* crown made up of the White Crown flanked by two plumes (a reference to *maat*, which was often denoted by a feather); sometimes Osiris's crown also had two curling horns emerging on either side of it, perhaps alluding to the god Khnum and to his role as the creator of the physical body and the *ka*. Osiris's flesh was shown as either black or green. The black referred to the fertile silt from the Nile's inundations and identified Osiris with the essence of the land of Egypt. The green symbolised the plants that were nurtured by the soil and presented Egypt at its most fecund and rich. Both colours were associated with the potential

Figure 83. Osiris was generally shown as a mummified figure with either green or black flesh, symbolising resurrection and rebirth, and a crook and a flail, expressing his dominion in the Afterworld. Photo Salima Ikram.

of the earth to bring forth life. The crook and the flail that Osiris carried were also allusions to the fertility and safety of the country's herds and crops. (Fig. 83.)

Osiris was mentioned as early as the Old Kingdom, but there were no complete written records of his myth until the Greek period, when the most coherent account was recorded by the Greek historian Plutarch. It is probable that the myth had evolved and changed over time, and that this Greek account was a modified version of the Egyptian original.

The Myth of Osiris

The story of Osiris, as derived from the Egyptian and Greek sources, has several variations, but can be summarized as follows. In the Golden Age, the gods ruled the world. Osiris ruled Egypt, with Isis, Great of Magic, his consort and sister, ruling beside him. As ruler, Osiris was associated with the physical land of Egypt. Thus the fertility and productivity of the land and its livestock were identified with, and derived from, the regenerative power of the king. This force was manifested in the *heb-sed* race and festival associated with divine kingship and the well-being of the country (see Chapter 6).

Osiris was an ideal ruler, good and just, beloved by all save for his brother Seth, who was jealous of Osiris's position. Seth plotted to overthrow his brother and rule in his place, so he conceived a wicked plan to murder Osiris. He had a richly decorated chest made to measurements that fit only his brother's body. Seth then hosted a magnificent feast to which he invited his seventy-two cohorts, as well as Osiris. At the end of the banquet, when everyone had indulged sufficiently, Seth presented the chest and offered it to anyone who could fit into it. Much as in the story of Cinderella, everyone tried to fit into the richly ornamented casket, but with no success. Finally, Osiris was persuaded to try it, and naturally he fit perfectly. Seth slammed down the lid and locked and sealed the casket. He then hurled this earliest of coffins, containing Osiris, into the Nile, where the king drowned.

The river took the casket to the Mediterranean Sea and thence on to Byblos (in modern Lebanon). There it lodged in a tree that was turned into a column in the local ruler's palace. Perhaps this is the inspiration for one of Osiris's symbols, the *djed* (eternal) pillar. Isis, mourning her husband's loss, went in search of him and eventually tracked his casket to Byblos, and brought it back to Egypt. In some versions, Seth, who had established himself in the interim as the ruler of Egypt, retrieved the casket. Opening the box, he removed Osiris's body and cut it into pieces that he scattered through-out Egypt. The number of pieces into which Seth divided Osiris's body was variously reported as from fourteen to forty-two (the latter figure being the traditional number of *nomes*, or provinces, of Egypt).[2]

Isis and her sister, Nephthys, who was Seth's consort, searched for Osiris's body parts. Isis gathered these together and reassembled her husband's corpse. But one crucial portion of his body was irretrievably lost: Osiris's phallus had been eaten by a fish. The fish that ate Osiris's member has been variously identified as the *Lepidotus*, the *Phagrus*, and the *Oxyrynchus* (genus *Mormyrus*), all of which were taboo foods in certain areas and at certain times. Isis manufactured a false phallus and attached it to her husband's reassembled body, successfully bringing about Osiris's resurrection. Then Isis turned her-self into a black kite (the bird *Milvus migrans*) and mated with her husband.

(Isis and Nephthys are commonly depicted as black kites in funerary contexts, acting as mourners and protectors of the dead. Perhaps the mournful cries of these birds recalled for the ancient Egyptians the wails of mourning women, hence the birds' identification with these goddesses.) After coupling with Osiris, Isis and Nephthys embalmed the body of Osiris, with the help of Anubis and Thoth.

Isis became pregnant as a result of her union with the resurrected Osiris, and she retired to the town of Khemmis, in the Delta, where she gave birth to her son, Horus. Horus grew to manhood here, nursed by his mother and by the goddess Hathor. When he came of age he emerged from the Delta and engaged in a series of dramatic battles with his uncle, Seth, in an effort to avenge his father and gain the throne of Egypt. This particular myth cycle is recounted in 'The Contendings of Horus and Seth', which, according to some sources, took place over an eighty-year period and was related to the Egyptian idea of divine kingship, which linked the ruler of Egypt to Horus. During their struggles, Horus and Seth battled each other in various guises, played tricks on each other, and were aided by different deities of the pantheon.

Horus was the victor in these contests against Seth, and was ultimately crowned king of the black land of Egypt. Thus this god is identified with the living pharaoh who becomes the manifestation of Horus on earth. Osiris became king of the dead and of the Underworld; as the prototype mummy, Osiris also was linked to deceased kings. Seth was given dominion over the red lands of the deserts, as well as over thunderstorms, both elements that were unpredictable and threatening, and that needed to be controlled. Thus, Seth was associated with the forces of chaos and disorder, while Horus and Osiris were associated with the maintenance of harmony and *maat* in the Nile Valley and in the hereafter.

Osiris ruled the Afterworld and judged the souls of the dead to determine who could be awarded eternal life. The deceased was conducted to the Judgement Hall of Osiris by Anubis, and his or her heart was weighed against the feather of *maat*. If the individual had lived a true and just life, the heart and the feather would balance and the person would be rewarded with eternal life in the realm of Osiris, a more perfect version of Egypt. If not, the deceased would be devoured by the monster Ammit and vanish forever. Egyptians also associated Osiris with Re, who vanquished evil and who entered the Underworld after the sun had set and rose again the following day.

Although Osiris was worshipped at many sites, his chief cult centre, and the focus of Egyptian funerary beliefs, rituals, and pilgrimages, was Abydos, where Isis allegedly buried his head. The route to the Otherworld was also thought to originate at a break in the cliffs here. By the Middle Kingdom, the Egyptians had identified the tomb of a 1st Dynasty ruler, King Djer, as that of Osiris, and the site became a major centre of pilgrimage. It was also at this time that it became common for any dead person to be given the epithet 'Osiris (Name of deceased)'. Previously, this term was reserved for royalty. Many Egyptians chose to be buried at Abydos, while others erected memorial stelae in a large area adjacent to the Osiris Temple at the site instead. This 'Pilgrimage to Abydos' was a key part of funerary belief and was featured in tombs in two-dimensional representations on the walls, as well as in three-dimensional wooden boat models that showed the bier being taken to Abydos, thereby further ensuring that the deceased would be reborn.

Funerary Texts

Egyptians believed that the journey to the Afterlife, an idealised Egypt where everything was perfect, could be eased by the use of funerary texts. These books were essentially guidebooks or crib-notes for protecting, provisioning, guiding, and helping the deceased to enter the Afterlife safely. They supplied spells that negated the threats and overcame the obstacles that riddled the way to the Afterlife.

The earliest funerary texts are called Pyramid Texts, as they were found inscribed inside pyramids. (Fig. 84.) They were exclusively for the use of royalty and were first inscribed in the subterranean burial chamber of the Saqqara pyramid of Unas (c. 2350 BC), the last king of the 5th Dynasty. They comprised some eight hundred spells or 'utterances'. The texts were carved in vertical columns in sunken relief. The spells were meant to aid the king in his ascent to the sky and ease his reception into the kingdom of the gods. Although the Pyramid Texts were a perquisite of royalty in the Old Kingdom, they were usurped extensively in their original format by non-royals in the Late Period, as well as by a few officials of the Middle and New Kingdoms, who used only a selection of these texts on their sarcophagi.

What are now called Coffin Texts were a development of the Pyramid Texts and were painted inside coffins of the First Intermediate period and the Middle Kingdom. They offered the guarantee of an Afterlife associated with Osiris for *everyone*, or at least, for everyone who could afford the necessary

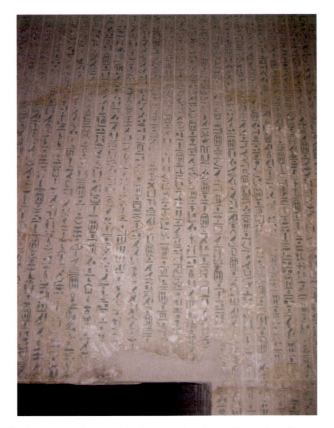

Figure 84. The Pyramid Texts in the burial chamber of Pepy I at Saqqara provided the king with a way to become one with the eternal stars. Photo Salima Ikram.

accoutrements for an Afterlife. The Coffin Texts contained at least 1,185 spells, often enlivened with vignettes. These spells were maps and guides to the hereafter. However, Coffin Texts were not restricted to coffins; they have been found on mummy masks, tomb walls, and sometimes even on papyri. Some of these inscriptions were identical to those in the Pyramid Texts, and their purpose was the same: to see the deceased safely through the tests and obstacles that marked the path to the Afterlife.

Perhaps the most famous of all Egyptian funerary books is the so-called Book of the Dead, which first appeared in the early 17th Dynasty and continued to be popular through the Late Period. Known more correctly as 'Coming Forth by Day', the book had about two hundred spells or chapters and was lavishly illustrated with obscure vignettes. Many were derived from the Pyramid and Coffin Texts, with new additions. Spells from this book

Figure 85. Funerary books were commonly interred with the deceased. This scene, from a papyrus in Berlin, shows Chapter or Spell 1 of the Book of the Dead. This text was the most popular funerary book and was used for several centuries. It consisted of several chapters, or spells, some of which were accompanied by vignettes. Photo Nicholas Warner.

were inscribed (generally in hieratic [see Chapter 8]) on papyri, mummy cloths, amulets, figurines, coffins, and even tomb walls. (Fig. 85.)

Several other funerary texts that date from the New Kingdom onward, termed the Books of the Underworld, also exist, primarily in a royal context. These include the Book of the Amduat (the Book of What Is in the Underworld), and the Book of Gates (named for the large gates that guard each hour). These two texts were organized according to the twelve hours of the night, with the ram-headed nocturnal form of the sun god located at the centre of each hour. The sun god illuminated each nocturnal hour, bringing life to the world and resurrecting the dead to be judged. These texts were distributed spatially in the tomb so that they started in the west and ended in the east, thus imitating the path of the sun god's barque on its route to rebirth. Later books, such as the Book of Caverns, replaced the division of the night into twelve hours with a division into six sectors. However, all of these books shared the idea that the deceased was to be identified with the sun god and, like him, must be safely steered through the perils of the night hours to ensure his safe rebirth, and that of the cosmos, on the following day. Ultimately, many of these royal texts were used by the elite in the hope that they too could support the sun god in his nightly journey and be reborn the next day. But regardless of the precise nature of any of these funerary texts, the desired result was the same: rebirth, resurrection, and eternal life.

6

Kings and Commoners

Egyptian Society and Government

Ancient Egypt was a stratified society, organized much like a layered pyramid, albeit with the possibility of social mobility from one level to another. Once established, the pattern of social and economic relations remained roughly the same throughout Egypt's history, with varying degrees of flexibility depending on the time period. Further vertical sub-divisions of the social pyramid divided society into broad groups, such as priests, bureaucrats, and the military, although these groups were interconnected: a priest could also be a bureaucrat, and a soldier could hold priestly and administrative, as well as military, titles. Each of these vertical groups contained representatives from all social echelons. (Fig. 86.)

The king was at the apex of the social pyramid, with everyone else below him and deriving most of their power directly from their connection to the monarch. In terms of administrative responsibility, the vizier (*tchaty*) was the next most important person in the hierarchy, followed by the most senior courtiers, who were the highest officials. In the early Old Kingdom, royal family members, aside from being wealthy and powerful by virtue of their family

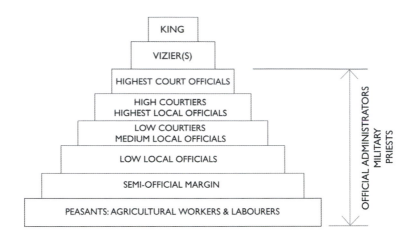

Figure 86. Egyptian society was organized in the form of a pyramid crowned by the king and his vizier. Official administrators and members of the military and the priesthood were drawn from all social strata. Drawing Nicholas Warner.

connections, also occupied key positions at the court. In later periods this changed somewhat; although their blood gave them many privileges, royal family members did not always hold high office – perhaps because the king was afraid that they might usurp his authority and pose a threat to his rule. The ancient Egyptians referred to the elite governing class as the *pat*, and the common people were referred to as the *rekhyt*. (Fig. 87.)

The organization of royal cemeteries, particularly pyramid cemeteries, reflected Egypt's social hierarchy. (Fig. 88.) The king's tomb was central, with the tombs of the king's family and courtiers clustered around it. The most important members of these groups were interred closest to the king. The status implied by this close spatial relationship was also reflected in the tomb's architecture, size, and decoration, as well as in the number and types of titles held by the tomb owner. The courtiers' dependents' tombs were clustered around their tombs, and people of lesser consequence were buried further away in smaller, less impressive tombs. Often portions of these cemeteries reflected one of the vertical sub-groupings, with priests of a certain type being buried in one place, butchers in another, and so forth. Sometimes these occupational groupings were familial as well, since titles were often hereditary. This model of mortuary space as a reflection of social organization broke down in the times directly preceding the Intermediate periods, in the Intermediate periods themselves, and in the New Kingdom, when the architecture of royal tombs changed (see Chapter 9). However,

Figure 87. The rekhyt-*bird on a basket, symbolising all the common people, praises Ramesses II's cartouche at Karnak Temple. Photo Nicholas Warner.*

the basic cemetery model of lower-status individuals and dependents clustering around tombs of higher-status people remained standard throughout Egyptian history and almost certainly echoed to some degree residence patterns in settlements.

Our understanding of social organization has been further elucidated by textual evidence. Certain texts, such as Papyrus Bulaq 18 (thus named because it was the eighteenth papyrus registered in the Egyptian Museum at Bulaq) and the archives from the funerary temples of Senusert II at Lahun and Neferirkare Kakai at Abu Sir, to name but a few, contain lists of people, with their titles and the amount of payment each received, depending on rank. Thus, the relative importance of different titles in certain contexts can be evaluated fairly precisely with the help of these documents.

The highest local officials and high courtiers occupied the next tier in the social pyramid, followed by medium-level courtiers and high-ranking local officials. In general, provincial officials, save for nomarchs (provincial governors) and high priests of important state gods, had a slightly lower status than their court equivalents. A lower level of courtiers in the capital were equivalent to medium-level provincial officials. Traders and merchants might also belong to this level of society, although individuals, depending on the degree of their commercial success, might occupy higher or lower positions. This level was followed by low-level local officials, and then by the semi-official margin. The base of the pyramid consisted of the largest part of the population, the peasants (agricultural workers and labourers). Enslaved persons also

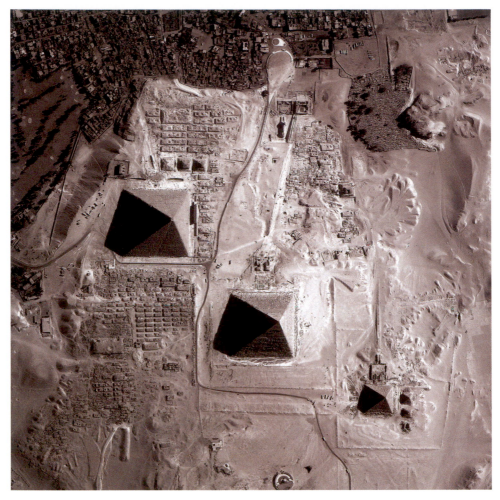

Figure 88. The pyramids of Giza and their attendant cemeteries reflect the social organization of the time. The king was the central, dominant individual, with members of the royal family buried in large tombs clustered in a special cemetery near the king. Elite members of society were also buried close to the king, but generally not in the same cemetery as royalty, and frequently in slightly smaller sepulchres. Photo courtesy S. Phillips, Space Imaging, Inc.

played a part in the Egyptian social structure, albeit a varied one, and had a surprising degree of social mobility (see following sections).

The King

The king was the central figure in the world view of the ancient Egyptians. He was the incarnation of the god Horus on earth (see Chapter 5, 'The Myth

of Osiris') and head of the social, political, religious, and military state. Upon his death, he became one with Osiris and Re, and ruled in the Underworld. Because of the king's divine nature, mere mortals could not touch him or his accoutrements without proper preparation or permission, lest they be destroyed. Rawer, an official who lived during the Old Kingdom, described the dangers of such an encounter in his tomb biography: Rawer had inadvertently touched King Teti's sceptre, and the king then had to recite spells and rituals over Rawer to save him from certain destruction.

The king acted as the chief link between the realms of the human and of the divine, and his titles and names emphasized his divinity. In addition to his birth name, a king acquired four additional names upon his coronation. The first name in the royal titulary is the Horus name that identified the king as the living Horus; this name initially appeared in Dynasty 0. It was written in a *serekh* and surmounted by an image of the Horus falcon, emphasizing the royal relationship with Horus. (Fig. 89.) A *serekh* is a palace façade that depicts the elaborately niched walls of the king's house frontally, with a rectangle behind it, indicating the palace enclosure from an aerial perspective. The king's name was written in the rectangle, signifying that he inhabited the palace. The second royal title and name to appear was the 'Two Ladies' or *nebty* name. The Two Ladies were Nekhbet and Wadjet, the goddesses of Upper and Lower Egypt, respectively, and their images directly preceded this name, indicating that the king ruled both parts of the land. The earliest example of this name dates to the 1st Dynasty. The third name is the gold name, whose meaning is harder to understand. It originated in the Early Dynastic period and was preceded by the hieroglyph for gold (*nub*); in the Middle Kingdom a Horus falcon surmounted the *nub* symbol. Perhaps the gold sign both invoked the sun's golden hue and symbolised the king's eternal divinity, as gold is everlasting and immutable.

The Egyptian king's fourth name is the *nsw-bity* name, literally, '[He of the] Papyrus and Wasp/Bee'. (Fig. 90.) In older books, scholars translated this title as 'King of Upper and Lower Egypt' and in more recent ones as 'He of the Sedge [papyrus] and the Bee', with the idea that this was a pre-unification Lower Egyptian title. However, this title might also reflect the idea of the king's power over the fertility of the land, with its two signs indicating a partnership between plant and pollinating insect. Although papyrus plants are pollinated by wind, it is possible that the Egyptians thought that, like most other plants, they benefited from insect activity. The fifth royal name is the *sa Ra* or 'Son of Re' name, and it stresses the relationship between the king and the sun god, Re. This name became common in the 4th Dynasty.

Figure 89. The earliest royal name was enclosed in a serekh surmounted by the Horus falcon, such as this one belonging to King Nebre, now in the Metropolitan Museum of Art, New York. The royal name is within the enclosure, and the serekh façade of the building is shown frontally. Thus, the owner of the palace, that is, the king whose name is inscribed within the enclosure, is the ruler. Photo Salima Ikram.

The fourth and fifth names are sometimes called the throne and birth names, respectively. The birth name was the king's 'real' name, or nomen, from birth, whereas the king took his *nsw-bity* name, or prenomen, upon his coronation. Both these names were enclosed in cartouches, which are elongated *shen* rings that are symbols of eternity. Writing the king's name in these symbols was a magical way of protecting him and ensuring that he lived forever. The encircling form of the cartouche, alluding to the sun's path, might also evoke control over terrestrial and cosmic territory. The first king to use a cartouche was King Huni, at the end of the 3rd Dynasty.

From the New Kingdom onward, other epithets were used for the king as well, the most notable being 'Strong Bull', perhaps acting as a complement to

Figure 90. The royal titulary of Ramesses III from a statue of the king at Karnak. Left to right: the king's nsw-bity title, followed by the epithet 'Lord of the Two Lands', and the king's prenomen, Usermaatre-meryamun, in a cartouche. This is followed by the title sa Ra (son of Re) and then the epithet 'Lord of the Horizons', and a cartouche containing the king's nomen, Ramesses Heka-Iwnw. The titulary is completed by the phrase, '[may he be/live] like Re'.

the *nsw-bity* promise of fertility. Additionally, the terms *ankh*, *wedja*, and *seneb* were inscribed after the king's name, meaning Life, Prosperity, and Health (abbreviated by Egyptologists as LPH). The title *pharaoh*, which literally means 'Great House', was not generally used to refer to the king until the New Kingdom.

Royal Iconography

Royal iconography, or the standard way in which the king was represented, was fairly well established by the start of Dynasty 1. The king's regalia included a shepherd's crook, symbolic of his function as caretaker and guardian of his land and people; a flail, representing his role as disciplinarian; a bull's tail, indicating his virility and the fertility of the land and its livestock; and a royal beard, the mark of divinity. A uraeus serpent (cobra with hood extended) appeared on his brow, an allusion to the uraeus as the eye of Re, which guarded the king by sitting on his forehead. Images of Nekhbet and Wadjet also sometimes adorned the king's forehead, reminding his people that he was ruler of the Two Lands. His crowns were manifestations of his right to rule: the Red Crown for Lower Egypt, presumably symbolising blood and power, and the White Crown for Upper Egypt, probably indicative of sunlight, fire, and purity. Additional crowns and headdresses were donned for special occasions: the *atef* crown, like that of the god Osiris, was worn for religious ceremonies; the *nemes* headdress was for daily wear; and the blue crown (*khepresh*) was most commonly used on the battlefield. The animals most closely associated with the king were the lion and the bull. With few exceptions throughout Egyptian history, the king was shown as eternally youthful and vigorous, a powerful being in the prime of life. Deviations from this standard – for example, during the 12th Dynasty and the Amarna period – illustrated visually significant ideological shifts in notions of kingship. (Fig. 91.)

Figure 91. King Seti I's coronation by Horus at Karnak Temple exemplifies many aspects of kingship. The king's importance and divine nature is emphasized by his being depicted as the same size as, and in physical contact, with the god; the king wears the bull's tail symbolic of strength and fertility; he is crowned with the double crown of Upper and Lower Egypt over the royal nemes *headdress; the divine beard is fixed to his chin; he carries an* ankh, *symbol of eternal life; and the sporran over the king's long kilt is embellished with uraei crowned by sun-disks, emphasizing the solar and divine nature of the king. Photo Salima Ikram.*

The king's role as Egypt's protector and caretaker, in both the physical and metaphysical realms, was pivotal to his position. He was the incarnation of the land, charged with recreating it every day by performing prayers and rituals in the temple; he was both high priest and a god incarnate – the preserver of *maat*. As such, the king initially 'owned' all of Egypt and then distributed its land, livestock, and goods to his family, courtiers, and the priesthood, albeit maintaining the lion's share for himself and his successors. Thus, his power was firmly rooted in his wealth, as well as in his divinity.

In addition to his religious role, an Egyptian ruler was expected to lead his troops in battle, inspired and emboldened by the gods. This was an important component of defeating cosmic as well as worldly chaos. Thus, the king was also the head of Egypt's military. He was also the ultimate arbitrator of justice in Egypt. When the usual courts could not resolve legal cases, the king made the final judgement; moreover, all of Egypt's laws (which were probably written by a committee of bureaucrats) were issued in the name of the king. Naturally too, in his political and administrative roles, the ruler dealt with foreign policy and diplomacy. The populace certainly regarded the king as ultimately responsible for whatever happened in Egypt.

Within a dynasty, the most common way for a king to ascend to the throne was through inheritance. Being the eldest born (or eldest surviving) son of the reigning king generally assured one's succession, unless the king favoured another male child, which sometimes occurred. This depended on the identity of the prince's mother – sometimes favoured wives' children took precedence over firstborns. Of course, power could also be seized by force, as it was, for example, at the start of the 12th Dynasty in the Middle Kingdom (see Chapter 4). In such instances, the new ruler made efforts to legitimate his claim to power, often by creating stories that stressed his divine birth or by putting about alleged predictions made by a seer. The Westcar Papyrus (see Chapter 4) linked the kings of Dynasty 5 to Re, while both Hatshepsut and Amenhotep III of the 18th Dynasty asserted that the god Amun-Re had had intercourse with their mothers (sometimes in the guise of the king, their biological father) and was their 'true' father. For Amenhotep III there really was no obvious need for this claim as his sovereignty was indisputable, but in his case the decision to invoke Amun as his father formed part of a shift in kingship ideology, stressing the divine nature of the ruler and his manifestation as a god on earth. Other legitimising strategies could cite actions by specific gods: Thutmose III, also of the 18th Dynasty, claimed that Amun, whose barque stopped before the young prince during a procession, chose him personally as ruler. Such strategies not only legitimated the right of a specific ruler to rule but also that of his lineage. The practice of co-regency, first formally established in the Middle Kingdom (see Chapter 4) also served to establish succession and strengthen a new king's claim to the throne.

All of Egypt's kings emphasized their legitimacy, as well as their divinity, by participating in royal ancestor worship linked to the royal *ka*. In a way, the royal *ka* was eternal, passing from the god Horus to each successive ruler of Egypt. This divine spark was venerated all over Egypt, and was a particular focus of the cult in Luxor Temple at Thebes. Kings also stressed their ties to Horus through their titles and in representations. A crown prince was referred to as 'Horus-in-the-nest', and when a king died and another took his place the cry went up, 'The [Horus] falcon has flown up to the sky and a new one has risen in his stead'. This was the ancient Egyptian equivalent of the phrase, 'The king is dead, long live the king'.

The two most important rituals of kingship were the coronation and, if a king ruled long enough, the *heb-sed*. The physical act of crowning the king and seating him on the throne gave him legitimacy. The crowns conferred divine power on the man who became king, with the royal uraeus on his brow referring to and commemorating the kingship of Re, who first wore the uraeus. The throne itself, *st* in Egyptian, was particularly important as it was also the name and symbol of Isis, the mother of Horus. When the king, Horus incarnate, sat on the throne, he was sitting in the lap of his mother, Isis, who empowered him. Coronation activities involved not only crowning the king and ceremonially seating him on the throne but also religious rituals that indicated the king's divinity, his willingness and ability to serve the gods, and the gods' acceptance and authorization of his rule. Nomarchs and nobles would formally give their allegiance to the new king, as would the common people of Egypt. Often royal progresses throughout the Nile Valley marked the accession of a new ruler.

If a king survived thirty years of reign, he would celebrate his first *heb-sed*. This translates as the Festival (*heb*) of the Tail (*sed*) and was probably related to the bull's tail that was part of royal regalia. This festival was presumably rooted in very early belief systems when the physical strength and ability of the king was thought to reflect the well-being of the land. The *heb-sed* was an opportunity to renew the land, the king's dominion over it, and the ties the king had made with the gods and his people upon his accession. The festival also stressed the unity of the king with Osiris, whose black skin personified the Nile Valley and its fertility. Images of the king engaged in the *heb-sed* depict him as a form of Osiris. The festival was a test of the king's strength, during which, to consecrate and protect the land, the king shot arrows in the four cardinal directions and ran four times (four was a sacred number for the ancient Egyptians) around an area that probably represented Egypt. Some scholars think that the king raced a bull along this course, and as long as the king kept up with or outran the animal, he had the strength and virility necessary to rule Egypt. This metaphorical encirclement of Egypt by the king both protected it and alluded to the sun god, who, according to Egyptian religious beliefs, literally encircled Egypt and safeguarded it. After the king successfully completed these trials of strength, the nobles, nomarchs, and images of divinities would renew their allegiance to him and endorse his rule over the land. Because the king's vigour was directly related to the well-being of the land of Egypt, the original idea of the festival was that if the king should falter during the physical tests or perform them badly, a younger and fitter ruler would replace him. After his first *heb-sed*, the king celebrated subsequent festivals every three years or whenever his popularity and authority needed to be boosted.

The Queen

The queen (*hemet nisw* in Egyptian) was the wife of the king. A king could have several wives, and the most important was the ruling queen, differentiated by titles such as 'Great King's Wife' (*hemet nisw weret*). Designations that were equivalent to kingly titles, such as 'Mistress (or Lady) of the Two Lands', or 'Mistress of Upper and Lower Egypt', were also used by queens, and in the Ptolemaic period the female form of the word for ruler was used (in the ancient Egyptian language this was done by adding a 't' to the end of the word). The king's mother, the dowager queen, also maintained a royal title: 'King's Mother' (*mwt nisw*). Like other royal women, her power was primarily derived from her relationship with the king. The high status of these women (the ruling queen and dowager mother) was manifested in their tombs, which were similar in style, size, and decoration to those of kings, regardless of the era. In the Old Kingdom, royal couples were frequently buried together, although this became less common from the Middle Kingdom onward, when queens sometimes had their sepulchres in separate cemeteries. (Fig. 92.)

Like their husbands, queens had a significant religious role, and were often depicted with the king in temples, praising the gods together, though they could also be shown on their own in religious contexts. They held priestly titles and took their position opposite the king as the female equivalent of the high priest. They were identified with several different goddesses, particularly Hathor, Isis, and Mut, and by the New Kingdom some of their titles, such as 'God's Wife of Amun', further emphasize their bond with the divine. Queens also were key participants in festivals associated with fertility and the protection and regeneration of the land.

Figure 92. Although queens were very important in Egypt, much of their power was derived from the king. This statue of Ramesses II and his daughter, Bintanat, at Karnak Temple shows the king wearing the double crown, the nemes *headdress, the royal beard, and the* shendyt *kilt. In his hands he holds the crook and the flail, symbolic of his roles as nurturer and disciplinarian, respectively. The princess stands before him and is much smaller in size. As is common with queens and important royal women, she is crowned with a modius topped by two feathers of* maat *and of divinity in general, with a uraeus serpent adorning her brow; she holds a lily, symbolic of rebirth and regeneration. This statue of Ramesses II was later usurped by Ramesses VI and later still by Pinudjem I. Photo Salima Ikram.*

At one time, scholars thought that Egyptian queens played a crucial role in royal succession – that succession was matrilineal, rather than patrilineal – although this does not now seem to have been the case. Of course, affiliation with the royal family was significant, and several kings who were not in the direct line of succession cemented their power by marrying women of royal blood. In fact, many monarchs married their (half-)sisters and had children by them; perhaps this custom evoked the gods, many of whom, at the dawn of creation, were said to have married their own siblings, such as Osiris and Isis. It is interesting that Egyptian royal women were never 'given' away as part of international negotiations, although Egyptian kings often took foreign wives to create or strengthen diplomatic ties. Perhaps there was a fear that foreign rulers would afterwards concoct some sort of legitimate claim over Egypt through such a relationship.

Early queenly iconography was relatively simple – the queen's position was indicated by a box throne and proximity to the king. However, starting in the 5th Dynasty the iconography became more complex. Queens wore either a vulture headdress that alluded to the goddesses Nekhbet and Mut or a crown that alluded to Wadjet as well as to the personification of the uraeus, the daughter of the sun and his protector. In the New Kingdom, queenly crowns bore double uraei. Other headdresses included diadems and a small hat known as a modius and surmounted by a pair of feathers. Queens often held lilies as symbols of rebirth, resurrection, and regenerative power.

It is difficult to assess the amount of political power actually wielded by queens. Obviously, some of their influence was unofficial and depended on their relationship with the king. Consequently, the influence of different queens varied significantly. For instance, Queen Tiye, the greatly beloved and respected wife of Amenhotep III, had much more political influence than many of her predecessors or successors. The only times when a queen's power was formally apparent was when she acted as a regent for her sons or took power for herself. Acting as a regent was a common and acceptable role for a queen. A queen's rule as pharaoh in her own right happened from time to time (e.g., Merneith, Nitokris, Sobekneferu, Hatshepsut, Tawesret, and some of the Ptolemies), but it was not quite acceptable because it did not fit the ideal of kingship wherein the position had to be held by a man. (Fig. 93.)

Queens were often very wealthy. They owned property, both land and palaces, as well as livestock, goods, and chattels. It has often been said that Egyptians queens lived in 'harems'. This term should be clarified. It is a loose translation of an Egyptian term, *ipt niswt*. It referred to where the royal family, particularly the female family members and the younger children, resided; basically, the term denoted the royal family's private quarters. Unlike harems in Islamic contexts, Egyptian harems had no sequestration of women or eunuchs. In fact, queens generally oversaw their harems and were responsible for all those within them.

The Royal Family

Besides the king, the queen, and their children, the royal family included the minor wives and concubines of the king and their offspring, as well as the king's brothers and sisters and various other relatives. Obviously, the importance of any particular family member depended on his or her proximity — either through blood or favour – to the king.

Until the 5th Dynasty, members of the king's family occupied most of the country's high administrative posts. Thereafter, perhaps owing to the potential threat that those who held them might pose to the king's

*Figure 93.   The very young king Pepy II sits on the lap of his mother, Queen
Ankhesenmeryre II. The pose alludes to the Isis–Horus connection and also establishes
Pepy's mother's position as regent. This statue, rendered in Egyptian alabaster, is marvel-
lously interconnecting, engaging the viewer on different planes, and displaying the skill of the
craftsman. Photo courtesy Brooklyn Museum.*

position, these jobs were given to people slightly removed from the royal
line. However, royal family members always remained important because
of their kinship with the king, and marriage to a royal person generally
elevated one's rank.

Other Egyptians who were closely associated with the royal family were
individuals who had shared the same wet nurse as the king or had been
brought up with him and shared the same tutor. Generally, these individuals wound up in trusted positions that were closely affiliated with the king,
acting as his 'companions', or bodyguards, or as tutors to his sons, as well
as holding key posts in the government. Royal wet nurses also held significant positions and in some ways were almost as esteemed as the kings'

mothers: King Tutankhamun's wet nurse was buried in a large decorated tomb that was probably given to her by her former charge, and her titles suggest that she was well loved and generously rewarded by him.

The Administration

Our insights into most other groups of ancient Egyptian society rest, to some extent, on the professional titles they held as preserved in texts from tombs, statuary, and documents. From these titles, we infer that the job of the civil service, under the direct authority of the vizier, was to ensure the smooth running of the country. This meant that the civil service was responsible for collecting taxes, administering justice, regulating agriculture, establishing land boundaries, and maintaining civic order. Thus, the administrative arms of the government included the treasury, the judiciary, royal mortuary temples (and sometimes cult temples), and even, to some extent, the military. The upper levels of the bureaucracy were occupied by the nobility, with the lower positions held by persons of less noble or of common birth.

The Vizier

In the Egyptian administration, the vizier followed the king in importance and undertook most of the actual day-to-day running of the country; basically, the vizier acted as the king's deputy and can be likened to a modern-day prime minister. The ancient Egyptian word for vizier was *tchaty*, and the position existed from at least the start of the 1st Dynasty, if not from the unification of the country. Men generally held this position, although there is an instance of a female vizier in the Old Kingdom. During the course of Egyptian history, the number of viziers varied from one to two (for Upper and Lower Egypt), depending on the configuration of the administration at the time. For the most part, the rank was not hereditary, but merit based, although there were times, such as in the 13th Dynasty, when the viziers became very powerful in their own right, and their positions were handed down from generation to generation.

Vizierial duties changed somewhat over time, but for the most part, their responsibilities remained the same. Rekhmire, a vizier who served under kings Thutmose III and his son Amenhotep II, inscribed his tomb (Theban Tomb 100) with a detailed text explaining the different aspects of his job. In the inscription he relates how he acted as the personal assistant and secretary to the king; managed the royal residence; organized 'works' (felling trees; constructing dykes, irrigation systems, and royal building works); oversaw the sealing and opening of storage areas; acted as head of the civil administration; communicated royal proclamations throughout the land; acted as chief magistrate, second only to the king; directed the tax levy and collection; examined and inventoried tribute; appointed the head of security, as well as many civil servants; and organized and despatched expeditions to mine, quarry, or explore. All in all, he asserted that he was the king's right hand and held significant power. It seems likely that, aside from the king, the only other officials who had the authority to check the vizier's power were the chancellor and the overseer of the treasury. (Fig. 94.)

Nobility and Officialdom

Those who were born into noble families generally occupied the highest positions in Egypt's administration, military, and priesthood. However, there are accounts of commoners rising to great heights through their merits alone. An 11th-Dynasty stela from Abydos (Stela 37) belonging to one Mentuhotep relates how he rose in the ranks, becoming a priest and notable cattle farmer, and Amenyseneb's stela (Louvre C12), also from Abydos, records how his priestly rank and responsibilities increased owing to his talents and honesty. Similarly, Senenmut, who became Hatshepsut's steward, chief architect, master of works, and close confidant (if not lover), was born of a common family from Armant and came to royal attention through his abilities. Amenhotep, son of Hapu, served King Amenhotep III so well, and his advice was valued was so highly, that he not only rose through the ranks during his lifetime but also achieved the status of a demi-god after his death and had a funerary temple constructed behind that of the king.

Treasurers (*imy-r per hedj*, or *imy-r pr wy nbw hedj*) were perhaps the most important national officials after the vizier. Often the post was divided between two people, one for Upper Egypt and the other for Lower Egypt. They were responsible for collecting, guarding, and disbursing royal funds. The most critical administrators on the provincial level were the nomarchs, or governors (except in the late 12th Dynasty – see Chapter 4); their regional administrative structure followed that of the capital. Other noteworthy posts included the Overseer of the King's Works (*imy-r kawt nisw*), who was in charge of building works; the Overseer of the Two Granaries (*imy-r shenuty*), who almost rivalled the treasurers because wealth was measured in grain; and

Figure 94.   The vizier Rekhmire's tomb at Thebes illustrates some of a vizier's duties. One important job was receiving and counting tribute and trade items. The top register shows Nubians bringing baboons, cheetahs, and tribute-filled bags; the next register shows either Minoans or Mycenaeans coming carrying vessels, followed by another group of Nubians bringing ebony, ivory, ostrich eggs and feathers, animal skins, more monkeys, and a giraffe. The bottom register shows peoples of the Levant bringing horses and jars that presumably contained wine or precious oils. Photo Salima Ikram.

the Secretary of the Great House (*sesh-shat n pr-a*), who was equivalent to a chief archivist. Below these people were several levels of officialdom.

Although generally officials were men, several women had titles suggesting positions of responsibility, as well as independent means. Naturally, all bureaucrats were literate and held the title or rank of scribe, a highly prized appellation. Many bureaucrats also possessed several priestly titles. One person could hold several titles, and accrue wealth from all of those positions – even though that individual might not actually perform those jobs. For example, the Overseer of the King's Butchers probably did not personally slaughter animals for the king's dinner; rather, his title conferred prestige and wealth upon him, and he oversaw other butchers who actually carried out the work, although he reaped most of the financial benefits connected to the post.

Temples were second only to the pharaoh in wealth, and they had large bureaucracies of their own, with influential priesthoods. High priests were chosen from amongst the elite and could be very powerful individuals – indeed, during the Third Intermediate period high priests virtually ruled the country. As was true for other areas of life, the most important priestly posts were held by the nobility, with the lowliest temple positions being held by commoners. Priests often worked for both the temple bureaucracy and the pharaoh, depending on which god they served and what position that they held. As with the post of vizier, at times the higher-level priests not only were selected from the nobility but also passed on their positions through heredity.

Magistrates and police were another part of the vast machine of Egyptian government and played an important role in both provincial and urban areas. The magistrates adjudicated land and water disputes, resolved inheritance problems, and administered justice to the people in their local area. Should their judgements be questioned, the people could appeal to the vizier or even to the king (for details on Egyptian law, see Chapter 8).

The upper echelons of the military were also made up of nobles, but these positions could also be won through merit. The autobiography of Ahmose, son of Abana, which is inscribed in his tomb at el-Kab, relates how he rose in the ranks of the military by serving his king, Ahmose, in Ahmose's struggle against the Hyksos. He also served Amenhotep I in various campaigns against the Nubians and was awarded the title 'Warrior of the Ruler'. In fact, the most socially mobile sector of Egyptian society was probably the military. If a soldier proved himself brave in battle, or had a particular talent in terms of strategy, even a raw recruit from the peasant class could eventually rise to great heights.

'The Satire of the Trades'

'The Satire of the Trades' is a text that was used to train scribes in handwriting and rhetoric. Like other works of its kind it also has an improving message embedded within it. This text elevates the life of the scribe above that of all others and gives us a view of what the administrators might have thought of others who were less qualified than they. It also emphasizes the importance and power of literacy in ancient Egypt (see Chapter 8). The text describes working as a scribe as 'the greatest of all callings', while everyone else's job is considered to be more lowly. A smith is described as having 'fingers like crocodile claws', the reed-cutter is devoured by mosquitoes, the potter 'grubs in mud like a pig', the mason is exhausted and filthy, the farmer suffers from swollen fingers and is always weary, and the washerman lives in fear of the crocodiles, as does the fisherman. The text is persuasive about the benefits of literacy, as all other professions are made to look painful and unattractive.

Non-Elites in Ancient Egyptian Society

The lower levels of the administration, military, and priesthood were occupied primarily by non-elites. For the most part, holders of these positions remained fairly static, although men of this social group could and often did rise in the ranks. Merchants and traders also numbered amongst this social stratum; if highly successful and crown employed, they too could achieve a higher level in Egyptian society. Thus, what might be termed a middle-class or an intermediate-level social group developed, made up of minor functionaries who worked in the priesthood, administration, and military, or as merchants, traders, or even artisans, particularly if they were favoured by the king (discussed shortly; see also Chapter 8), as well as residents of towns or cities unconnected either to agriculture or to the bureaucracy. Artisans such as carpenters, sculptors, and painters were a part of this group, although those who enjoyed royal favour and were directly attached to the court enjoyed more wealth and status than did those without royal patronage.

Thus, the craftsmen who lived in the workers' village of Lahun and were employed by King Senusert II to work on his funerary monument, or those who carved the statues, stelae, and tombs at el-Amarna for Akhenaten, or the inhabitants of Deir el-Medina in Thebes who made and decorated tombs and funerary equipment not only in the Valley of the Kings but also for the New Kingdom nobility constituted an elite group amongst artisans. Potters and builders were included in this group, and in the one below it. Obviously, architects involved with royal projects tended to be members of a more elite group.

Strikes in Ancient Egypt

Royal necropolis workers, such as the inhabitants of Lahun and Deir el-Medina, were a special class of craftspeople and had a definite sense of what was their due. They had a contract with the king to decorate his tomb and fill it with beautiful items; he, in turn, would provide them with special status, houses, and regular payment. During the reign of Ramesses III, when Egypt was beset by economic and military troubles, the workers of Deir el-Medina were not being regularly paid and they staged the first sit-in strike ever recorded in history. The hungry workers refused to go to work and protested at the mortuary temples of Thutmose III, Seti I, and Ramesses II. That strike was successful, but for the remainder of the 20th Dynasty they were paid only intermittently because of the deteriorating economic and political conditions.

Peasants (agricultural workers), with the exception of certain types of slaves, formed the majority of the lowest level of Egyptian society. Although agricultural wealth and, consequently, labour formed the basis of the Egyptian economy, farming was not considered a prestigious occupation: 'The Satire of the Trades' declares, 'A peasant is not called a man, beware of it!' Some peasants may have owned small parcels of land, although most either worked the land for landowners and took a percentage of the yield as payment or leased land from elite landowners or temples, and also probably paid taxes on their produce to the king. Scholars believe that sometimes in lieu of paying taxes, peasants engaged in corvée labour for the central government. Thus, building the pyramids, cutting large canals, and constructing dykes were other jobs that peasants carried out.

Peasants traded their surplus and supplemented their income on a modest level by carrying out tasks for others. Members of the peasantry also engaged in relatively unskilled labour, such as digging canals or fetching and carrying on building sites. They also could be soldiers, and, in times of military emergency, peasants may have been conscripted into the army. Many might also have served temples as workers or at the most basic level of priests, as a *waab*, or pure one. A particularly gifted peasant might be able to move up in the temple's social hierarchy.

Slaves

The most common Egyptian words for 'slave', *hem* or *bak* (*fem.*, *hemet* or *baket*), were, in fact, used to describe anyone who was a servant. Thus, many priests were called *hem-netjer*, or servants-slaves of the god (or the pharaoh), and anyone working on a nobleman's private estate was called a *bak*. It is sometimes difficult therefore to determine who might have been enslaved in the modern sense: individuals who work for another without payment and who are the property of their owners and can be disposed of as the owners wish.

As far as scholars understand the subject, slaves in ancient Egypt were prisoners of war or possibly were provided as tribute by vassal countries, although slave traders might acquire people through other means. In Egypt slaves primarily came from the Near East, Libya, and Nubia/Kush. Male slaves were generally pressed into hard labour and would be sent to work in the inhospitable environments of stone quarries and mines to extract stones and ores. This back-breaking work ensured that most slaves had short and fairly hard lives. They, like the peasants, but with less recompense, also worked for the state, cutting canals, building roads, and constructing royal edifices. If they had special skills, these might be exploited and they might be spared hard labour. If they were house slaves, their lives would be far less arduous, although this also depended on their owner.

Slave owners had specific responsibilities to their charges, at least in domestic contexts. They gave slaves names and an identity, and were responsible for the upbringing of their children, perhaps to the point of educating them. Slaves could even own property and have possessions, and could trade legally. Obviously, many slaves were dissatisfied with their lot, particularly if they were engaged in hard labour, and there are reports of slaves trying to run away, and sometimes succeeding. However, it seems that being a slave in ancient Egypt might have been preferable to being a poor peasant, particularly if one were a house slave.

Female slaves generally had a better life than their male counterparts. Most were taken into domestic service, although some, no doubt, were purchased to work at manufacturing textiles, producing beer and bread, or cultivating the land. Others might have functioned as a combination of concubine and domestic worker, and would have had a higher status than those female slaves who served as domestic workers alone. Most information concerning domestic slaves dates to the New Kingdom. Texts show that these slaves were often freed by their owners and sometimes adopted into their families, and that they even inherited goods and property from their erstwhile owners. One elderly lady was so annoyed by her own children that she left everything she owned to her manumitted slave!

Little information has come down to us concerning captured children. Presumably, they also worked as slaves but were probably treated leniently, as is indicated by the text of an 18th-Dynasty letter that discusses their treatment and education. Such children might have had the best chance of eventually being freed and absorbed into Egyptian society.

Foreigners

In addition to slaves, free-born foreigners lived in Egypt, particularly from the Middle Kingdom onward. How the Egyptians viewed them depended on whether the foreigners had become acculturated to Egypt or maintained their own traditions and language. The Egyptians had an extremely ethnocentric view of the world: they were the central power and had the superior culture and the most powerful gods. According to them, Egyptians were the chief of the four peoples of the world, the others being Nubians, Libyans, and Near Easterners, all of whom could be, and sometimes were, subjugated by the Egyptians. This superiority of Egypt was partially formulaic, as it was a way of demonstrating the country's security and autonomy: in temples, the king was shown smiting foreigners; foreigners were shown bound and being brought as gifts to the gods; and the Nine Bows, emblematic of the traditional enemies of Egypt, were represented on the king's footstool, so that every time he placed his feet on the stool it symbolised Egypt's victory over its enemies. However, foreigners who settled in Egypt and took Egyptian names, learned the language, prayed to Egyptian gods, and were absorbed into the culture were regarded as honorary Egyptians; they could integrate effectively into society and could enjoy social mobility. Even Egypt's rulers could be of foreign origin: King Amenemhat VI and King Hornedjhiryotef, rulers during the 13th Dynasty, were of Asiatic origin, as their sobriquet, *aamu* (Asiatic), suggests. A slightly later ruler within the same dynasty, Khendjer, was a Syrian mercenary. (Fig. 95.)

Additionally, from the New Kingdom onward, foreign princes were taken captive and held in Egypt or were kept as diplomatic hostages, indoctrinated and raised in the Egyptian way so that later they would be sympathetic to Egypt. The Romans later adopted this scheme to bring people into their Empire and to promote and maintain the Roman way of life. Egyptian royal

Figure 95. Although many foreigners emigrated to Egypt, particularly during the Middle Kingdom, many others came as prisoners, such as these Libyans and Near Easterners who are shown in abject poses in the Memphite tomb of Horemheb at Saqqara. Photo Salima Ikram.

diplomatic marriages meant that many queens of Egypt were foreigners, bringing with them their own entourages, whose members also settled in Egypt and married Egyptians. It is possible that in addition to their ladies- and gentlemen-in-waiting these foreign queens brought artisans to Egypt who painted frescoes or produced specialised crafts and thus influenced Egyptian art and technology.

Many foreigners in Egypt were part of the army. Mercenaries from Nubia and Libya were taken into the army from the Old Kingdom onward, and Near Easterners and even Greeks were employed in later periods of Egyptian history. Nubian Medjay people, who were famed for their prowess with the bow, were an important corps in the Egyptian army. Later, the word *medjay* was used to describe the Egyptian police force. How allegiances held when Egypt's foes were Nubian is unclear – perhaps for mercenaries the enemies were less important than their pay. Foreign interpreters were also used for trade and military expeditions.

The other large influx of foreigners into Egypt came because of trade. Until about 600 BC the majority of traders and merchants came from the south, the east, and, to a lesser degree, the west. Subsequently, these groups were joined by Greeks, who even established major trading posts/cities in the Delta, such as Naukratis. They were at least partly responsible for the complex cocktail of Egyptian culture that characterises the Late and Graeco-Roman periods.

People often immigrated to Egypt from Libya, the Near East and Nubia. This was especially true in times of famine, as Egypt was more agriculturally stable than the surrounding areas, and also had reserves of grain to see it through times of scarcity. Once settled in Egypt, the immigrants tended to stay and could be totally integrated into Egyptian society. Presumably, it is such settlers who introduced their gods into the Egyptian pantheon to be worshipped by foreigners and Egyptians alike. Thus Astarte, Baal, Anath, and other divinities became part of Egypt's religious landscape from the second millennium BC onward.

Once foreigners had been acculturated, they could work in diverse areas and enjoyed the same social mobility as Egyptians. They might start as peasants and rise to be landowners or serve as priests and end their careers as administrators. The vizier Aperel, who served Amenhotep III and had an elaborate tomb at Saqqara, was Asiatic in origin, as was Paser, who was a vizier to both Seti I and Ramesses II. There is evidence of foreigners working as goldsmiths, architects (there is a record of one Pasbaal, who worked in the temple of Amun at Karnak in c. 1470 BC), and scribes. Foreign scribes were particularly important in the New Kingdom when Akkadian became the lingua franca of the Near East and all diplomatic correspondence was carried out in Akkadian. Thus, depending on their desire and ability to 'become Egyptian', foreigners might enjoy the same privileges as native-born Egyptians.

7

Town Life and Country Life

Current knowledge of Egyptian settlement sites is limited because so few have been excavated. The primary reason for this is that many of these sites remain inhabited to this day, and it is not feasible to displace entire villages and towns in the quest for their ancient predecessors. What information has been gathered is gleaned from those sites that we have been able to investigate (the largest expanses of which survive because they were special-purpose settlements located in the desert), from texts, and from the application of common sense and ethnographic extrapolation.

Town Life

The most modest sort of human settlement in ancient Egypt would have been a hamlet, followed by a village, then a town, and finally a city. The ancient Egyptians also built specialized settlements associated with particular projects, such as pyramid building or military fortresses, or ones constructed for a specific group of people, such as the craftsmen who decorated the New Kingdom royal tombs at Thebes. Other state-organized settlements were associated with mining and quarrying activities or other short-term projects. The majority of settlements that were established by the state show evidence for orthogonal town planning, in that the streets were laid out on a grid with arrangements made for drainage and possibly for waste disposal. Hitherto such town planning had been attributed to the Greeks, but there is plenty of evidence from Egypt to indicate the establishment of such urban organization as early as the Middle Kingdom, if not before, at the Giza Workmen's Village. (Fig. 96.) Within these planned settlements, areas for administrative and religious buildings were allocated, with the layout of domestic plots being less carefully monitored.

In contrast, non-state-sponsored towns or cities presumably grew organically, with only limited planning and organization. Other types of communities might have been of more ephemeral duration and size, such as those associated with seasonal occupations, such as netting migrating birds or caring for herds.

As the majority of the Egyptian population consisted of agriculturalists, it is logical to assume that most Egyptians lived in a rural rather than an urban setting. Thus, the most common types of settlements were small hamlets or villages dispersed throughout the country and associated with fertile land. The hamlets consisted of a few houses clustered together, with agriculture being the inhabitants' main activity. In the case of the villages, some craft specialisation, such as pottery and textile production, would have been present as well. These settlements would have grown organically, with little or no planning, and consisted entirely of mud-brick constructions with reeds or wood used for such elements as roofs, doors, and window frames. Domestic shrines or even small community-supported chapels served religious needs. The restricted size, population, and relationships found in an ancient Egyptian village were reflected in the Egyptian term for village, *wehyt*, which was also related to the word for family, kindred, or tribe (also *wehyt*, but spelled slightly differently).

Settlements with significantly larger populations and more buildings, temples, and administrative centres can be defined as towns (*demi* in Egyptian, though this word can also mean abode or neighbourhood). In their most expanded form, large settlements might be considered cities (*niwt* in Egyptian). In some texts, the Egyptians did not differentiate too closely between town and city, using the word *niwt* for both – it seems that in principle any large urban centre was regarded as a city. The hieroglyph for *niwt*, an 'X' within a

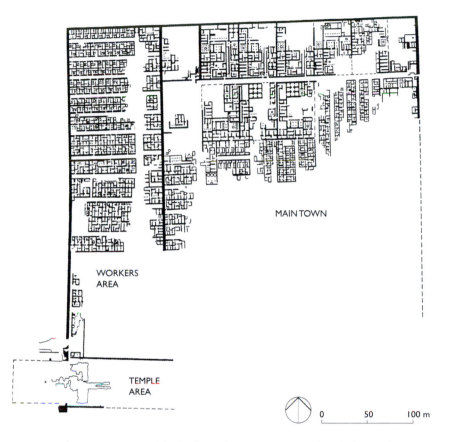

MAIN TOWN

WORKERS
AREA

TEMPLE
AREA

0   50   100 m

*Figure 96. Lahun was presumably built as the town associated with the nearby pyramid
of Senusert II. A higher temple area was situated at one corner, and the rest of the town was
divided into two main portions, one for the workers and one for the elite. Orthagonal town
planning is obvious here. Drawing Nicholas Warner, after Petrie.*

circle, represents an encircling wall around the city's main cross-streets. This
hieroglyph drew on reality: early settlements at Abydos and Hemamieh were
constructed in this manner.

In the earliest years of Egyptian history there were probably few cities as
the term is defined today, that is, a dominant urban settlement with a significant population supported by food supplies brought in from the hinterland,
serving a multiplicity of functions (commercial, religious, administrative),
with a varied economic and social profile. The capital would have been the
pre-eminent city for the entire country, with the pre-unification capitals
continuing to be important centres. Some of these retained the position of
towns, with only the largest and most economically active ones achieving
the status of cities. Indubitably, the number of cities increased over time.

Also of importance were the nome capitals and major religious centres; indeed, these might have formed the cores of significant settlements. The Great Harris Papyrus now in the British Museum (named after its first modern owner and reflecting its dimensions) records 160 towns in Egypt that Ramesses III gave to various temples; clearly, there was a large number of towns and cities in Egypt to house an increasing population. The number of urban centres probably increased still further in the Late period, when more trading centres were needed.

Sites for towns and cities were chosen because of their access to water, fertile land, transport routes, economic promise, and defensibility. Some places might also have been selected for religious reasons because the Egyptians believed them to be locations significant in their cosmology: the burial place of Osiris, the birthplace of Horus, and so on. Religious reasons would certainly also have been a factor in the size of the settlement and its economic importance.

For much of Egypt's history, Memphis was the administrative capital, although the principal royal residence, and thus effectively the country's political centre, was at various times located at Itj-tawy (near Lisht?), Thebes, El-Amarna, Tell el-Dab'a, Qantir, Tanis, Sais, and Alexandria. A modern capital city is generally regarded as the seat of government, with the head of state and most of the administration in residence. However, in ancient Egypt, while the bulk of the administration was situated in the 'capital' (i.e., Memphis), the king moved about the country and probably had palaces in several places. The court, which would have included some of the senior ministers, moved from place to place with the king: similar itinerant court systems can be observed in historic Ethiopia, as well as in countries in medieval Europe.

Memphis was allegedly founded specifically as the capital of a united Egypt at the beginning of Dynasty 1. Sadly, excavations at Memphis have not revealed as much as one might have hoped concerning the layout and evolution of the ancient city; many of the stone elements were quarried to build the medieval and modern city of Cairo, and much of the mud brick has fallen prey to the *sebbakhin*. It seems also that the course of the Nile shifted substantially over the millennia and may have obliterated some of the city's earliest levels. However, some of the mud-brick buildings in Memphis have been excavated, revealing the presence of palaces and residential buildings. Texts and scanty physical remains indicate that the city contained the great temple of Ptah, a palace, and administrative areas, all surrounded by a white wall. Perhaps the city's earliest form inspired the layout of royal cemeteries: in Memphis, the king's palace and major administrative buildings occupied the central space (equivalent to the pyramid), with less important administrative buildings and residential areas spreading outwards from the royal focal point (corresponding to the tombs of individuals of lesser importance).

Of all of Egypt's capitals, el-Amarna (Akhetaten) and Tell el-Dab'a (Avaris) have thus far revealed the most about Egyptian cities. Tell el-Dab'a started as a planned settlement under 12th-Dynasty pharaohs and continued to grow thereafter, becoming the Hyksos capital in the Second Intermediate period, and subsequently a major Egyptian royal city in the 18th Dynasty. Significant features of the site are of course its size, the number of palaces and large administrative buildings, and the richness of imported finds that include a series of Minoan frescoes that might have once adorned a queen's apartments in a palace. A curious feature about the site is that it was built on a series of turtlebacks and thus was connected by a system of watery 'paths' suggestive of the Italian city of Venice.

Akhetaten provides significant insight into Egyptian urbanism, particularly as it covers a specific period and shows a snapshot in time, having been occupied for no more than two decades. Furthermore, it was designed specifically as a capital city, much like the twentieth-century and earlier capital cities of Brasilia, Canberra, Islamabad, and Washington, DC. This is both an advantage and a disadvantage: on the one hand, it illustrates certain Egyptian ideas concerning town planning, but on the other hand, this means that it is an atypical example, as compared with 'organically' developed cities elsewhere in Egypt. Fifteen boundary stelae delineated the area of the city, which was located on both sides of the Nile. Not only did these stelae mark the borders of the city, but they also named some of the buildings within, such as 'The Mansion of the Sun-Disk' and the 'House of the Sun-Disk', both of which were temples to the Aten. Most of the city was located on the river's east bank, with agricultural land on the west. The area of the city was about sixty-one square kilometres, laid out in the shape of the Egyptian symbol for city, *niwt*, a circle with a 'X' within it. The city was arranged on a north–south axis and divided into several portions connected by a road some seven or more kilometres in length. It was not enclosed by a mud-brick wall, perhaps because of its size and the fact that the cliffs on either side of the river established its limits. Its total population in its heyday is estimated to have been between twenty thousand and fifty thousand individuals. (Fig. 97.)

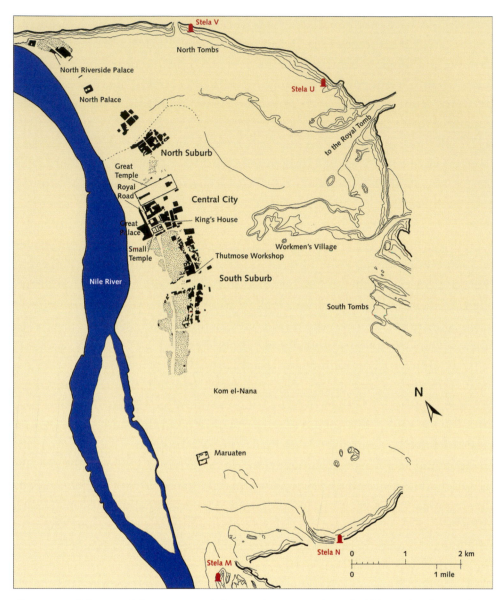

Figure 97. The city of Amarna extended over a large area along the Nile, with stelae marking the city's boundaries. Royal palaces occur in more than one place, as do temples to the Aten. Smaller settlements, such as the Workmen's Village that housed the men and women who worked on carving and decorating the tomb, are located at a slight distance from the main city, closer to the workplace. A network of roads connected the different parts of the city. Drawing by Peter Der Manuelian.

In the north, from whence the royal road originated, lay the North Riverside Palace and some ancillary buildings, perhaps related to supplying and administrating the area. This palace was probably the main residence for the royal family. Other houses were built across the road from the royal residence. To the south lay the isolated North Palace, which may have been exclusively for the queen's use, and still farther south was a mainly residential area, the North Suburb. About another two kilometres south lay the area known as Central City. This was probably the administrative centre and included the major Aten temples, places for food storage, the temple middens, an official palace where the king conducted state business, archives, offices for bureaucrats, barracks for the police and their animals, and some residential blocks and their associated rubbish dumps. The Southern or Main City contained the bulk of residential and administrative quarters. Butchery yards, breweries, and bakeries that served officialdom were probably located here as well as in Central City. Workshops for artisans, including that of a royal sculptor, Djhutmose, were also located here. Farther to the south lay the site of a temple at Kom el-Nana, and still farther a site known as the Maruaten, which was associated with queens and the worship of the Aten.

The dead were not ignored – a large cemetery divided into northern and southern halves was located in the eastern cliffs, bracketing a wadi in which the royal tombs were located. Symbolically, this mortuary landscape was considered to be part of the city plan, as were a separate walled town housing the tomb workers (see later in this section) and another crude stone village located on the outskirts of the city, perhaps to monitor the surrounding roads.

Although Amarna was an intensely planned new royal city, there is, aside from the administrative buildings and barracks area in the Central City, limited evidence for purely organic growth in the residential areas in the North Suburb and the Main City. Small houses were inserted haphazardly into the interstices between larger villas and their surrounding gardens; perhaps these houses came after the villas were constructed and belonged to those dependent on the residents of the more opulent houses. It is also possible that the king granted courtiers tracts of land but did not specify the precise layout of the plots, thus creating an organic city within and beyond a planned one.

Other settlements that were not capitals and have also been (partially) excavated include Kom el-Hisn, Merimde, Buto, and Mendes in the Delta; Lahun (Kahun) in the Fayyum; Abydos (particularly the area of Kom el-Sultan) in Middle Egypt; and Medinet Habu/Jeme, Deir el-Medina, Tell Edfu,

Figure 98. The walled village now called Deir el-Medina was home to the workers who decorated and equipped the tombs of the New Kingdom pharaohs. The houses were laid out along streets and were fairly regular in plan, although some houses were larger than others. Photo Salima Ikram.

Hierakonpolis, and Elephantine in Upper Egypt. Many of these urban centres shared standard features, such as being enclosed within mud-brick walls and having houses arranged along streets. With the exceptions of Lahun and Deir el-Medina, which were royal foundation, the other sites grew organically, and there is little indication of any formal town planning with streets laid out on a grid. The size and layout of houses also yield evidence of social differentiation within residential areas. City plans show some basic zoning according to use: some areas were dedicated to food production, industry, and crafts, whereas others were administrative, religious, or residential in nature. (Fig. 98.)

A great deal of information concerning royally sponsored settlements in Egypt has been derived from special villages, such as the Workmens' Village at el-Amarna, the Old Kingdom pyramid town at Giza, the Middle Kingdom towns of el-Lahun and Hetep Senwosret, and the New Kingdom craft settlement at Deir el-Medina, as well as from towns established inside the fortresses that the Egyptians built in Nubia. All of these sites were built purposefully and expeditiously by royal command and paid for by the state.

Thus, all these settlements shared several characteristics: an enclosure wall (although less true thus far for Giza), an orthogonal street layout, some form of drainage, standardisation of houses, and defined quarters dedicated to administration, religion, industry, and food production. These settlements were much more controlled than were the majority of Egyptian towns and cities whose layouts were less carefully organized, although most became somewhat less rigidly arranged over time.

Houses and Palaces

Our knowledge about Egyptian houses (*per*, in Egyptian) and palaces (house of the king, so *per-nsw*, or Great House, *per-aa* and *per-wer*) comes not only from excavated sites but also from wooden and ceramic house models found in burials or given as votive offerings, images of houses found in tombs, descriptions of ideal dwellings recorded in religious and literary texts, and references to houses and household economy found in archival documents. In addition, tombs were regarded as houses of eternity (*per-djet*), and they frequently reflected aspects of house design; in Dynasty 2 they even contained toilets!

Houses

The Egyptians regarded houses for the living as temporary structures since people were sure to die, and thus they built these houses out of perishable materials. It did not matter if the resident was a king or a commoner, the basic building materials used for palaces or more modest houses were the same. For most of Egyptian history mud brick was the primary component in any construction, with mud plaster added as a finishing touch. (Fig. 99.) Reeds, palm leaves, and wood (palm, acacia, and tamarisk, in particular) augmented the brick and were most commonly used to construct roofs if they were flat and not barrel vaulted. The Nile silt used in the bricks was not only plentiful thanks to the annual flooding of the river (see Chapter 1) but also practical as a building material. Thick mud-brick walls functioned as insulation, keeping houses cool in summer and warm in winter, as did the substantial roofs made of palm (or other) logs and covered by reed and palm-leaf mats, alternating with mud plaster. In wealthy houses, occasional elements such as thresholds, lintels, window frames, and pillar bases were added in stone, and pillars in timber. Only houses for eternity, that is, temples and the tombs of the elite, were built from more enduring materials. (Fig. 100.)

Figure 99. Brick-making scenes such as this one in the tomb of Rekhmire at Thebes (TT100), together with actual bricks, tell us how bricks were made. Silt from the banks of the Nile or from canals was mixed with chaff, sand, dung, and other temper and then put into a form to give it shape and left to dry in the sun. At different periods of Egyptian history, bricks were made in different sizes, and the temper used varied depending on where the bricks were made. The scenes here show other industries as well, such as metalworking, woodworking, and leatherworking. Photo Salima Ikram.

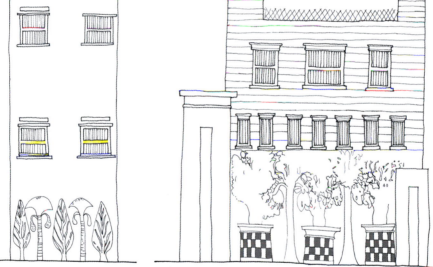

Figure 100. Houses are sometimes represented in tombs or on papyri, giving us a sense of what the façades on a street might look like. From the top left, moving clockwise, *houses belonging to Nebamun, Nakht, Mosi (TT 254), and Thay (TT 23) are shown. The triangular shapes are the* malqaf. *Mosi's roof-space is shielded by a reed enclosure, and the trees in front of his house, between the front and back doors, are protected from goats and dogs by low brick enclosures. Drawing by Nicholas Warner, after A. Badawy.*

Because of the seasonal temperature differences in Egypt, the houses of rich and poor alike were carefully oriented to take advantage of the environment, sharing architectural features that made for maximum comfort. The houses of the wealthy might even have had, when possible, separate summer and winter quarters, much as is found in Arab houses of later periods. Where possible, doors and openings might have been oriented to the north to catch the cooling breeze that ran through the entire country. Wind scoops, also found in later Arab houses and called *malqaf* in Arabic, helped funnel these breezes through the house during the hot months and were sealed off during the winter. The wealthy enhanced the 'natural air-conditioning' of their *malqafs* by digging ponds to the north of their front doors so that the breezes would be doubly cooling. The thickness of walls and ceilings acted as additional insulation. In winter, poorer people, especially those in less urban areas, brought their animals into small courtyards within the house to help keep both them and the humans warm. Windows were small and high up, letting in a minimum of direct sunlight in the summer and cutting down on cold air in the winter.

As in any period of architectural history, wealth determined the size and the components of different dwellings. It was common for the elite to own a country house located on their estates, as well as one, if not more, dwellings in towns. People could also own or lease land in several different parts of the country, as is made clear in the Middle Kingdom letters of Heqanakht, a man who lived in Thebes but owned or leased properties not only there but also in the Delta, near Lisht and the Fayyum.

Country estates, called *huwt-aat*, were often far more complex than were houses in towns. In addition to domestic quarters, estates included workshops for weaving, woodwork, and possibly pottery, as well as places for bakers, brewers, butchers, and perhaps even vintners to ply their crafts. The gardens might contain shrines to a preferred deity, ponds for fish that were both ornamental and edible, and pigeon towers for birds that provided both food and guano for fertilizer. The attached lands could include vast tracts for growing major crops, such as grain, as well as orchards, vineyards, large-scale vegetable plots or smaller kitchen gardens, and ornamental gardens surrounding the house.

The houses of the rich shared many features. In 'The Story of Sinuhe', a Middle Kingdom tale, Sinuhe, the protagonist, describes an ideal Egyptian house as containing gardens, bedrooms, and bathrooms – clearly the high points of his ideal house. In general, an encircling wall defined the area of a wealthy person's house, whether the dwelling was in the country or the city.

Often a small room for a doorman guarded the entrance. A courtyard, sometimes with a pond, lay in front of the house over which the 'sweet breezes of the north' blew into the dwelling, cooling it during the hot months.

A portico marked the front of the house architecturally and provided shade. Roofs show evidence of drain spouts, indicating a wetter climate or at least intermittent rains. Larger houses tended to be divided into two main sections: public and private. In some publications, the latter areas have been called the 'harem', although there is no indication that Egyptian women lived the sequestered life implied by this term in modern usage. Rather, these were the family quarters, not to be accessed by the majority of people who visited the house.

The main feature of the public area of a wealthy Egyptian's house was a large room, often columned, and sometimes lined with mud-brick benches. An ideal place to receive important guests and to conduct business, this room was frequently associated with a courtyard and was surrounded by a few smaller rooms. The remainder of the house and the upper stories tended to be devoted to family life. Bedrooms, often painted with images of household gods such as Bes and Taweret, living rooms, lavatories equipped with latrine seats and pots in which waste was collected, bathrooms, kitchens with mud ovens and granaries, and storage areas (some subsurface to maintain a cooler temperature), made up the remainder of the house.

It is difficult to assign particular activities to most rooms of excavated houses; kitchens, lavatories, and reception areas are easily identifiable, as are bedrooms enhanced by painted decoration. However, other rooms are less clearly characterised, and it is probable that a multiplicity of activities took place within them, perhaps varying with the seasons. Many houses had two storeys; the stairs were made of mud brick and sometimes equipped with wooden treads. Roofs were also used for storage, for cooking in summer, and for sleeping during the hot summer months. The number of rooms in a house depended on an individual's wealth and position. Ceilings and walls were often decorated with paintings on the mud plaster, or walls were covered with reed mats that would serve as further insulation. Tomb decoration offers clues as to how houses might have been decorated. (Fig. 101.)

Houses that were a part of a special royally sponsored settlement tended to have regularized plans. These units were repeated over and over with some variation, and were tidily arranged along a gridded street system. Occasionally, larger houses with gardens belonging to overseers or senior

Figure 101. Meket-Re, a vizier who worked for the kings of the late 11th Dynasty and perhaps even for the first kings of the 12th Dynasty, was buried in Thebes. When, under the direction of H. E. Winlock of New York's Metropolitan Museum of Art, Meket-Re's tomb was being cleared in order to document the plan, the tomb was thought to have been emptied by thieves. However, as one workman was clearing the floor of the tomb, he felt it give way. Beneath lay a small chamber, or serdab, *containing several wooden models that depicted Meket-Re's considerable estate and belongings. These models included workshops for carpenters, weavers, butchers, bakers, and brewers; granaries; cattle stalls; pleasure and fishing boats; and images of Meket-Re's houses. The models were distributed between the Egyptian Museum, Cairo, and the Metropolitan Museum. This model, in the collection of the latter, shows the façade of a house fronted by a portico and a pond surrounded by trees. The pond and the shade of the fig trees kept the house cool in the summer. The presence of drain-spouts on the roof indicates a wetter climate. Photo Salima Ikram.*

officials interrupted the pattern. At Deir el-Medina, the entrance courtyards contained a curious feature: a large raised and enclosed bed or bench made of mud brick that was frequently painted with convolvulus vines. This has been variously identified as a place for the confinement of women during childbirth or as a platform for the household's gods, with the latter option seeming more feasible. (Fig. 102a, b, and c.)

Houses belonging to less wealthy Egyptians had the same basic components but on a much more reduced scale and with less differentiation of special purpose space. Rooms for doorkeepers and formal reception rooms were generally absent. In towns and cities, particularly during the later periods of Egyptian history, people lived in multi-storey dwellings that were often crowded together, in many cases lacking the basic necessities that might have been enjoyed by their rural contemporaries. (Fig. 103.)

Palaces

King's houses were just larger versions of wealthy homes and were made predominantly of the same materials and used the same technologies. Most of the Egyptian palaces that have been excavated date to the New Kingdom. Some that were ceremonial were attached to royal funerary complexes, particularly those at Thebes, and they presumably housed the king when he came to oversee the building of his tomb and funerary temple, his 'Temple of Millions of Years', or whilst he officiated at ceremonies. Other palaces were clearly parts of a living city. The best preserved of the former type is the palace of Ramesses III at Medinet Habu, while the palaces at Deir el-Ballas, Malqata, el-Amarna, Tell el-Yahudiya, Memphis, and Pi-Ramesses are particularly good examples of the latter.

As one might expect, the formal reception rooms in a palace were far larger and more numerous than those found in private homes. The king's throne room would not have had places for people to sit – just a dais for the royal throne. An element that New Kingdom palaces shared is a place where the king would appear before the populace: a window of appearance. This was a popular feature of the Amarna palaces; from it, the king could reward his courtiers, utter proclamations, and be adored by his people.

Egyptian queens are known to have had separate palaces. Architecturally, these were similar to the main royal palaces, albeit a bit smaller. These buildings might have housed one or more royal wife, as well as the king's concubines and children.

102a   Entrance   Entrance

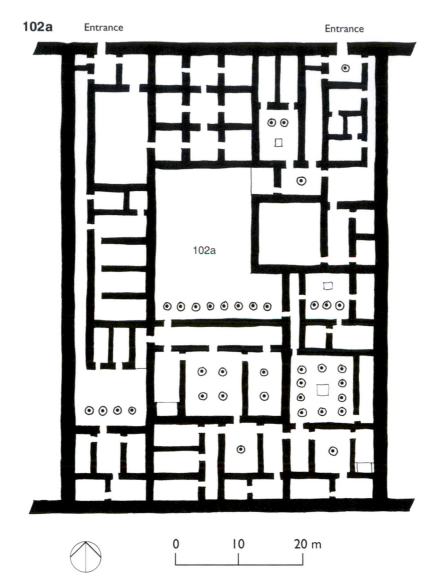

0   10   20 m

Figure 102. Houses varied depending on the owner's social status. They could be simple and fairly linear, such as those belonging to the workmen at Deir el-Medina (102c), complete with cellars and house shrines, or they could be larger, such as the houses of the elite, with several courtyards embellished by small limestone containers suggestive of ponds, storage rooms, and public and private areas, like those found at Lahun (102a). Lavish dwellings or estates were found at Amarna (102b); the houses were set in large gardens with shrines and sometimes equipped with wells or ponds. In addition to a large house with public and private areas, and perhaps having two storeys, such estates also had animal pens, storage facilities, and a separate wing for servants. Drawing Nicholas Warner, after A. Badawy.

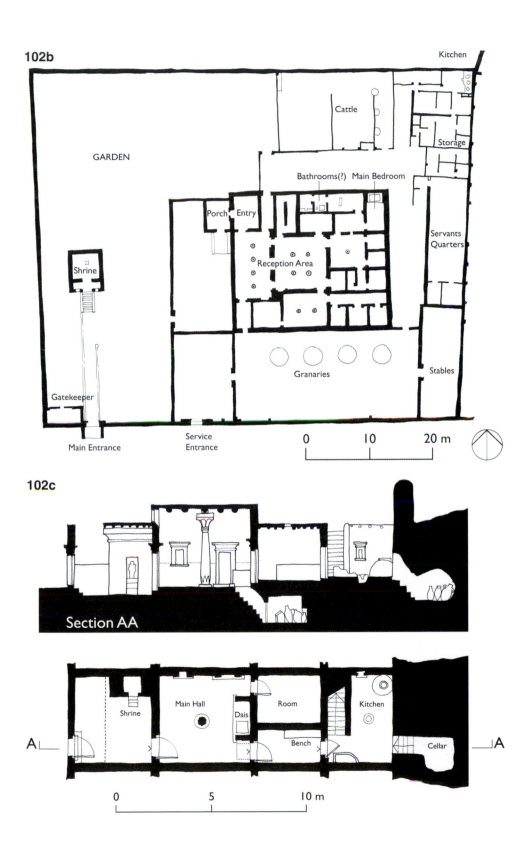

102b

GARDEN

Kitchen

Cattle

Storage

Bathrooms(?) Main Bedroom

Porch Entry

Reception Area

Servants Quarters

Shrine

Granaries

Stables

Gatekeeper

Main Entrance

Service Entrance

0   10   20 m

102c

Section AA

A — A

Shrine

Main Hall

Dais

Room

Kitchen

Bench

Cellar

0   5   10 m

Figure 103. A limestone toilet seat from Amarna and now in the Cairo Museum. It would have been balanced on parallel stacks of bricks with a pottery vessel placed beneath the hole. The contents of the vessel would be covered with sand or perhaps even with lime, and then disposed of. Photo Ahmed Amin.

The decoration of palaces was quite different from what was found in private residences. Thus, floors, ceilings, and walls were painted. Faience tiles made in a variety of shapes and colours enhanced columns and other architectural features. Windows were always constructed so that they let in only a limited amount of light; the windows were made of elaborately carved pieces of limestone and often included the king's name or images of deities. In addition to decorating palaces for aesthetic appeal, artists employed iconographic devices to protect the king and to emphasize his royalty. Thus, painted ceilings, such as those found at Amenhotep III's palace at Malqata (Thebes), show images of bulls, a royal symbol, while the floor of the royal dais, where the king placed his feet, was painted with images of nine prisoners, representing the 'Nine Bows', the traditional enemies of Egypt. Instead of plain slats, windows were carved with the king's name or with images of the 'Two Ladies'. Other motifs, such as symbols of the people of Egypt praising the king, or of protective vultures, were also featured in the decorative scheme of palaces.

Households and Families

Founding a house, taking a wife, and begetting a family were regarded as the proper duties of every Egyptian man. The sage Ptahhotep wrote: 'When you prosper and found your house, And love your wife with ardour, Fill her belly, clothe her back . . . .Gladden her heart as long as you live, She is a fertile field for her lord.'[1] The size of a household is difficult to define. The 'ideal' family that is shown in Egyptian art consists of a husband, a wife, and two children. (Fig. 104.) But textual and other artistic data shows evidence to the contrary – Paheri's

Figure 104.   The dwarf Seneb is shown here with his wife, Meritites, and his two children. Men and boys are coloured brownish-red as they spent more time in the sun, while women and girls are yellowish-white. The children are shown as small-scale adults, with their fore-fingers to their lips in a typical pose, and Seneb's son has the side-lock of youth, which would be cut off when he reached maturity. Photo courtesy Sandro Vannini and Egyptian Museum, Cairo.

tomb at el-Kab contains depictions of five generations of his family with many more than two children appearing throughout. Although Egyptian marriage was monogamous, a man might have one or more concubines, depending on his wealth, inclination, and the tolerance of his wife. Often an Egyptian family had many children, particularly in rural areas where they would help to work the land. Children were important as they inherited from their parents and were responsible for them in their old age. They were also duty bound to bury their parents and to keep up their funeral cult (see Chapter 9). Sons took care of supporting their parents, but if the eldest child were a daughter, she would have the responsibility. In Egyptian art, children were portrayed as miniature adults, except that they were shown unclothed, indicating their youth, and holding a finger to their lips. This gesture can be interpreted in a variety of ways: that children should be seen but not heard, that children are young and suck their fingers or thumb, or that children show their respect for their parents by such a gesture. Young prepubescent boys, particularly if they were from wealthy families, were also depicted with a side-lock of hair that was cut off when they reached maturity. Possibly the removal of the side-lock was associated with male circumcision ceremonies that seem to have occurred when the boys were quite old – probably between the ages of six and eleven. As far as we know, girls were not circumcised, although this is difficult to determine from female mummies. Texts mention only male circumcision.

A household consisted of more than just the immediate family. Older parents from both sides of the family, distant relatives, and servants also formed part of a household. In palaces, the number of dependents rose dramatically, especially as it included females who were unmarried or widowed. Perhaps this is why so many 'harem' or family palaces were constructed – to take care of the many royal dependents. The Heqanakht letters indicate that his household contained at least eighteen people in addition to Heqanakht himself. Presumably, his married children and their offspring made up part of this group; the letters show that households consisted of extended family groups and their various dependents and servants, all living together, sometimes in crowded circumstances.

Country Life

The majority of ancient Egyptians lived in the countryside, and their daily life was regulated by the natural and agricultural cycles. The two most important natural features were the Nile and the sun. The entire Egyptian agricultural cycle was dominated by the Nile, which also determined the three seasons of *akhet*, *peret*, and *shemu* (see Chapter 1). It was perhaps the management of water and land that led to the birth of writing, the bureaucracy, and ultimately, the Egyptian state.

The Egyptian language has many words for the different types and qualities of land that reflect their physical relationship to the Nile and its floods. The best type of land was known as *tepw* or *nekheb*, and consisted of relatively virgin soil, capable of producing significant amounts of grain, the main measure of wealth in Egypt. This type of terrain was related to *mawt*, or new but untried land. There were several names for arable land, no doubt reflecting subtle differences in quality: *aht*, *ineb*, *ifed*, *kayt*, and *meqeq*. Land abutting the river (or canals) was not as valuable as it might over-flood, but it was judged better than land located at the desert edge, perhaps equivalent to areas that were situated at the utmost reach of the inundation and were sometimes fertile. The worst kinds of land for cultivation were *teni*, or old and tired land; un-watered land; or *mast*, land on which crocodiles slept. Land that was used exclusively for grazing was called *mehr*.

For the most part, a person's wealth was measured in land and livestock, as Egypt had no monetary system until the Persian period. Only the king and the elite calculated their wealth in gold. Land was measured in units of *arouras*, 2,735 metres square. A piece of rope, knotted at regular intervals, was used to measure out a field and to establish its area. The Wilbour Papyrus, a ten-metre long hieratic document named after its purchaser, records the measurement and assessment of the different types of land in Middle Egypt for taxes during the reign of an unnamed king who might be identified with Ramesses V (c. 1143 BC). Tax was determined by calculations involving field size, the type of land, and the level of inundation. The height of the Nile was one of the most important and variable elements in agriculture and taxation. If the river was too high or too low, the land would not yield optimally, and taxes would have to be adjusted accordingly.

> ## Measuring the Inundation
> The Nilometer, a vertical slab of stone marked in cubits, was the basic tool for measuring and recording the height of the Nile. Nilometers were mainly located in temples. At the same time every year, the priests would mark the height of the inundation on the temple's Nilometer. Over the years, priests and bureaucrats had calculated the optimum height of the Nile for the land to prosper, and by judging from the Nilometer whether the river was too high or too low, they could calculate taxes accordingly. The most important Nilometers were located at Elephantine, where the inundation first struck Egypt, and at Memphis, before the waters dispersed into the different branches of the Nile.

Irrigation

Arable land consisted not only of areas adjacent to and flooded by the Nile River but also of land that was made cultivable by basin irrigation and a loose system of canals, which were also dependent on the annual inundation of the Nile. A complex system of canals, often terminating in pond-like reservoirs, fed water from the river and through the land away from the Nile, significantly increasing the area Egyptians could cultivate. The basins, which lost some water through evaporation, served as reservoirs after the flood's subsidence. Dykes and barrages were also constructed in order to regulate water supply throughout the year.

In addition to siphoning off water from canals by creating smaller ones, Egyptians took water from the river and canals manually. The most basic method involved dipping buckets into the water and carrying them away, either by hand, by donkey, or on a yoke that fitted over a man's shoulders. The tool to draw water most commonly used from the New Kingdom onward was the *shaduf*. An upright frame from which a long pole was suspended, with one side projecting farther than the other, the *shaduf* worked like a see-saw. A receptacle (bucket, pot, basket, skin bag) hung from the

Figure 105. Saqia (waterwheels) were used in Egypt probably from the fifth century BC,
if not a bit earlier. These were animal powered and raised the water using pottery jars.
Apart from shaduf, *these were the main mechanical means of obtaining water.*
Photo Zangaki, courtesy Susan Allen.

long end of the pole, while the short end carried a weight that acted as a counterbalance. This permitted the user to swing the bucket down and easily draw up a full bucket, using the weight as a balance. The water brought up using a *shaduf* could be emptied into small runnels that ran through fields or into larger receptacles to be taken further distances. Much later on, perhaps during the Persian period, a new device, the *saqia,* was used in Egypt. This was an animal-powered (donkey or ox, generally) rotary waterwheel that raised water in small pots and emptied it into tanks or runnels. (Fig. 105.) The Archimedian screw, a machine that transfers water from a larger, low-lying body of water to smaller irrigation ditches located higher up, was not introduced into Egypt until the Graeco-Roman period. These last two devices significantly increased the cultivable land available in Egypt in that era.

Additional agricultural land in Egypt was located in the oases that to this day are supplied with 'fossil' water that is trapped between the sandstone layers that form the floor of these depressions. Natural springs that bubbled out of fissures provided water for agriculture, as did wells. From the 26th Dynasty, an additional form of irrigation was used in the oases of Baharia and Kharga: underground aqueducts, known in Arabic as *qanat* or *manawir*. These were underground tunnels dug through the water-bearing strata that, using the natural topography and slopes, brought water to the surface to irrigate large tracts of land. The tunnels were maintained by gangs of workmen who accessed them through vertical holes that punctuated the roof of the tunnel and were secured by stone slabs. The oases were exploited for both growing crops and grazing herds. The most famous agriculturally based product of the oases was wine – an item that is no longer produced there today.

Cultivation and Crops

The Egyptian year had three seasons and started in June with the advent of the Nile's flood (*akhet*). *Akhet* ended in September/October, once the flood had run its course. During these months fields lay fallow or under water, and flood-water was collected in basins and canals for use throughout the remainder of the year. While the fields were flooded peasants could do little work except for ensuring that the canals were viable. It is probably during *akhet* that most corvée labour took place, as it provided employment for those who would otherwise be idle. The next season was *peret*, meaning 'coming forth', and indicating that the land was rising up out of the receding flood-waters, new and fresh, drenched with water, covered with rich silt, ready for cultivation. This season lasted from October to mid-February. The farmers prepared the fields for planting using hoes, mattocks, and ploughs to break up the soil. The ploughs could be pulled by people or by cattle. Once the ground had been prepared, the seeds were strewn upon the ground, and in some instances trampled into the earth by herds of sheep, goats, and pigs. In smaller plots, particularly where vegetables were cultivated, planting was done by hand. The crops were then left to grow, some being watered as necessary. Vegetable patches were occasionally weeded, and when the grain began to ripen, young children were stationed in the fields to scare away birds and other pests. Scarecrows, or their equivalent, also might have been employed to guard the crops.

The final season, *shemu*, meaning 'drought' or 'dryness', was harvest time, when all signs of flood-water had vanished. This period lasted from mid-February to June, with April being most active. Peasants harvested the grain by hand, using wooden sickles with flint blades (which were replaced by metal tools in the Roman period); they then tied the grain into sheaves and loaded them into sacks that were transported by donkeys (or people) to the threshing area. There, the grain was processed. The threshing floor usually consisted of a slightly depressed circular area of earth with a shallow lip around the edge. The grain, still in its husks, was piled on the floor, ready to be threshed. In larger establishments animals were driven over the grain to separate the wheat or barley from the chaff, while in smaller farms this was done by people beating the grain with sticks, often in time to music played by other workers. The chaff was removed by winnowing, which was done by both men and women. Using winnowing fans, they would throw the threshed grain into the air. The grain would fall to the floor, while the lighter chaff would be carried away by the wind. Threshing and winnowing was extremely tiring, hot, dusty work. After the grain had been processed, it was put into sacks, baskets, or pots and taken to granaries for storage, or measured and exchanged at the going rate. (Fig. 106.) The granaries or silos were made out of mud brick or wattle and daub. There was a hole in top through which the grain was poured, and a door at the bottom from which it was extracted, thus ensuring that the older grain was eaten before the newer. The granaries were built so that they were off the floor, making it harder for mice and rats to raid them. These vermin were so ubiquitous in their houses and granaries that Egyptians protected these areas with magical spells and, more prosaically, with mousetraps. By the Middle Kingdom, when domestic cats are attested to in Egypt, these animals also served to protect the Egyptians' food supplies.

It is unclear when the Egyptians started to grow two cycles of crops, but in the Roman period two harvests of many crops were common. The second crop had to be manually watered with water carried from the Nile, as by the season of *shemu* the water in the canals and basins had already been emptied. Presumably, in earlier periods, only certain areas that were closer to the Nile were capable of supporting two crops a year.

The mainstay of the Egyptian economy and diet was grain, which was augmented by legumes, vegetables, and fruits. The main cereals that the Egyptians produced were wheat, most commonly emmer (*Triticum dicoccum*),

Figure 106. These registers from the tomb of Mena at Thebes show part of the agricultural cycle. On top, a man and a woman are offering a fertility symbol and food and drink to the man (not in the picture) who is assessing the amount of the harvest. The bottom register shows men using nets attached to poles to transport the harvested grain for preliminary threshing. The middle register shows cattle trampling the grain to free the wheat kernels, and then a group of people wearing kerchiefs winnowing the wheat. Photo Salima Ikram.

although some scholars have also identified cultivated and wild einkorn (*Triticum monococcum, Triticum boeoticum*), and barley (*Hordeum vulgare*). These grains were used to produce bread and beer, and were staples of the Egyptian diet. The vegetables, fruits, and herbs cultivated in Egypt changed over time as new plants were introduced through trade, conquest, and immigrants. The list of vegetables included onions, leeks, garlic, peas, lentils, chickpeas, various types of beans, radishes, cabbage, cucumbers, cress, a kos-type lettuce, and perhaps some form of marrow. Fruit included grapes grown on arbours for eating or wine production, and the yield from orchards filled with fruit trees. The most common fruit trees included dates of several different varieties, sycamore figs, figs, pomegranates, dom-palm nuts, *nabk* berries, persea, and melons. Apples, pears, apricots, and peaches were cultivated in the Graeco-Roman period, and possibly earlier. Although olives were cultivated, they did not thrive in Egypt, and therefore formed only a small part of the food and oil industry. Egypt's major oil-producing plants were sesame, castor, and flax. Vegetables and fruits were grown in both large and small gardens. They were harvested by hand, although there is a tomb scene at the site of Beni Hasan showing apes being used to help in the harvesting of figs.

Flax was valued not only for its oil but also as the main raw material in the textile industry. Egyptian linen was made of flax. Like grain, flax was grown in large fields. It tended to need more water than cereals did and therefore was planted in the wetter Delta area, as well as in plots that were within easy reach of generous irrigation. Flax was harvested by being pulled up by hand before being processed so that its fibres could be used to make cloth. Some of the flax was allowed to go to seed to produce oil.

Papyrus was also assiduously cultivated in the marshlands of the Delta. It was used for making paper, boats, baskets, mats, sandals, and ropes. Its tubers were edible, and thus it also served as food, particularly for the poor.

Livestock

In addition to agriculture, the Egyptians depended on their livestock for food and as a source of raw materials and draft animals. Cattle were the most valuable of all domestic animals. The king counted his wealth not only in the amount of gold and grain he had but also in heads of cattle. Every two years the king's cattle were counted as a measure of his wealth. Whenever records of this biennial cattle count, or cattle census, have been found in King Lists or other texts, they are used to try to calculate the length of a king's reign. Egyptian breeds included long-horned cattle (*nigiw*, in Egyptian) and short-horned ones (*wendjw*), and even polled animals. There is some debate as to when and whether zebu (humped cattle) were used in Egypt, although most scholars agree that they were introduced into Egypt in the New Kingdom. In addition to milk and meat, these animals provided the raw materials for leatherwork and served as draft animals.

Lesser livestock, called 'small cattle' by the Egyptians, included sheep, goats, donkeys, and pigs. Several different breeds of sheep and goat inhabited the Nile Valley. They, together with pigs, provided much of the meat consumed and were useful in trampling grain into fields. Horses arrived in Egypt only with the advent of the Hyksos, and they became valuable commodities, most useful in military or elite contexts. The donkey remained the main beast of burden throughout Egyptian history, until the advent of

Figure 107. *Draft animals were kept at the farm to carry out necessary work, whereas cattle that were to be eaten might be kept in a distant pasture and brought back to the homestead only near the time they were to be slaughtered and consumed. To fatten these animals, they were tethered close to ever-full troughs. Once they stopped eating by themselves, they were force-fed by hand, as is seen in the rear of this wooden model from Middle Egypt now in Munich. Photo Salima Ikram.*

the camel. The camel was not common in Egypt until the Persian period, although examples must have been seen earlier, as is attested to by images on pottery dating to the New Kingdom. Camels revolutionized transport and facilitated long-distance desert travel and trade.

The smaller livestock could be pastured along the outskirts of villages. Goats and pigs were particularly well adapted to urban life, as they could eat almost anything. Indeed, pigs were probably used to help clean the streets, as they could be let loose to eat the rubbish that was left lying around. Large herds of cattle, and sometimes of ovicaprines (sheep and goats), were probably kept in the countryside, the oases, or even in greener areas of the desert where they could find pasturage. They would be brought back to their owners when they were needed for consumption. If cattle belonging to different individuals were herded together, they were distinguished by brands. (Fig. 107.) Archaeologists have identified branding irons, as well as tomb scenes showing people branding cattle. In some instances, horns were etched with signs showing ownership. Cattle rustling was a problem in ancient Egypt; the Varzy Papyrus documents how a cattle thief placed his own brand over the original one in an effort to make off with several head of cattle. He was unsuccessful.

When animals were sick, veterinarians tended to them. The veterinarians were priests of the goddess Sekhmet, and they also acted as physicians for people. A papyrus found at the site of Kahun discusses diseases that were specific to cattle. Clearly, these animals were the most important creatures in the Egyptian economy.

8

From Sunrise to Sunset

Daily Life of the Ancient Egyptians

Although Egypt's state and provincial administrations, as well as its temples, employed a portion of the population, many other jobs needed to be filled for the smooth running of the country and the comfort of its inhabitants. Ironically, the most crucial, but least prestigious, work was that of the peasant, who provided the food that gave the nation its wealth and ensured the people's survival; the most revered work was that of the scribe, who could be employed in the government or by the priesthood. The text called 'The Satire of the Trades', which was used to teach young scribes the finer points of grammar and calligraphy, also expands on the hierarchy of occupations in ancient Egypt (see Chapter 6).[1] Naturally, as it was written for scribes, the text glorifies scribes and their work at the expense of all other occupations. However, it is clear even from this biased text, and from the artefacts and images that the Egyptians left behind, that society and daily life functioned effectively when all Egyptians did their jobs.

Language, Literacy, and Literature

The earliest evidence we have of the Egyptian language dates to c. 3250 BC, when a simple pictorial script was used to label commodities that were placed in the tombs of Egypt's earliest kings at Abydos. Its final manifestation was Coptic, the language used by Egypt's Christian population starting in the first century AD, which is now used only in church liturgy. Arabic, introduced in the seventh century, is the language of modern Egypt.

Egyptian is a member of the Afro-Asiatic or Hamito-Semitic language group. Other languages that fall into this group are the Semitic languages, such as Akkadian (the language of Mesopotamia), Hebrew, and Arabic, and the Hamitic languages, such as Berber (spoken in North Africa going west from Siwa Oasis in Egypt), and Cushitic (spoken in portions of Sudan, Somalia, and Ethiopia), to name but two. All of these tongues share grammatical features that link them together, and it is far easier to learn Egyptian using the grammar and approach of a Semitic language than those of a European language. Indeed, his knowledge of Hebrew and Arabic helped Champollion in his understanding of Egyptian grammar when he deciphered the Rosetta Stone.

The grammar and vocabulary of the ancient Egyptians' language changed during the course of its more than three-thousand-year history, and the language is divided into five stages of development. Old Egyptian was commonly used in the Old Kingdom for all types of texts. Middle Egyptian, the most standard form of Egyptian, was used for monumental inscriptions and formal documents until the 18th Dynasty, and in religious and certain literary texts until the Roman period. Late Egyptian served as the vernacular during the New Kingdom and Third Intermediate period, and was used in more formal contexts from the end of the 18th Dynasty. In Late Egyptian foreign words appear more frequently and letters are added, such as 'L', to accommodate new sounds. Demotic was used from the Late Period onward. It contained many loan words from Greek, Semitic, and other languages, and it had grammatical peculiarities that were not shared by earlier incarnations of the language. It was a very vernacular form of the language; its name, 'demotic', was derived from the Greek word *dimotika*, which means 'of the people'. Coptic was the final form of the Egyptian language and was used by everyone until the advent of Arabic. Thereafter, Coptic was used primarily by the Coptic Christian community, although by the nineteenth century it appeared only in liturgical texts. During the Ptolemaic era, Greek was generally used by the ruling elite and thus was the language of administration, but hieroglyphs continued to be used in religious contexts. Even under Roman domination, Egyptians rarely used Latin; the main language for administration remained Greek, as it was still the language of the ruling elite.

Hieroglyphs

The Egyptians regarded writing as a sacred activity filled with magical power. To write something down and to say it out loud made it happen. One Egyptian creation myth focuses on how a god thought things and then reified them by speaking them out loud. The power of the word and the ability to control the world by naming things in it is shared by many cultures to this day.

Hieroglyphs (from the Greek *hiero*, meaning 'sacred', and *glyphika*, meaning 'writing') were always used in monumental inscriptions, whereas hieratic, the quick and easy cursive form of the language, was common for matters pertaining to daily life. The former tend to be found on temple and tomb walls, statuary, and stelae, while the latter most commonly appear on papyrus and on ostraka (*sing*. ostrakon), the small fragments of stone or potsherds that were used for notes or the temporary storage of information. The earliest hieroglyphs appear in the fourth millennium BC, and the latest, on the island of Philae, in AD 394. Although over six thousand glyphs exist, most of which were introduced during the Ptolemaic and Roman periods, only eight hundred or so were commonly used throughout Egyptian history. As new words, often with foreign origins, were introduced, new signs were added. Hieroglyphs are written from right to left, left to right, or top to bottom. The way to orient a text is to read into the front of the sign, most easily identified if it is an animal: one reads into the face of an animal. Sometimes the signs are grouped together aesthetically, making reading them a bit of a challenge.

Hieroglyphs were an offshoot of pictorial art and were derived from the physical world that surrounded the ancient Egyptians, including elements from the environment and objects made by humans. One sign can stand for a single sound, a set of sounds (bi- or triliteral signs), or a whole word, or can give a sense as to what type of word it is (determinatives). Thus, sound signs can be viewed as phonograms, and determinatives as ideograms. Phonograms are generally used to spell a word. However, the Egyptians did not use vowels (the equivalent of Arabic diacritical marks) when writing, thus similarly spelled words that are easily differentiated in speech cannot be separated when written, save by the determinative placed at the end. In some cases the determinative might be used for the word with no phonograms at all; thus, an image of a sheep might simply mean a sheep. It is difficult to know what rules for spelling were established and followed at any one time.

Because hieroglyphs are both visual and aural, they lend themselves to puns. The Egyptians were inveterate punsters, and their texts and wall decorations were riddled with jokes that were accessible mainly to the literate, and some even to those who were not. Scribes sometimes wrote crypto-graphic texts, limiting themselves to certain signs; an example is the texts in Esna Temple, which are written primarily with crocodile glyphs. No doubt these kinds of texts contributed to Egypt's image as the home of esoteric learning. (Fig. 108.)

Hieratic, Demotic, and Coptic

The most common cursive writing is known as hieratic, the term deriving from the Greek word *hieratikos*, meaning 'priestly'. Hieratic was written from right to left in horizontal lines or vertical columns. Old, Middle, and Late Egyptian were written in this script. Some religious texts written on papyrus, such as funerary books, were in hieratic, although this form was generally reserved for letters and legal and administrative texts. The earliest surviving example of hieratic dates to the 5th Dynasty, and the latest to the third century AD. Demotic was written in a cursive script that ran in horizontal lines from right to left. It derived from hieratic and was faster to write. Most demotic texts were written on papyrus, although some funerary stelae and administrative texts, such as that appearing on the Rosetta Stone, were in demotic.

Coptic was written using twenty-four letters of the Greek alphabet in addition to six demotic signs that provided sounds not found in Greek but present in Egyptian. Coptic was always written in horizontal lines from left to right. Unlike the other forms of Egyptian, Coptic is purely alphabetic. By about the twelfth century many secular Coptic texts were written using the Arabic rather than the Coptic script. Spoken Coptic is the closest that we can come to hearing ancient Egyptian; the fact that there are several Coptic dialects suggests that there were several regional variations in spoken Egyptian. Some of these variations persist in the colloquial Arabic spoken in Egypt today.

Sign	Object Shown	Transliteration	Approximate Sound
	vulture	ꜣ	a
	reed	i̯	i
	reeds	y	y
	arm	ꜥ	eye-in
	quail chick	w	w
	leg	b	b
	stool/mat	p	p
	horned viper	f	f
	owl	m	m
	water	n	n
	mouth	r	r
	reed enclosure	h	h
	rope	ḥ	emphatic h
	placenta?	ḫ	kh, like in Scottish *loch*
	animal's belly	ẖ	gh, Arabic *ghain* or German *ich*
	folded cloth	s	s
	door bolt	ś, z	z
	pool	š	sh
	hill	ḳ	qw
	basket	k	k
	jar-stand	g	g
	bread loaf	t	t
	tethering rope	ṯ	tj, tsh, or th
	hand	d	d
	snake	ḏ	dj
	lion (later addition)	rw, l	l or rw

Figure 108. *The hieroglyphic alphabet. Font courtesy G. Camps and J. Kamrin.*

Daily Life of the Ancient Egyptians

Literacy

Despite being surrounded by monumental inscriptions on temple walls, the Egyptians had a low literacy rate. However, those who could not read hieroglyphs could easily interpret the large-scale images on temples and understand the main message that was being transmitted. Throughout Egyptian history, the elite was literate, as were most people who were involved with administrative work at a reasonably high level. Presumably, the literacy rate rose over time, along with the development of the Egyptian language and the decrease in the rigid social structure that had been typical of Egypt during the Archaic period and early Old Kingdom.

Although scribal titles were clear indicators of literacy, other people who might not have been as well-versed in the use of the language or have worked officially as scribes could still be counted amongst the literate. Fewer women than men were literate, although this was probably not the case amongst the upper classes, where women had to manage huge estates and conduct business. Certainly, funerary literature has been found in the tombs of women of varying rank, indicating that they were capable of reading the texts themselves, and fully intended to do so in their Afterlife. Casual notes to women, such as the workman Neferhotep's message to his wife asking for beans as well as bread for lunch, indicate that basic literacy was not limited to the upper classes. Indeed, some form of literacy and ability to do arithmetic might have been far more widespread than has been thought by scholars.

Scribes and Scribal Training

> ...Scribedom...
> It is the greatest of all callings,
> There is none like it in the land.
> Lo, no scribe is short of food
> And of riches from the palace.
> > From 'The Satire of
> > the Trades'

The Egyptian word for 'scribe' was *sesh*, written with a scribal palette and a man-sign, or with the feminine 't' ending and a woman-sign when the scribe was female. Being a scribe was a sure way to social and financial success, as is stressed in the section on scribes in 'The Satire of the Trades'. The most

Figure 109. Heti is shown as a seated scribe in this statue in the Hildesheim Museum (No. 2144). His kilt is pulled taut over his crossed legs to support the papyrus roll, and he holds a reed pen in his right hand. Photo Nicholas Warner.

traditional jobs for scribes were within administration, whether working for the bureaucracy, the military, or the priesthood. Although being a scribe first and foremost meant that one was literate and adept with words and numbers, scribal work was not limited to copying texts and filing them. Rather, it could be the initial step on the path to a high administrative position. In addition, scribal training opened the way to other positions, including estate manager, personal secretary, itinerant letter writer, or even teacher. Professional letter writers were especially important because they composed and wrote letters and other necessary documents, often legal in nature, for the illiterate. Large villages and towns might have one or more resident letter writers, whereas smaller hamlets might have to make do with an itinerant writer whose appearance coincided with market day, a time when the demand for contracts and records would be high. (Fig. 109.)

Scribes were probably trained in schools of some sort. Schools tended to be associated with temples, perhaps attached to the House of Life where scholarly investigations were carried out. Official state schools, offering more specific scribal training, might also have existed, although these too might have been run through the temples. There is evidence that school-rooms were not restricted to the temples: sometimes tombs may have been used as they contained excellent illustrations of the art of writing. One tomb in Asyut is inscribed with fragmentary texts that appear to have been made by a teacher illustrating specific points to his students.

Writing Implements

The English word 'paper' was derived from the Greek *papyrus*, the word for ancient Egyptian paper. Papyrus rolls were made from the stems of the *Cyperus papyrus* plant that grew at the edge of the Nile and in the marshy areas of the Delta. After being harvested, the hard green exterior covering of the stems was cut off, and the softer beige pith was thinly sliced, then kept in water to maintain their flexibility and natural adhesiveness. These strips were laid side by side, slightly overlapping, and then a second layer was placed over the first at right angles. The starch from the plants sufficed to stick the layers together. The paper was then either placed in a press of some sort – perhaps between two blocks of stone – or hammered with a wooden mallet to make the pieces adhere to each other and to smooth them out. Following this procedure, the paper was left to dry. Finally, the dry paper was polished with a burnishing stone to smooth out all the ridges. To make a long roll for lengthy texts, several papyrus sheets were attached to one another.

Ink came in two colours: black and red. The former was made out of charcoal, and the latter of ochre. Black was used to write down most things, although chapter headings and important statements were written in red ink. The ink was kept in dry pats in scribal palettes, which also contained fine reed pens or brushes. A complete scribal kit consisted of a scribal palette with prepared inks and pens, an extra bag of pigments, a water container (often a shell), and a stone or ivory burnisher to smooth the papyrus and to correct mistakes.

In addition to using papyrus, the Egyptians sometimes wrote on leather rolls, although this custom seems to have been uncommon. The Egyptians rarely used the clay tablets that were common in Mesopotamia where papyrus was unavailable. The only Egyptian examples of clay tablets come from Dakhla Oasis. One set dates to the Old Kingdom and was found at the administrative centre at Balat; the other example comes from the Graeco-Roman–period town at Amheida. Perhaps the use of clay was unique to this oasis, where papyrus did not flourish as it did in the Nile Valley.

Education consisted of rote learning, reading, writing, calculating, accounting, and perhaps some basic science, such as astronomy. Examples of texts used in teaching have come down to us, sometimes as student copies of texts that illustrated the finer points of composition and grammar, as well as others that provided improving moral literature for the young scholars. The earliest such text dates to 2200 BC, suggesting that schools had been established some time before that date. Students probably practised with writing boards and ostraka before they were allowed to write on valuable papyrus. Writing boards were the equivalent of slates and were made from smooth planks of sycamore wood, often covered with a thin even wash of clay or gypsum in preparation for receiving the text. These planks could be washed, or rubbed clean with a stone, and used again and again. Once a pupil was adept at writing, he or she might be given papyrus.

Two divinities were associated with writing: the god Thoth and the goddess Seshat (whose name incorporates the sound for the word for scribe and scribal palette, although it is not written using that symbol). Thoth invented writing, the 'words of God', and was shown holding a papyrus roll and a reed pen, writing a sacred book or recording a significant event in the divine world. As the goddess of recording and of history, Seshat was most often depicted writing the name of a king on the leaves of the sacred persea tree, thereby lengthening his life, or recording royal tribute or acts of valour. Images of Thoth as an ibis or baboon were particularly popular, and several scribes showed themselves at their work, with a statue of a zoomorphic form of Thoth above them.

Literature

Set your heart on books! . . .
There's nothing better than books!

Literature is generally defined as 'belles lettres', or creative forms of writing. Literary texts certainly existed in ancient Egypt, although there were a great many other types of texts as well. In addition to creative work, the ancient Egyptians' written output included historical records, autobiographies inscribed in tombs, legal documents, medical treatises, temple records, lists of temple and royal holdings, the disbursement of commodities, bills of sale, letters, and notes. Religious texts, such as funerary texts, form a group unto themselves.

The 'belles lettres' group of texts includes stories, poems, hymns, and a set of texts called Wisdom Literature by Egyptologists. Wisdom Literature encompasses ethical texts with rules for the kind of proper behaviour that will bring rewards in both this life and the next; these dictates are a combination of moral admonitions and advice. For example, the texts advise, 'Beware of stealing from a miserable man/And of raging against the cripple';[2] 'Do not eat a meal in the presence of a magistrate, Nor set to speaking first';[3] and 'If you are with the people, Gain for yourself supporters who are trustworthy'.[4] The tone of this genre of Egyptian literature changed over time, presumably reflecting changes in mores and values.

Surprisingly few stories have come down to us from ancient Egypt, and some of those that have may have been propagandistic literature designed to bolster or facilitate the rule of a particular dynasty or king, rather than be a work of entertainment. Perhaps this paucity of literature from ancient Egypt is due to the fragile nature of papyrus or to its outright destruction: in ancient times papyri were erased and reused or were burnt as fuel or used to make cartonnage (a form of papier mâché used to make coffins and other funerary coverings), or used as stuffing to maintain the natural shape of mummified crocodiles. Two Egyptian tales that do seem to have been told purely for entertainment are 'The Shipwrecked Sailor', and 'The Doomed Prince'. Unfortunately, no intact copy of either tale has survived; consequently, Egyptologists and fiction writers have created several endings for these stories.

Compared to stories, a wealth of Egyptian poetry, including religious hymns, has survived. Many are love poems with a very lyric quality, while others, such as Akehnaten's 'Hymn to the Aten', are reminiscent of later biblical psalms. The love poems are particularly charming, and unlike the majority of Western love poems, the Egyptian poems are composed from both male and female perspectives, and they share similarities with love poems the world over.

> Would that I were her signet ring
> Which is upon her finger,
> For I would see her love every day,
> And it would be I who would touch her heart.[5]

And,

> He gazes at me whenever I pass by,
> And I keep my joy to myself.
> How with bliss is my heart delighted,
> For my lover is in my sight.[6]

Maintaining Law and Order: The Judiciary and the Police

Much of Egyptian law was regarded as divine law, with the basic precepts against murder and theft that are found in any of the monotheistic religions, and the injunction to uphold *maat*. Additional behavioural codes were embedded in Wisdom Literature. Ancient Egyptian law could be loosely divided into three categories: criminal, consisting of offences against the king and state; sacral, which were offences against the king and the gods; and civil, relating to matters between private citizens. Certain offences might be a combination of these. It should be remembered that no complete law codes have survived. One fragmentary text remains, the Code of Hermopolis, named after the city in which it was found. This demotic text dates to the third century BC and deals mainly with arable land tenure, property rights, and inheritance. The majority of what we know of Egyptian law comes from surviving legal documents, moralistic tales, and royal decrees.

One royal decree that survives is that of King Horemheb. This edict was aimed at rectifying the administration's abuses against the people, particularly those associated with tax collection, by reorganising the courts and dismissing corrupt judges and palace administrators. The decree defined unlawful appropriation of goods, ranging from vegetables to wood to hides, by soldiers and tax collectors, and the punishments that were meted out to the offenders. The contents of the decree were announced throughout the land, and the text was inscribed on a stela erected in front of the tenth pylon at Karnak. Other royal decrees that have been found tend to cover specific infractions, generally against temples that were dear to that particular king. Thus, the Nauri Decree issued by King Seti aimed at protecting the property owned by the temple of Osiris at Abydos and outlined punishments for anyone who tried to wrongfully appropriate the temple's wealth.

Stories that convey details about law courts (*kenbet* in Egyptian) include 'The Eloquent Peasant' and 'The Contendings of Horus and Seth'. These show how human law courts emulated the divine model, with a judge (*saab*) and a council that acted as a jury. Legal procedure is also illuminated by these tales: defendants could plead for themselves, and the more eloquent a defendant was, the better that defendant's chance of being exonerated; defendants could call witnesses to testify in their support; and defendants could have others plead on their behalf. If the defendant was not satisfied with the court's decision it could be appealed again and again. Ultimately, some Egyptians turned to the gods for a decision in their cases, and oracular judgements were well respected.

Funerary beliefs also provide insight into the legal world of the Egyptians. The ancient Egyptians believed that the dead were tried in the court of Osiris, where they underwent a cross-examination and were judged. Those deemed to have been worthy or innocent were allowed to live forever in the Afterworld; those judged guilty were devoured by a monster and eradicated from existence.

Most of what we know about the Egyptian legal system comes from texts that pertain to court cases. For example, the Tomb Robbers Papyrus (Leopold II-Amherst Papyrus) deals with the trials of a group of tomb robbers at the end of the 20th Dynasty who violated the royal tombs in the Valley of the Kings – a criminal and sacral case. The Harem Conspiracy case, recorded in the Turin Juridical Papyrus, concerns conspirators who were attempting to depose Ramesses III through murder and magic, which was both a criminal and sacral offence. The Turin Indictment Papyrus has to do with the priests in the temple of Khnum at Elephantine who were accused of theft, fraud, bribery, and even violence. Other trial records cover cases of adultery, drunken and disorderly behaviour, and theft. The non-payment of taxes is often the subject of tomb scenes and accompanying texts. Most judicial texts, however, are civil documents between men and women. These include private contracts of sale and employment, endowment of property, marriage contracts, wills, and manumission. Such documents provide a remarkable insight into the daily life of the ancient Egyptians.

Punishment for different crimes varied. In many of the civil cases, it was simply a fine or the restoration of property. In criminal or sacral cases, the punishment could be far more severe. Depending on the seriousness of their crimes, people were punished by whippings or by more severe beatings administered to the feet (bastinado). An even harsher punishment was the Five Bleeding Cuts, which involved severing the nose, ears, and lips. The ultimate punishments were impalement, enforced suicide, and the destruction of a person's name, which eradicated that individual's existence completely, in this world and in the next.

The Police

The police, sometimes aided by the military, were involved with maintaining civil order. Their jobs can be loosely divided into two categories: enforcing justice and inflicting punishment, and protecting and guarding. Images

Figure 110. This large male baboon is held securely on a leash by a policeman. Baboons were used to apprehend thieves and are frequently shown in marketplace scenes, such as this one from the causeway of Unas at Saqqara. Photo Salima Ikram.

of policemen patrolling market places, sticks at their sides, to stop thieves and brawls and to settle disputes have been found in Old Kingdom tombs. Some scenes show the policemen with their police-baboons, fierce animals who were trained to chase after and seize wrongdoers. Such animals seem also to have been used as guards in palaces; the body of a large male baboon with enormous canine teeth was excavated near a palace guardhouse at Tell el-Dab'a (ancient Avaris). The police also administered punishments, including beatings, to tax evaders. (Fig. 110.)

Guarding temples, palaces, cemeteries, desert roads, mines, quarries, and outposts also fell under the purview of the police. These forces, known as *nww, menie tjesenw* (in the mines and quarries context), or *medjay* (special mercenary troops), patrolled vulnerable areas, often with trained dogs, to protect them against any form of attack. No doubt traders with large amounts of stock and wealthy nobles also hired people to protect their caravans, businesses, and homes.

The Military

The Egyptian military consisted of an army and a navy. In addition to fighting battles, the army was garrisoned in forts along Egypt's frontiers, carried out exploratory trips, led mining and quarrying missions, protected and escorted merchants and travellers, and went on foreign expeditions, either military or peaceful. The army initially comprised groups of infantry equipped with different weapons (bows and arrows, spears, maces, swords, and knives). After the introduction of the horse and chariot in the Second Intermediate period, a section of chariotry became part of the fighting force. Both horse and driver of this elite strike force were protected by leather armour. Proper mounted cavalry did not feature in Egyptian warfare until the eighth century BC.

The navy was most active on the Nile, whether engaged in royal business or in military pursuits. Naval actions in the Mediterranean Sea are not well recorded, although the navy may have been more involved in expeditions in the Red Sea, particularly expeditions to Punt, a country rich in incense that was probably located on the coast of East Africa in the region of modern Somalia.

The size of an army contingent varied over time; in the New Kingdom fifty soldiers seem to have made up the contingent, headed by a non-commissioned officer. A company was made up of five contingents, led by a troop commander. A division consisted of five thousand soldiers. Divisions were often named after divinities: Amun, Re, Ptah, and Seth were mentioned in the Ramesside period. In addition to fighting men, the army had scribes, grooms, armourers, cooks, and other support staff. Mercenaries were also recruited during troubled periods to enlarge the army; Nubian archers were particularly sought after as their prowess with the bow was renowned.

Although people often chose (or were born into) the army as a career, mass conscription existed. Any draft dodger was severely punished, as was his family, often being forced to serve long terms at state labour. The length of time that a soldier had to serve is unknown, but presumably it was not less than ten months. This training ensured that a reserve group of fighting men was available whenever Egypt went to war. Tomb scenes, such as one in the tomb of Userhet (TT56), show new recruits being barbered before starting their service. The army offered one of the most socially mobile career paths in ancient Egypt.

Military weapons included bows and arrows, spears, javelins, maces, clubs, daggers, axes, scimitars, and swords. Over time, with improved metallurgy as well as the introduction of new forms from the Near East, the efficiency of these increased. Body armour, made of leather and bronze, was minimal; shields of cowhide, turtle shell, and possibly crocodile-skin helped protect soldiers. Aegean helmets made of slices of boar's tusks were imported during the New Kingdom. (Fig. 111.)

Figure 111. Soldiers were trained to fight in a variety of ways, including hand-to-hand combat. This group of wrestlers at Beni Hasan might be soldiers training to fight hand to hand. Other portions of these scenes show soldiers attacking fortresses and battling their enemies. Military training included archery, running, and the use of maces, swords, daggers, and spears. Photo Salima Ikram.

Sustaining the Body: Food Producers and Food

Although food was the basis of existence, the majority of those who were engaged in food production did not rank high on the Egyptian social scale. 'The Satire of the Trades' describes a particularly harsh existence for gardeners and farmers.

> The gardener carries a yoke,
> His shoulders are bent as with age . . .
> He works himself to death
> More than all other professions.

The poor farmer with his swollen fingers 'wails more than the guinea fowl. . . . He is weary'. The lives of those tilling the fields, harvesting the grain, and tending the orchards and vegetable plots was harsh indeed, involving long hours and physically draining labour. However, it was not much easier being a fisherman, whose life was daily threatened by crocodiles and hippopotami, or a bird catcher, who spent his life trying to capture birds in the marshes and raise them in confined spaces. The lives of brewers, bakers, and vintners were better, particularly if they did not work independently, but for a large estate, be it royal, sacred, or noble. Butchers were more favourably regarded, as they had access to the food with the highest status – beef – and were wealthier than other food producers.

The diet of the wealthy in Egypt was richer and more diverse than that of the poor. Texts suggest that all Egyptians ate three meals a day. Peasants probably had a large meal in the morning to energize them for the work ahead, a modest lunch, and a slightly more generous early dinner after sunset. For those who did not have to engage in vigorous physical labour, it was probably more common to eat a light meal in the early morning, followed by a large lunch and dinner. Celebrations were marked by banquets, and the food for the poorer classes was augmented by gifts from the king and temples during festivals.

The two staples of the ancient Egyptian diet were bread and beer. These were eaten by the entire population, and supplemented by various other types of foods: meat (including poultry and fish), vegetables, pulses, fruits, dairy products, grains, oils, butter, eggs, and honey and other sweets. The elite would obtain much of their food from their own estates, trading with one another and occasionally with professional manufacturers for special or rare foodstuffs. The remainder of the population would obtain different foods through trade. (Fig. 112.)

Bread and beer production often took place in the same or in adjoining premises, as the raw materials needed for both were identical. Bread was generally made of emmer wheat, although barley was occasionally used, as was lotus or tiger-nut flour for special loaves. Flour, made by grinding or pounding the grains in saddle querns, was kneaded with water or milk and salt, and spices such as cumin, anise, cloves, or cinnamon may have been added for flavouring before baking. Although when yeast was first used in bread is unknown, it would probably have been added at this point in the process; alternatively, natural airborne yeasts (as in sourdough) might have been used to make the bread rise.[7] The dough was either shaped into loaves or placed in pottery moulds and then was baked inside an oven. Bread was generally round, oval, baguette shaped, or triangular. Sometimes it was made in the shape of cows, gazelles, or even people. Bread could be eaten as a dessert by adding honey, dates, lotus flour, or tiger-nuts. Some Egyptian bread was extremely gritty as the grit from the querns was mixed with the flour. Perhaps this accounts for the extreme tooth wear seen on Egyptian mummies.

Beer was made by kneading roughly ground flour and water into dough and allowing it to ferment. After basic fermentation, the watery mixture

Figure 112. Bread and beer were typically produced in the same or adjoining work-shops as they used the same ingredients. The Meket-Re brewery and bakery model in the Metropolitan Museum of Art, New York, shows the grinding of grain, kneading of dough, and subsequent preparation of bread and beer. This model is so detailed that the artisans painted the hands of some of the workers white to indicate that they were handling flour. Photo Salima Ikram.

was passed through a sieve and put into coarse pottery jars and sealed. The beer's flavour might be varied by the addition of spices or fruits, such as coriander or dates. Egyptian beer was of the consistency of gruel and was highly nutritious. The elite poured their beer (and sometimes wine) through fine sieves so that the more chewy parts of the beer could be ignored. One such sieve has been found amongst Tutankhamun's belongings. Many Egyptian workers were paid in bread and beer so that they did not have to produce it at home.

The most prestigious meat eaten by Egyptians was beef, followed by mutton, goat, and pork. Hunted animals were commonly consumed in the Predynastic period. After the domestication of animals, wild game ceased to be a crucial source of food but continued to provide luxury and exotic meats. However, small desert game, such as hare, would have augmented the peasant diet. Cattle were owned by the very wealthy. Because one animal produced sufficient meat to feed a few hundred people, cattle were slaughtered most often for use in palaces and temples rather than in an individual's home. A text (Papyrus Boulaq 18) inscribed with temple accounts records that the excess from butchered offering meats was sold in the market. Once a cow was slaughtered, its meat had to be processed and preserved by salting or drying, or sold off before it went bad. Mutton, goat, and pork were more commonly eaten by the nobility, and occasionally by the less privileged classes. The fat from sheep was used for cooking as well as in medical remedies and cosmetics. Pork was probably the most common meat to be consumed by the poor, as pigs were easy to raise, ate almost anything, and reproduced rapidly. Milk from cattle, goats, and sheep was used for drinking and as the basis for simple cheeses and yogurt.

Poultry and fish also provided rich and poor with regular food. Nobles might stock ponds on their estate with fish or purchase fish from fishermen. Poorer people could catch their own fish in the river or in canals. Fishermen caught fish using nets and traps, although both professional and amateur fishermen also used fishing poles. Large catches of fish were preserved in salt and sold in pottery jars. The Egyptians also enjoyed a type of caviar: mullet roe. The roe was removed from the fish, washed, and then laid in layers of salt. Each layer was separated by planks and then weighted down with stones until it was dry. The processed roe was then sliced up and eaten with bread, much as caviar is today.

Bird catchers using nets or traps captured wild birds, particularly during the birds' migration seasons in November and April. Birds were also confined in poultry yards and thus available year-round. The most commonly consumed birds were ducks and geese, although cranes and other water birds were eaten. The chicken was not common in Egypt until the late Persian or the Ptolemaic period. The eggs of many birds, including ostriches, were also consumed.

In addition to eating bread and drinking beer, poorer people depended on vegetables, pulses, and fruits for regular nourishment. Onions, garlic, lettuce, radish, celery, cucumber, and, perhaps, squash were regularly cultivated and consumed. Legumes were represented by lentils, fava beans, lupines, lobia, and chickpeas. The word for 'chickpea' in ancient Egyptian, *hr-bak*, translates as 'hawk-face' and alludes to the beak-like point of the chickpea. Fruit, such as grapes, pomegranates, dates of several varieties, dom-palm nuts, persea, figs (the usual type, as well as sycamore figs), *nabk* berries or jujubes, and melons were standard features of the Egyptian diet. Exotic fruits, such as apples, pears, plums, and peaches, became common only in the Ptolemaic period, although apples were known in the New Kingdom. Whereas onions and garlic could be stored year-round, as could most of the legumes, fruit was more seasonal, although dates, figs, and grapes could be dried and thus were available out of season.

Beer was not the only alcoholic beverage produced by the Egyptians. Date wine, made by steeping dates in water and then pressing out the liquid and leaving it in a jar to ferment naturally, was easily made at home. Palm wine was made from the fermented sap of the date palm and obtained by incising the top of the palm tree at the base of the fronds, and collecting the sap that issues from these incisions and leaving it to ferment. The Egyptians may also have made fig wine, as well as wine from pomegranates; perhaps the word *shedeh* means 'pomegranate wine', although 'juice' has been suggested as another possibility. Grape wine was produced all over Egypt, although the main production centres were the Delta and the western oases, particularly Kharga and Bahariya. The Egyptians took their wine making seriously and labelled different vintages, not only with the *domaine* of origin and production date but also with its quality. Wines were 'good', 'very good', or 'very very good'; a few wines were 'to be merry'. Naturally the wines' prices reflected their qualities. Both red and white wine could be produced in a similar fashion. Workers gathered the grapes and then trampled them in large emplacements, where the juice ran off into another container. The must was squeezed in linen cloths. The wine was then put into amphorae, sealed, and labelled.

Figure 113. *The top register from the tomb of Rekhmire at Thebes shows bee-keepers smoking out the pottery hives and then collecting and storing the honey. The register below shows storerooms, with their contents piled alongside of them. Photo Salima Ikram.*

Honey and carob were the most effective sweeteners apart from fruits and their juices that were available to the Egyptians. Honey was the main sweetening ingredient in ancient Egypt. Bees were bred in special pottery hives, and their honey was collected from the hives (after smoking out the bees), as was the beeswax, which was used for many medical and practical purposes. (Fig. 113.) Honey was a precious commodity and available only to the wealthy; the poor used dates for a sweetener or did without. The other sweetener in ancient Egypt, carob, was a dark brown pod that grew on a tree. The hieroglyphic symbol for 'sweet', *nedjem*, took the form of the carob pod. Nowadays, health food stores market a form of chocolate made out of carob.

Over time, owing to trade and emigration, variations in the Egyptian diet occurred. New foods, such as apples, were introduced. Exotic spices, such as cinnamon and peppercorn, became part of the elite's fare. Possibly, new recipes were also introduced, and older ones modified, in response to the food traditions of newcomers.

Cooking was a relatively simple affair. Meat, fish, and poultry were stewed, boiled, grilled, fried, or roasted. Vegetables were eaten raw as salads

or stewed with meat. Herbs, including marjoram, purslane, dill, fenugreek, coriander, celery, anise, fennel, mustard, basil, cumin, and rosemary, would have been used to add flavour to any dish. Vegetable oils as well as animal fats were used in cooking, and each imparted a distinctive flavour to the food. Oils included those produced from safflower, balanos, sesame, lettuce, and radish. Beef and sheep fat were the most commonly used, and jars that once contained fat have been found at settlements such as Deir el-Medina, Malqata, and Tell el-Amarna. Breads and cakes were baked in clay ovens; when travelling, Egyptians spread flour and water mixtures on hot stones to bake. In poorer homes, family members cooked, whereas wealthier Egyptians employed cooks, both men and women, to prepare their food. The larger and more populous the estate, the more numerous the cooks and domestic staff.

Maintaining the Body: Doctors, Dentists, and Health

While the judiciary and police were intent on protecting the rights of the people, doctors and dentists in ancient Egypt were engaged in caring for the people's health. On the whole, the elite were healthier than the peasants as they enjoyed a better diet, better living conditions, and better hygiene. Nonetheless, both the rich and the poor had shorter lifespans than their modern counterparts. The average lifespan in ancient Egypt was between thirty-five and forty. Women tended to die younger because many died in childbirth, a fairly common occurrence in antiquity. However, there were some amazingly long-lived individuals, such as Pepy II, who lived for approximately ninety-six years, and Ramesses II, who died when he was in his late eighties.

Egyptian physicians and dentists were probably trained in the *per-ankh*, or 'House of Life', a sort of research center and school, of a temple and retained some sort of affiliation with it, even when practicing privately. (Fig. 114.) Veterinarians also were attached to temples, particularly to the temple of Sekhmet. Some of the earliest titles we have from ancient Egypt belong to people in the medical profession.

In the ancient world, the Egyptians were famous for their medical knowledge. There are documented occasions from 1500 BC onward when Syrian princes, Palestinian kings, and Hittite rulers received or requested Egyptian physicians and their medicines. Egyptian doctors (*suwnw*) had a reputation for curing their patients – or at least for not killing them. In his tomb, the doctor Nebamun, who lived and died in fifteenth-century BC Thebes, recorded the generous reward he received from a Syrian ruler whom he had cured. Later on, Persian kings, such

Figure 114. Hesire, a 3rd-Dynasty official, was, amongst other things, a dentist. The symbol for dentist was an elephant's tusk (second symbol from the top of the right-hand column). He was also a scribe, and his scribal equipment can be seen hanging over his shoulder. Photo courtesy Sandro Vannini and the Egyptian Museum, Cairo.

as Cyrus, had Egyptian physicians at their courts, as the Egyptians' reputations were far superior to those of all other healers. Indeed, Greek medicine, the precursor to modern medicine, has its roots in the medical traditions of ancient Egypt, and Alexandria's medical school was the site of many medical experiments and of the exchange of ideas concerning medicine.

Fractions and the Eye of Horus

According to Egyptian myth, Horus's eye was ripped to bits by Seth, and then was reconstructed and healed by Thoth. The healed eye was called *wadjet*, meaning 'the sound eye'. Egyptian physicians used the different parts of the eye as the basis for their calculations, in fractions, when they made up medicines. Each portion of the eye symbolised a different amount, all totalling 63/64, an incomplete number, with the missing amount representing what had been magically restored by Thoth in the healing process. Thus, the eye became associated with physicians and pharmacists, and became the root for the modern symbol 'Rx' in references to drugs. The *wadjet* was a favoured protective amulet for both the living and the dead. (Fig. 115.)

Figure 115. The eye of Horus that served as a basis for measurements in medical recipies. Drawing Nicholas Warner.

Illnesses such as migraines were first identified, described, and prescribed for by the Egyptians, who also named the condition. The Egyptian word for a migraine, *gs-tp*, meant 'half the head', as in 'half the head hurts'. This definition moved into 'half the head' in Greek and later in Latin, with *hemicrania* ultimately turning into *migraine*. The word 'cataracts' and the description of the condition is also Egyptian in origin. In Egyptian, cataracts were *akht net miw*, literally, 'gathering of the waters', which accurately described the condition.

The Egyptians' reputation for being good doctors may have had something to do with mummification. Certainly, the process gave Egyptians an insight into the human body, although they were not always clear as to what each organ did. The medical texts that have survived give us an idea of the Egyptians' attitudes towards disease and their approaches to its cure. Many of the medical papyri that we have deal with specific sorts of diseases, thus implying that Egyptian doctors specialized. These texts were organized according to human anatomy, going from head to toe. One significant medical papyrus is known as the Edwin Smith Surgical Papyrus. The copy of this papyrus might date to the end of the Second Intermediate period or the early 18th Dynasty, although the original text might have been composed earlier. Physicians probably annotated and amended their copies of medical texts depending on the success or lack thereof of the treatments. The Edwin Smith papyrus deals primarily with surgical matters – broken bones, external pathologies, and bone surgery – and must have been quite useful for the military and the police. The Papyrus Hearst covers wounds from animal attacks and cures for the bites of different creatures. Both the Kahun Papyrus and another papyrus in Berlin focus on gynaecological issues, including

Figure 116. Teams of fishermen, such as these featured in the tomb of Mereruka at Saqqara, were used to wield large nets to catch a vast variety of fish. Fish were a source of ingredients used in medicines as well as a source of food. Photo Salima Ikram.

contraception and ways to detect cancer of the uterus and to determine the sex of unborn children. The Ebers Papyrus deals with general medicine: it covers headaches, eye diseases, coughs, asthma, stomach trouble, and even aids for hair loss. The main text that deals with dental health is the Papyrus Chester Beatty.

The general attitude towards diagnosing and treating illness is the same throughout the medical texts, regardless of their specialty. The Egyptian doctor was advised to first talk to the patient to find out what was wrong and then to examine the person. After that, the doctor was to choose the likeliest from a series of possible diagnoses and then treat the disease, keeping check on the patient's response to the treatment. If the cure was unsuccessful, another treatment was to be tried.

Egyptian medicines were made from a variety of materials, including herbs, animal fats, and minerals. (Fig. 116.) Some curious ingredients were used at times, such as dung, blood, and hairs or scales from different animals.

One of the strangest cures for baldness called for tying a live lizard to the sufferer's scalp. In addition to administering medicines, Egyptians also turned to religion and faith to effect cures, especially when the patient seemed beyond saving. The idea that faith might cure someone when pure medicine could not was familiar to the ancient Egyptian physicians. Thus, the Egyptian healing tradition included spells to be worn as charms by the patient; having the patient drink or bathe in water that had been poured over an inscription, thereby absorbing the power of the words; and having the patient sleep in a healing shrine in order to be cured by the god through dreams (incubation).

The gods most closely associated with disease and its cures were Sekhmet, (goddess of plagues), Isis, Hathor, Anubis, Ptah, and Imhotep. The Greeks and Romans adopted Imhotep as the founder of the medical profession, and from the Ptolemaic period onward his cult flourished in Egypt, as well as abroad. He was associated with the Greek god of medicine, Aesklepios. Certain statues of deities also enjoyed a reputation for curing diseases. Thus, Ramesses II sent a statue of the god Khons the Provider to a Hittite princess to cure her ailment. The god was successful, earning Ramesses the loyalty and friendship of the Hittite king. Ramesses also sent the king Egyptian medicines to further cement the bond.

Adorning the Body: Barbers and Beauticians

> The barber barbers till nightfall . . .
> He moves from street to street . . .
> He strains his arms to fill his belly,
> Like the bee that eats as it works

Although 'The Satire of the Trades' did not have anything very complimentary to say about them, barbers played a useful role in Egyptian society, together with others involved with cosmetics, manicures, and coiffures. Not only were barbers and the others critical to beautifying the Egyptians, but they also helped Egyptians maintain their hygiene and health. Barbers seem to have been a common feature in any settlement, although they do not appear to have had fixed shops; instead, they might go from house to house or set themselves up under a convenient tree. Whether they engaged in any surgical activities, as their later Western counterparts did, is unknown, although it is probably unlikely, given the number of medical practitioners in ancient Egypt. Tomb scenes show barbers cutting hair in the open air, often providing fresh army recruits with the equivalent of a buzz cut. This gave the troops a uniform appearance, as well as reduced the chance of nits. Barbers were in charge of clipping hair on both the head and the face, and they might also act as manicurists. Certainly, the elite employed manicurists and hairdressers (*neshet*); those who served the king in these capacities rose high at court and often had splendid tombs, such as the double sepulchre of Niankhkhnum and Khnumhotep at Saqqara. Anyone involved in the royal toilette had to rank high in royal trust and esteem and to enjoy a certain level of ritual purity, for they touched the royal person, not only with their hands but also with sharp metal and stone instruments. They also had access to the king's hair and nail clippings, which were powerful tools in certain types of magic, similar to what is employed in voodoo. Therefore, these individuals had to be totally loyal to the king and above reproach.

Artefacts, mummies, and tomb and temple scenes show that beautification was equally important to men and to women. Both enjoyed elaborate toilettes, wore complicated wigs, used cosmetics, and anointed themselves with perfumes and unguents. Bathing was common. For the elite, servants would slowly pour vessels filled with water over the bather, rather like a manual shower, while commoners would carry out the pouring themselves. Soap could be made out of a mixture of natron, fuller's earth, and maybe pounded lupins (*Lupoinus albus*). Natron was also sometimes used to clean teeth, having the same effect as baking soda would. Natron is used to this day to launder clothes. Hair was also washed using soaps. Deodorant in its simplest form consisted of chunks of alum that were dampened and then swiped over the armpits. More complicated mixtures included the addition of resins or sweet-smelling oils.

Throughout most of Egyptian history, men tended to be clean-shaven, save for during the Old Kingdom when moustaches seem to have been the norm. Occasional instances of bearded men are found in the Middle Kingdom, with this becoming a common phenomenon in the Graeco-Roman period. Copper razors and flint or obsidian blades were used for shaving. Women tweezed with copper or bronze tweezers, and recipes for depilatories have also been found in medical texts such as the Papyrus Hearst.

Particularly in the Old Kingdom, both men and women had short hair and wore different wigs, depending on the occasion. The short hair would have been cooler and would also have diminished the possibility of lice, examples of which have been found on some wigs. Wigs were made of human hair and were elaborately curled, waved, and braided affairs, often secured with bone or ivory hairpins. A wig workshop has been excavated at the site of Deir

Figure 117. Both Egyptian men and women had elaborate toilettes using oils, unguents, and make-up. Hair, most frequently in the form of wigs, was elaborately curled, as is shown here on the sarcophagus of a princess of the Middle Kingdom, now in the Egyptian Museum, Cairo. Jewels were worn and often affixed to the coiffure. Toilette kits included mirrors, tweezers, and jars of oils, unguents, and perfumes. Photo Salima Ikram.

el-Bahari. Particularly in the Late Period, hair and nails were sometimes dyed using henna, a colouring extracted from the dried and powdered leaves of henna (*Lawsonia inermis*). Medical texts provide recipes against baldness (as noted earlier), as well as for blackening white or grey hair, for which various ingredients (often extracted from black animals) were boiled with oil and applied to the hair. (Fig. 117.)

Oils and unguents were applied to the face and the hair to prevent dryness and to stop ageing. Those who could afford it would use elaborate concoctions made of fats, oils, and scents, while the less affluent would manage with simpler and less fragrant mixtures. Oils made of sesame, castor, moringa, or almond were commonly used throughout Egyptian history. Recipes to prevent wrinkles appear in the Ebers Papyrus and employ ingredients such as resin, oils, and different plant juices.

The use of cosmetics focussed on enhancing the eyes with kohl, which was made of ground-up galena. This powder, stored in slim vessels of bone, ivory, wood, or glass, was applied to the eyes with a thin stick. The kohl not only enhanced the eye by highlighting it in black but also provided some protection against eye diseases. Pulverized malachite was used as eye shadow and might also have protected the lids from the sun. Rouge and lip-colouring have been detected on mummies and were probably made from powdered red ochre in an oil or fat base, as has been successfully re-created by experimental archaeology.

Perfumes were the crowning glory in any toilette. The Egyptians were famous for their perfumes, which they made from essential oils and fats impregnated with the essence of different plants. A room in the temple of Dendera was devoted to the manufacturing of perfumes. The seeds, flowers, bark, or leaves of plants were crushed and used to infuse oils or fats, or the essential oil of the plant itself was mixed with less fragrant oils and fats. Ingredients for perfume might include lotus, lily, cedar, cinnamon, thyme, coriander, marjoram, iris, or roses. Resins such as frankincense and myrrh were also used in perfume production. Egyptians also used a curious type of perfumed fat cone at banquets. The cones appear in Egyptian reliefs and paintings of the New Kingdom and look rather like brightly coloured party hats perched upon wigs. Scholars think that these cones were made of fats impregnated with sweet-smelling perfumes that would gradually melt during the party. These would not only have emitted a pleasant scent, but also might have helped keep away mosquitoes and flies, depending on the mixture of herbs used. A few scholars suggest that these cones were never really used, but that they actually were a symbol for scent.

Some cosmetics and oils might have been made in the home, particularly on a nobleman's estate, where much of the raw material might have been available. Certainly, temple estates were large-scale producers of oils and perfumes, as these were crucial to temple ritual, whether to be used on the image of the god or to be used by the priests who served the deity. Royal estates also produced a significant quantity of the more valuable perfumes, some of which might have been sent as diplomatic gifts or even sold commercially. No doubt commercial enterprises also existed, with their owners being quite wealthy, and the workers less so.

In addition to using paints and perfumes, the Egyptians also adorned their bodies with tattoos. Tattoos appear to have been used most commonly by entertainers such as singers, dancers, and musicians. In works of Egyptian art such women are shown with images of the god Bes tattooed on their thighs, along with elaborate designs picked out on their arms, ankles, and legs and around their waists. One Middle Kingdom mummy from the mortuary complex of Mentuhotep II at Thebes shows evidence of tattoos. These were presumably made with needles and soot.

Clothing the Body: Weavers, Tailors, and Cobblers

The main fabric used by the Egyptians for clothing, sheets, towels, soft furnishings, sails, mummy bandages, and shrouds was linen. Wool was less frequently used and was more often made of sheep fleece than of goat hair, although the latter was not unknown. Wool production is attested to at Kahun as well as at the Workmen's Village at Amarna. Examples of cotton have been found in Ptolemaic contexts, but cotton was commonly produced in Egypt only from the Roman period onward. Only occasional examples of imported silk have been found from the Ptolemaic period.

Linen was made from the flax plant (*Linum usitatissimum*), which was farmed throughout Egypt, although most successfully in the Delta. Flax was harvested at different times of year, depending on its prospective use. The young stems were used to make fine thread; as the plant matured and became yellow, the stronger fibres could be used for sturdy linen cloth; mature flax provided the tough fibres for rope and mat making. Once the flax had been harvested, it was processed to release its fibres by being rippled (pulled through a wide-toothed comb-like tool) and then retted (soaked to separate the fibres). The fibres were beaten and scraped to free them from the woody stem, then re-combed using a finer tool, after which the spinning and weaving process could begin.

Weaving workshops were part of royal, temple, and noble estates, with the weavers working as employees. Excess cloth would be bartered for other commodities. Presumably, independent commercial weavers also existed to provide those who did not have their own production centres. Both men and women spun and wove, although it was probably more common for women than for men to spin thread. It is probable that spinning was carried out in small-scale domestic workshops (maybe by the peasants who had helped grow the flax or, more likely, by their wives) that supplied larger estate or commercial cloth producers. (Fig. 118.) Just as it had concerning the butchers, 'The Satire of the Trades' is once again uncomplimentary about weavers' work, calling attention to the close, dark quarters in which weavers laboured, often choked by the fine dust produced in processing flax.

> The weaver in the workshop . . .
> He cannot breathe air.
> If he skips a day of weaving,
> He is beaten fifty strokes.

Figure 118. This painting, a copy of a scene from the Middle Kingdom tombs at Beni Hasan, shows a floor-loom operated by two women, and the spinning of linen thread, all under the watchful eye of an overseer. Painting Nina de Garis Davies, courtesy Metropolitan Museum of Art, New York.

The Egyptians recorded four qualities of cloth: royal cloth, which was the best and was produced mainly in the royal workshops; fine thin cloth; thin cloth; and smooth, or ordinary, cloth. Until the end of the Middle Kingdom, all these varieties were produced on a ground loom; thereafter, vertical looms were used, although the ground loom was never abandoned. Indeed, ground looms are still used today by Bedouins, as well as by some Egyptian villagers, for home-produced carpets and cloth. Excavations have revealed loom emplacements in Thebes that confirm two- and three-dimensional representations of weaving workshops. The archaeologist Flinders Petrie also found a cloth-dyeing workshop dating to the Graeco-Roman period near the temple of Athribis. The dyers were clearly temple employees, and the cloth that was dyed was not only used in the temple but also sold. The Egyptian dyers used natural dyes: blue ingotin or woad (*Isatis tinctoria*) for blue, madder (*Rubia tinctorium*) or ochre for red, safflower (*Carthamus tinctorius*) for yellow and red and acacia pods for brown. Mixing the colours together in different proportions made greens, purples, and browns.

Once the cloth had been made, it could be turned into garments, left in long pieces for sheets and towels, or used for furnishings and sails. There is little evidence for professional tailors in ancient Egypt, although some tailors surely existed, perhaps within the group of weavers. All types of garments were made of cloth: loincloths, kilts, tunics, aprons, dresses, cloaks, shawls, gloves, and socks. Some garments were dyed different colours, and others, using the technique of tapestry weaving with multi-coloured threads, were covered in elaborate patterns or were enhanced with attractive borders. The tools for tailoring were simple: metal or bird-bone needles, thread, and thimbles. A sandstone thimble was found in the excavations at Lisht.

Over time, Egyptian fashion became increasingly elaborate. The sheath-like dresses with shoulder straps that women commonly wore in the Old and Middle Kingdoms gave way to elaborately pleated tunics and a proliferation of fringed shawls and scarves that were tied in a variety of ways to enhance the figure. Men's dress also changed radically in the New Kingdom, with more layers appearing, many of which were tightly pleated.

The rich stored their clothes in wooden chests, and the poor kept their garments in pottery containers. Some storage boxes belonging to kings and the elite were made of cedar imported from Lebanon. The cedar not only imparted a pleasant scent to the clothing but also deterred moths and other insects. Clothes were kept clean by washing them in the river. Large households had a group of washermen or washerwomen who were responsible for the laundry, and professional groups also existed. In smaller domestic contexts this job fell to the women. Natron-based soaps that also bleached the fabric were used for the washing, and wooden paddles were used to beat larger garments and sheets and towels. According to 'The Satire of the Trades', washermen had a job that stretched their nerves as it involved contact with dangerous creatures: 'The washerman washes on the shore / With the crocodile as neighbour'. Laundry was a serious business: many ostraka inscribed with laundry lists have come down to us, and sheets and garments bore laundry marks so that they would not go to the wrong owners and be lost.

Several different people were responsible for producing footwear as it was made of a variety of materials including leather, papyrus, palm leaves, and fibres. The most common sandals were made of vegetal materials that were gathered at the appropriate season and then woven into footwear. Footwear styles changed over time, although not radically, with the earliest sandals being flat thongs; later versions were protected on either side and

Figure 119. Papyrus was harvested by teams of men who either pulled it up or cut it near the root. These bundles were transported to different workshops where the plant was turned into boats (shown here), paper, sandals, mats, baskets, or other objects. People who worked as papyrus harvesters, as well as others who worked in areas with still water, often contracted bilharzia (shistosomiasis), a disease caused by a parasite that lived in the snails that infested still water. These workers, from the tomb of Nefer at Saqqara, exhibit the characteristics of bilharzia sufferers: baldness, distended bellies, and enlarged genitalia. The lower register shows the force-feeding of cattle prior to their being eaten. Photo Salima Ikram.

were more a shoe than a sandal. People who wove sandals from reeds and palm also produced the baskets and bags that Egyptians used for storage and transportation, as well as the mats that covered the walls and floors of their houses, and were sometimes used in roof construction. Life was not easy for reed cutters; they were prey to mosquitoes and gnats and suffered cuts from the sharp edges of plants, and they ranked fairly low on the Egyptian social scale. (Fig. 119.)

Leather shoes were more expensive than those made of papyrus or palm, and were more commonly used in the winter in outdoor contexts, whereas sandals were worn indoors, as well as outdoors in the summer (depending on what one could afford). Cobblers produced not only shoes but also other leather goods, such as leather aprons and loincloths used by hunters, cloaks, tents, bags, and raw materials for chariots (including the wheels), furniture, weapons, and tools. 'The Satire of the Trades' is eloquent on the cobbler's miserable lot:

> The cobbler suffers much
> Among his vats of oil;
> He is well if one's well with corpses,
> What he bites is leather.

Leather was made from the hides of juvenile and adult cattle, sheep, goat, and gazelle. The latter produced the particularly soft and resilient leather that was often used for the loincloths favoured by hunters and soldiers. Calf-skin also yielded softer leather; a pair of King Tutankhamun's sandals have been found that were made of calf-skin. Once the hide had been dried, the hair was removed and the hide was tanned using a variety of techniques: drying, smoking, salting, and coating in ocherous earths. Dung, fat, and urine were used to soften the hide, followed by oils and alum for tanning. Acacia (*Acacia arabica*) pods produced tannin for the curing process. Leather was also dyed with plant dyes: some boots were brightly decorated with red and green geometric shapes, and the leather tent of Lady Isetemkheb D was coloured in pinks and greens, and enhanced with elaborate cut-out work, as were chariots.

Metal Work and Jewellery

Metalworkers, particularly jewellers, had more prestigious jobs than many other craftsmen, particularly if they worked with gold or silver. Of course, some of the more menial but necessary tasks involved in preparing the metal before turning it into objects were less attractive and prompted the author of 'The Satire of the Trades' to comment that the smith had 'fingers like claws of a crocodile' and that he 'stank more than fish roe'.

The basic metal that the Egyptians used was initially copper, followed by bronze. Frequently, the Egyptians made objects from copper-bronze alloys. Iron was not produced in Egypt until the sixth century BC; before that the few iron items that have been found were imported from the Near East and Anatolia, or were made of meteoric iron, such as a bead recovered from a Predynastic tomb. Precious items were made of gold and silver. The latter was not available in Egypt and had to be imported.

Prospectors identified mining sites, and then expeditions would move into camps there. The crude ore was extracted from open cast or underground mines in the Eastern Desert and Sinai using stone and sometimes metal tools. It was processed on site by being crushed into small pieces and then winnowed, or in the case of gold, sometimes washed, to purify it. The ore was then smelted in furnaces that became increasingly sophisticated with time. Copper and bronze ingots were formed on site and then transported by donkey caravan to the Nile Valley. By the Roman period large carts pulled by bullocks or horses were used to transport the material back to the Nile. The miners who obtained the raw materials from the mines had a most unpleasant job involving back-breaking labour; moreover, they had to live in stone huts in a harsh environment, subject to wind, sand, heat, scorpions, and serpents. Many labourers involved in mining were prisoners of war or convicts. Most mining operations were run by the military on behalf of the king, or sometimes the temples; as far as we know, mining was never a non-state activity.

Once they arrived in the Nile Valley the ingots were broken up and then melted in crucibles that were fuelled by wood and heated with blowpipes or bellows. Workers then worked the hot metal. The most common ways of working metal involved casting it or hammering it into the required shape; complex objects were soldered together. As a final touch, objects were polished and sometimes engraved. (Fig. 120.) A vast range of objects were made of metal, including needles, adzes, knives, razors, tweezers, scales, hinges, vessels, chariot parts, musical instruments, statues, and jewellery.

Jewellery makers, especially those employed by the king, were probably the most highly regarded of all metalworkers. They fashioned the exquisite beads, rings, pectorals, bracelets, anklets, collars, girdles, and earrings that adorned Egyptian men and women. Jewellers worked primarily in gold that was mined in Egypt or traded for from Nubia. Silver was rarer and had to be imported from the Near East. Electrum, an alloy obtained by mixing gold and silver that was also found in nature, was occasionally used for jewellery, particularly in religious contexts. Texts indicate that a thin coating of electrum that caught the sunlight and dramatically reflected it back originally covered the pyramidions that capped pyramids, as well as those topping obelisks. The stones used in jewellery tended to be semi-precious and most came from the Eastern Desert or Sinai. The most popular stones were turquoise, malachite, agate, hematite, jasper, quartz, and carnelian. Most of these were favoured throughout Egyptian history, although some stones were particularly fashionable during certain periods; for example, amethyst

Figure 120. Jewellers would carefully heat the metals prior to working them into elaborate designs. As is seen in this scene from the tomb of Mereruka at Saqqara, dwarves were frequently employed in jewellery making, presumably because of their small, nimble fingers. Interestingly, dwarves are also considered good miners and jewellers in European folk tradition. Photo Salima Ikram.

had its heyday in the Middle Kingdom, and the striking blue lapis lazuli, imported from Afghanistan, was valued for its colour as it often contained streaks of a golden hue, thereby combining two elements (blue and gold) that the Egyptians associated with their gods (see Chapter 5). Other materials, such as mother of pearl, shell, ostrich egg shell, horn, bone, coral, pottery, glass, and faience, were also used for jewellery from the earliest times. (Fig. 121.)

The basic technologies used in goldworking were similar to those employed for other metals, with additional techniques employed to produce special effects. In addition to hammering and casting, techniques such as repoussé, engraving, incising, chasing, granulation, and cloisonné were used to produce exquisite pieces of jewellery or to adorn dagger sheaths and royal vessels. A special feature of jewellers was that many of them were dwarves whose dextrous fingers could create the elaborate and intricate forms required for this work.

Every Egyptian, from newborn infants to people in their dotage, wore jewellery. The wealthier a person was, the more valuable the jewellery that

Figure 121. Broad collars were popular pieces of jewellery. This example comes from the tomb of Hapyankhtify at Meir and is now in the Metropolitan Museum of Art, New York. Collars could be made of gold, but they were more commonly made of faience, a highly fired and glazed ceramic that was far more affordable. Bracelets and anklets were also popular. Photo Salima Ikram.

they owned. However, even kings like Tutankhamun, who could afford gold, wore simple shell and bone jewellery. People wore jewellery not just to display their wealth or to look attractive but also to protect themselves. Amuletic jewellery in the form of the protective eye of Horus (*wadjet*), *tyt* knots sacred to Isis, or *djed* pillars indicative of strength and a symbol of Osiris, was supposed to shield the wearer from harm, and perhaps, if the wearer were ill, even help effect a medical cure. (Fig. 122.)

Woodwork: Carpenters and Boat Builders

Egypt produced only a limited number of types of wood: acacia, sycamore fig, tamarisk, persea, willow, and palm. All of these woods were used in making furniture, coffins, chests, boxes, weapons, sticks, doors, ceilings, sculptures, and boats. To make large objects, such as huge temple doors and large boats, exotic woods with longer and thicker trunks had to be imported into the country; juniper and cedar wood were imported from Lebanon as early as the Old Kingdom. During the New Kingdom, ash, boxwood, yew, and oak were also brought in from the Near East and Asia Minor to produce objects

Figure 122. The workshops that Rekhmire oversaw included jewellery making (top and bottom registers), as well as woodworking (center) and leatherwork (second from top). These scenes in Rekhmire's Theban tomb depict the processing of raw materials into finished products. Photo Salima Ikram.

for royalty and the elite. Ebony (*hebny*, in Egyptian) came from Punt and more southern parts of Africa and was used primarily as an inlay.

Because wood was scarce, Egypt's skilful carpenters often made larger objects by piecing together smaller bits of wood as though putting together enormous three-dimensional jigsaw puzzles. Coffins, statues, and boxes could be made of many tiny pieces of wood cleverly joined with dowels. Like the tools of so many other workmen in Egypt, carpenter's tools were relatively simple. Axes, initially of stone and later of copper-bronze alloys, were used for cutting down trees, and saws, adzes, chisels, and wooden mallets were used for everything else. Joints were secured by lashing the wood together with leather or gut thongs or by inserting wooden dowels. Sophisticated furniture, such as that belonging to Queen Hetepheres, was fabricated using mortise-and-tenon joints. The oldest folding camp bed ever found, made for Tutankhamun, had hinges to help fold it into three pieces.

Some carpenters worked independently, but many were attached to large estates. The tomb of Meket-re, a nobleman who lived during the Middle Kingdom, contained wooden models of the different workshops on his estate. One of these models included a carpenter's workshop, complete with miniature tools. The carpenters were shown in the process of making Meket-re's coffin. It is possible that once the workshops associated with noble houses or temples had completed the work for their estates, the carpenters were interested in working for others as well.

Specialised craftsmen made wooden boats. These artisans may have been associated with carpentry workshops, but they clearly devoted themselves only to producing boats. Scenes show boat builders working at sawing and hammering planks, and then joining the planks together with ropes and wooden nails, often helped by a trained baboon. (Fig. 123.) Wooden boats plied the Nile for long distances, transported large quantities of goods and people, and travelled the seas. Large boats were commissioned by the state and were made of imported cedar. Both of the boats buried with King Khufu at Giza were made of cedar. Smaller crafts, made of bundles of papyrus stems lashed together, were more common; they were used for transport over short distances, pleasure outings, duck hunts, and fishing on the Nile.

Constructing Containers: Ceramics, Faience, and Glass

The potter is under the soil . . .
He grubs in the mud more than a pig . . .
He grubs the yard of every house
And roams the public place.
From 'The Satire of the Trades'

Pottery has been the most commonly found artefact in excavations in Egypt. Potters were the main producers of all containers, whether jars for beer, pots for cooking, or coffins for burial. Egyptian pottery was made of two types of soil: Nile silt and marl clay. The silt formed a part of river or canal banks, whereas the marl was mined in the desert, where it could be found trapped between limestone layers. Silt is more porous and permeable than marl, and when it is fired it is red or black. Marl clay generally fires to pale pinks and

Figure 123. The tomb of Nefer at Saqqara contains a series of scenes connected to woodworking. The central scene shows men chopping down trees with axes and preparing the wood. The upper register depicts boat building, with a trained baboon helping by fetching and carrying. In addition to showing that the animal is working, the baboon in the scene is also an allusion to the sun god, who traverses the sky in a boat. The register below shows workers sawing planks and making a coffin for the deceased. Photo Kent Weeks.

greens, and was used more often to contain precious liquids or, as it was slightly more robust than silt, for materials that had to be transported great distances.

Potters' workshops have been found from the Predynastic period onward. One of the earliest such ateliers was located at Hierakonpolis; the potter had misjudged the location of his kilns in relation to the wind and his atelier and house burnt down. Luckily he survived and went on to rebuild both house and workshop (at safer distances) down the road from his old studio.

Although wealthy estates might produce their own pots, it was probably more common for them to obtain these objects from commercial potters. Perhaps this was because of the special needs for a pottery workshop: it had to have easy access to water and a source of a large amount of fuel. Thus, kings and temples might have their own production centres, but it is less likely that nobles did. The first step in pottery production was to mix the mud with water and to make the mixture malleable by trampling or kneading.

It was then mixed with temper – chaff, sand, crushed sherds, pebbles, dung, or shells – which strengthened the mixture. After this, the mixture could be transformed into vessels, lamps, toys, or coffins.

Basic pot-making technologies included coiling (coiling long rolls of clay into the shape of a pot), slabbing (constructing a vessel or coffin with slabs of clay), pinching (building a vessel by pinching the walls up), or using a wheel. The earliest representation of a kick wheel in Egypt dates to the sixth century BC and was found at the temple of Hibis at Kharga. In the Old Kingdom, potters constructed the pot on a rotating table made of stone or wood; by the Middle Kingdom, they had invented a wheel that was spun by one person, while the other worked on constructing the pot. Moulds were used to make toys, lamps, some pots, and later on even figurines.

Once a vessel was made, it was dried. When leathery it might be polished with a pebble or a bone tool to impart a shine, as well as to reduce its permeability. Vessels and objects might be enhanced with a slip, an application of liquid clay, or be painted after firing. Some vessels were further decorated with appliqué work, the addition of clay gazelle heads to handles, or the addition of facial features and a mane to make the pot look like the god Bes. The more strenuous work of kneading and softening the raw material, as well as of throwing on the wheel, was probably restricted to men. However, polishing, burnishing, and painting probably utilised both men and women.

In addition to professional potters who produced a vast range of objects, some ceramic manufacture was done in the home. Mud ovens, troughs for animal fodder, and granaries or large storage jars might have been produced by the women of the household, much as is done today. All of these objects were made of Nile silt mixed with chaff and dung and were built up, piece by piece, as well as maintained, by the householders. (Fig. 124.)

Faience and glass vessels were also used as containers. Faience is a type of ceramic made of crushed quartz or sand with small amounts of natron, ash, or lime mixed into it. It was covered with a glaze, and fired at a very high temperature. The finished vessel was white with a glossy coloured glaze. The glazes often took the colour of semi-precious stones, giving the illusion that the objects were made of those rather than of more base materials. The most common colour for the glaze was a turquoise blue, although darker blues, yellows, reds, greens, and even purples were used. Faience was used to make small vessels, particularly those intended for cosmetics and perfumes; figurines; gaming pieces; tiles to enhance palaces and sometimes homes; amulets;

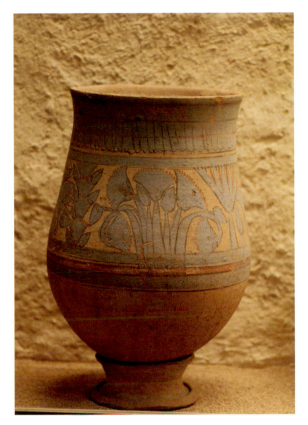

Figure 124. For the most part, Egyptian ceramics are plain, with little embellishment. However, some vessels, made in the late 18th and early 19th Dynasties, are decorated with vegetal motifs picked out in blue paint, such as this one from Thebes, now in the Munich Museum. This wide-mouthed jar is painted with lotuses, lilies, papyrus, and other plants, and rests on a jar stand. Photo Salima Ikram.

and jewellery. Frequently, poorer Egyptians wore only faience jewellery as opposed to jewellery made from the more costly semi-precious stones. However, faience was also worn by the wealthy – Tutankhamun had several rings and some broad collars made out of it.

By the New Kingdom, the Egyptians were manufacturing glass objects. Glass was made with silica (sand or powdered quartz or flint), alkali (plant ash or natron), and lime and was fired at a very high temperature. Glass and faience were often produced near each other as they required similar firing temperatures. Glass was used for luxury vessels, generally those for perfume; as inlays in jewellery and amulets, or as decoration on coffins. Many of the eyes used in statues and coffins were made of glass.

Art, Artisans, and Artists

The Egyptians were enthusiastic about the enhancement and adornment of not just themselves, but of everything around them. They decorated all sorts of surfaces: tombs, temples, houses, stone slabs (stelae, *sing.* stela), boxes, and pots. In addition to sculpting images of gods, people, and animals, they carved ordinary objects into beautiful shapes: *kohl* containers in the shape of young monkeys, lion's feet on chairs, and vases in the form of flowers. All these objects have been studied as examples of Egyptian art. However, the ancient Egyptians may not have regarded these creations simply as beautiful images to be admired or as an expression of their wealth or culture, as the pieces served several purposes, beauty being but one of them.[8] The context of each object, be it a painting, a relief, or a sculpture, helped define its purpose, and the images that adorned it conveyed specific meanings. It should be remembered that for the ancient Egyptians an image had magical properties and with the recitation of the right prayers and spells could be reified. Statues in tombs were conduits for the soul, while effigies of gods in temples were worshipped, and statues of people in temples acted as eternal worshippers.

Most of our evidence comes from religious contexts: temples and tombs. The images shown on their walls were meant to express eternal verities, and following the Egyptian idea that once recorded something becomes real, these images were reflections of an ideal world, an eternal cosmos ruled by *maat*. Thus, the depictions tended to show people in their prime, the marshes devoid of mosquitoes, and existence to be fairly idyllic. These images can be read like giant hieroglyphs that express a complex idea in shorthand, using a single picture.

The major characteristics of Egyptian art were established by 3000 BC and are exemplified by the Narmer Palette, a ceremonial slate palette depicting the victory of a southern ruler over the peoples of the Delta. (Fig. 125.) Variations occurred in the style and subtleties in depictions, the use of line and colour, and poses throughout Egyptian history, but within the confines of the artistic canon. The official canon was applied in contexts where the images were depicting eternal verities, particularly for the images of divinities, royalty, or the elite in temples and tombs. Rules were bent and artists expressed their range of techniques in informal sketches, including images of incidental workers and peasants in tomb scenes, and perhaps on papyri and other materials that are now lost.

Figure 125. The Narmer Palette is an artefact with both historical and artistic significance. Historically, it commemorates a battle that contributed to the first unification of Egypt. Artistically, it is the first example of the canon of Egyptian art that persisted throughout Egyptian history. Photo courtesy Sandro Vannini and Egyptian Museum, Cairo.

The Narmer Palette is a good example of all that was typical of Egyptian art, particularly two-dimensional art. Register lines that divided the palette into different zones provided an organizational framework for the image. The most important person was always the largest depicted, with the sizes of other figures dependent on their social importance. A canon of proportion governed Egyptian art. This was a regularised system of measurements so that all figures would have the same proportions. A grid was laid over the surface to be painted or carved, and the drawing was made using the grid as a guide. Over time, the canon of proportion changed, and it is possible to date pieces based on the proportions used within it. The standard set of measurements divided the human figure into eighteen squares from the hairline to the groundline (e.g., 1 square from the sole to the ankle, 6 squares from the sole to the knee, 12 squares from the sole to the waist, and 18 squares from the sole to the hairline). (Fig. 126.) The drawings would be made by an artist in the atelier and would be corrected by the chief artist before the images were carved.

Figure 126. This carving, dating to the Ptolemaic period and coming from Tuna el-Gebel (now in the Hildesheim Museum), shows the grid marks used by artists in composing or copying paintings, reliefs, and sculptures. The proportions varied over time. Photo Salima Ikram.

People and animals were shown in a conventional manner so that they were easily recognised: the head was in profile, the torso was frontal, and the legs and arms were in profile. The eye was shown fully frontally, not because the Egyptians did not know how to depict it as it naturally would be in such a pose, but because it was easily recognisable, and might also serve a magical purpose of emphasizing identity. Anyone or anything that was important was provided with a groundline; a way of indicating disrespect or a sense of chaos was to omit a groundline. Thus, on the Narmer Palette and elsewhere the enemies of Egypt were shown flailing about with no groundline giving solidity to their existence.

Sketches found on ostraka prove that the Egyptians could make perspectival drawings; however, perspective was not used in formal representations. Instead, registers sometimes provide a clue as to how a scene was laid out: upper registers or sub-registers within a scene show that someone was behind and to the left or right of the main figure, such as the sandal bearer of Narmer. If a container was shown, its contents were often depicted in the register above. (Fig. 127.)

Statuary followed slightly different principles. Chief among these was what was called the 'Law of Frontality', which meant simply that the image,

Figure 127. The unfinished tomb of King Merneptah (KV8) in the Valley of the Kings shows us how tombs were decorated. Initial drawings in red ink would be corrected in black, and artisans would then begin to carve away the background, creating the bas-relief. This portion of the tomb indicates that the carving could start at the bottom, while other areas show the carving beginning at the top, or even in the middle of the wall. Photo Salima Ikram.

regardless of its position (sitting, standing, lunging, kneeling), faced forward, with its most important features clearly visible to anyone standing before it. This law held true for most stone sculpture. Wooden models, common in the Middle Kingdom, had a somewhat different function from most formal sculpture: they were three-dimensional equivalents of wall reliefs that provided for the deceased in the hereafter. As such, they were less formal and showed a certain liveliness from any angle. Formal statues, fashioned from stone or wood, tended to be expensive and were generally made for royalty and the elite. Even figures of servants, such as those first found in tombs of the late Old Kingdom and continuing through the 12th Dynasty, were commissioned and paid for as tomb equipment by the wealthy, who believed that the images would come to life and serve the deceased.

Iconography was heavily employed in Egyptian representations and provided a quick way of conveying complicated ideas. Of course, the modern viewer does not always know or understand Egyptian symbolism, and can sometimes miss information. It would be as difficult for someone unversed in biblical stories and iconography to interpret the decoration of a medieval church as it is for us to interpret all the symbols used in an Egyptian temple or in any Egyptian representation.

On the Narmer Palette, the king is shown four times. On each side he is shown twice, once in human form, and once as an animal: a falcon and a bull, respectively. These animal icons imply that he has dominion over all the creatures of the earth and the sky. In his human form he is immediately recognisable by his size and because he wears all the accoutrements of royalty: crown, beard, tail, and the special *shendyt* kilt. He is also identified by what he is doing: smiting the enemies of Egypt and keeping the country safe. These motifs reoccur in Egyptian art and immediately convey the idea of perfect kingship. Two enemies flail below the king's feet on the palette, the implication being that they have been effectively subjugated. The king is depicted again, in the form of a raptor, the manifestation of the god Horus, dominating the people of the Delta, who are shown as marshlands with a human head. The other side of the palette shows the king, the largest figure in the register, with his trusted companions going to inspect his fallen enemies. All of the enemies, save their chief, have not only been beheaded but have also been deprived of their manhood, proving that they were truly defeated and subjugated by the Egyptians.[9] The centre of the palette shows a pair of serpopards, mythological beasts with the bodies of big cats and the necks of serpents, twined together, symbolising the union of Upper and Lower

Egypt. The final image of the king on the palette shows him as a bull, on a groundline, destroying towns and trampling on Egypt's enemies. The message is clear: the king in both his human and his divine forms, blessed by the gods (the goddess Bat, in the guise of a cow, surmounts the palette, sanctifying the activities shown on it and guards the king's name, which is written in a *serekh*), has been protecting his country and his people.

Egyptian tombs scenes that appear to be straightforward representations of daily life activities can be interpreted on many levels. At their most basic, they were narratives of activities that occurred in this life and that by being represented in the tomb will magically continue in the hereafter. However, these narratives were not like comic strips with every action recorded; rather, the most important events that made the activity recognisable were shown, with the understanding that the viewers, who knew what was going on, could fill in the blanks. On a deeper level, the images can be understood as metaphors. Thus, pictures of the tomb owner hunting wild creatures can also be viewed as the tomb owner's controlling chaos and establishing and maintaining *maat*. Images of papyrus marshes not only depicted the world of the tomb owner but also evoked Osiris, who made Egypt green and whose presence was sometimes symbolised by a papyrus plant.

Even paintings in houses served more than a decorative purpose. Often images of divinities and their symbols were used to protect the inhabitants from evil or to encourage wealth and good health. Of course, other paintings might have been present just for their colour and beauty, but more often than not, an additional meaning was provided with every decoration.

The artisans who created the statues, carved the reliefs, painted the walls, and made objects beautiful held different ranks, depending on their prowess and on whether or not they enjoyed royal favour. The best artisans worked for the king (or for temples) in ateliers or workshops. They were highly regarded and well paid. Several ateliers might serve the king, and each might be known for a certain style of depiction. The king could favour his chosen courtiers by giving them access to his workshops, and quite possibly, the royal artists, if they had the time, might hire themselves out to a chosen few. Also, nobles might have artists associated with their households; this was less common, although it increased during the Intermediate periods when nomarchs assumed quasi-royal status. Ateliers filled with artisans of lesser talent served the needs of the majority of the population, and itinerant artisans might have occasionally provided their expertise in the smaller villages.

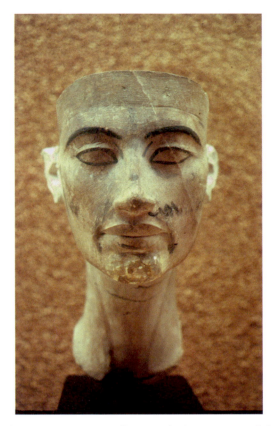

Figure 128. Several practice pieces as well as roughed-out images of the royal family were found at Amarna in the studio of Djuthmose, the artist. This sculpture, possibly of a royal woman, shows the ink guidelines that the artist was to follow. Photo Salima Ikram.

The ateliers probably functioned in similar ways throughout the country, with a chief artist teaching the less qualified. Textual evidence from the Workmen's Village of Deir el-Medina indicates that teams of artists worked on a single scene or image. Presumably, some individuals specialised in carving hands and feet, while others did heads, or furniture, or hieroglyphics – some incomplete tomb walls exhibit this degree of specialistion. Those junior artists who were not the son of the chief artist but who had achieved a certain level of prowess might either start their own ateliers or work as itinerant artists along the Nile Valley.

For the most part, the names of the sculptors and painters in ancient Egypt are unknown: their creations were regarded not as artistic works to be signed, but as images that would serve an eternal religious purpose. However, a few artists have become known by name as their homes and workshops, complete with unfinished works, have been found. Djuthmose, who carved the famous painted bust of Queen Nefertiti, is one such artist. Several others, who carved and painted many tombs in the Valley of the Kings and Queens, as well as many of the New Kingdom elite tombs in Thebes, have also been identified because they served the king and lived in a special workers' village in Thebes. The ancient walled village of *set maat* (Place of Truth), modern Deir el-Medina, was established during the reign of Thutmose I. The houses, furnishings, tombs, and texts that have survived provide a rare insight not only into village life but also into how tombs were cut, carved, and decorated. Artistic training was provided within an atelier, and the job of artist was generally handed down from father to son, barring the youth's extreme ineptitude or talents in other directions. (Fig. 128.)

Architects and Architecture

Architects and directors of works held important and respected positions in the Egyptian social order. Indeed, Imhotep, the alleged architect of King Djoser's Step Pyramid, ultimately rose to the level of a god. The title of architect, or master of the king's works or buildings, appeared in many tombs from the Old Kingdom onward, clearly indicating that this was an occupation for the elite. Designing tombs and temples was the purview of royal architects. Senenmut, the chief steward and architect of Queen Hatshepsut, was responsible for the design and decoration of her funerary temple at Deir el-Bahari, just as Amenhotep, son of Hapu, was responsible for that of Amenhotep III at Thebes. The majority of cult temples seem to have followed templates that, once established, showed only limited variation (see Chapter 5). It is possible that palaces also benefited from the attention of architects. However, we do not know if houses were designed by architects, or if houses followed a vernacular model, with differences dependent on the size of the family and wealth of the owner.

Architects were trained not only as scribes but also in mathematics, and they had to have some sense of design and innovation. There are no records of the formal training received by architects, nor do we have many elaborate plans left by them, although some must have existed. A few sketches on ostraka and some drawings on papyrus, such as the Papyrus Turin 1885, which shows the tomb of Ramesses IV, indicate how buildings were planned and surveyed. Inscriptions from the temples of Edfu and Dendera gave the dimensions of certain rooms and explained how these rooms come

Egyptian Art

At first glance Egyptian art looks unchanging over some three thousand years of Egyptian history. Yet although the canons and conventions were observed at the dawn of Pharaonic history, variations and innovations occurred over time and can be used to date objects produced in different periods. These changes included variations in how eyes were depicted, how the royal beard was detailed, figure poses, and the location and manner of indicating physical details such as knees, nipples, and navel. In addition to stylistic changes, the types of clothing, hair, and jewellery that are depicted help scholars date the images.

Some of the most interesting variations in Egyptian art occurred in the Old Kingdom, when artists were still experimenting with the canon. For the most part, both two- and three-dimensional royal images showed the king as a youthful, athletic, and majestic figure. Images of the king's facial features varied somewhat, which might be attributed either to actual renderings of the royal visage or to the hand of the sculptor. There was a greater range in depictions of the elite and of commoners, with certain features typical of an individual (dwarfism, a hump, a pronounced nose) sometimes being emphasized. Sculptures of the 4th Dynasty frequently showed some evidence of portraiture, albeit with a certain degree of the idealisation that is found even in modern portraits. The statues of Ankhaf and Hemiunu are particularly remarkable examples of this trend. By the end of the Old Kingdom, however, the personalisation of images had decreased significantly.

In the First Intermediate period, save for Thebes and Herakleopolis, there were few courts able to provide patronage for artists, and thus this period saw an overall decline in the quality of art. The canon of proportions was often ignored, resulting in depictions of people with disproportionately long arms, overly large hands, and goggling eyes, and standing at different levels without benefit of a groundline. The colour palette also changed with the addition of a pale green that was used for texts, food, and clothing indiscriminately.

By the Middle Kingdom, artistic order had been restored, together with political stability. Once again, kings and nobles were shown as youthful and athletic beings, although often with slightly different proportions than those followed in the Old Kingdom. However, this shifted again in the 12th Dynasty, perhaps reflecting the political turmoil attached to the royal succession. By the middle of the dynasty, the king was no longer depicted as an untroubled youth; instead, his brow was furrowed, he had bags under his eyes, his lips sometimes drooped, and his mouth was bracketed by naso-labial furrows. Although the pharaoh's body was still strong and muscled, he was often shown wearing a protective amulet, indicating that he, like other mortals, was in need of divine aid. Kings' ears were now generally much larger than those depicted for previous monarchs, and they stood away from the king's head; perhaps this was an actual physical trait of these rulers or maybe they were shown thus so that they could better hear the pleas of the populace. Queens' images did not look as troubled as kings', but did share their large ears. They also sported a new hairstyle typical of the period: rising high up from a central part, flanking the face, and flipping up in an exaggerated curl, reminiscent of Western hair styles of the 1960s.

These modes of depiction were adopted by the elites, who always emulated royalty, especially if they were employing the same artists. A new statue type called a 'block statue' also emerged at this time. As the name suggests, it consisted of a block of stone, surmounted by a human head, in the pose of someone seated with his or her knees to the chest and a robe or tunic pulled over the knees. This kind of statue was much quicker to carve and also provided a great deal of space for inscriptions.

New Kingdom art continued to use the innovations in poses and styles of its predecessors, as well as adding its own. There is a greater fluidity in the art of this period, as well as more variations in the types of scenes found in tombs and temples. The major innovations of this era started in the Amarna period with the exaggerated proportions of the head, chin, belly, and buttocks, coupled with slender arms, legs, and neck. After the Amarna period the style became less extreme, but it left behind a legacy of changes in proportion, and new poses for kings and commoners.

For the most part, the art of the Third Intermediate period was blockier and more stolid than that of the New Kingdom. An increase in covering surfaces densely with text and images of deities was typical of this era. The 25th Dynasty saw innovation and change with the introduction of ideas from Nubia, most often manifested in the so-called Kushite fold flanking the nostrils, and in a double uraeus on kings, indicating their dominion over Egypt and Nubia. Another feature of the period was the start of a new tradition of archaizing. Thus, Late period art hearkens back to the art of the Old, Middle, and New Kingdoms, and sometimes it is difficult to distinguish the archaizing pieces from the originals. This trend ceased during the 27th Dynasty (Persian period). The final stages of the Late period saw a rounding and softening of features and more traditional poses for royalty and the elite.

The last phases of ancient Egyptian art were the Ptolemaic, followed by the Roman. One hallmark of Ptolemaic art, the mixture of Egyptian and Hellenic motifs, is regarded by some scholars as vulgar, and by others as an entertaining cocktail of styles reflective of the tastes of Egypt's diverse population at that time. Images showed Egyptians with protruding breasts, stomachs, and buttocks, and with chubby faces and rounded chins, and wearing clothing that was a mixture of Egyptian and Greek. Also, there was an increase in the use of the colour pink and of gilding. The presence of pink and gold persisted into the Roman period; however, the exaggerated proportions of breasts and buttocks were abandoned during this time, with figures reverting to a more sedate silhouette. Coptic art was based on Egyptian art, and its styles, techniques, and motifs were borrowed and adapted in the final flowering of Egyptian art.

together to form a harmonious whole.[10] Presumably, in addition to designing buildings, architects actually oversaw their execution and had some knowledge of construction methods and materials. The tool-kit of an architect was simple. Some have survived intact from the tombs, such as that of Kha, at Deir el-Medina. They held a cubit stick for measuring, set-squares, plumb bobs, and a knotted rope for longer measurements.

Entertainers and Entertainment

Although the wealthy had more time for leisure activities, all Egyptians liked to relax and be entertained. Active pursuits included a variety of games and sports, as well as hunting and fishing, while listening to musicians, singers, and story-tellers and watching dancers provided more sedate entertainment.

Group sports, depicted in tomb scenes, included leapfrog and tug of war. It is possible that some form of hockey – or some game played with a curved stick and a ball – was enjoyed. Boat jousting was also popular, often as a spectator sport. It involved groups of men on papyrus boats who would try to push each other off their respective crafts into the water with a stick. Games involving long jumps, akin to the modern Egyptian *khazza lawizza*, were also very popular, as were games that involved throwing balls. Some ball games also had religious overtones and were associated with defeating the enemies of the gods or protecting Osiris; these were played with a bat and a ball – perhaps an early form of baseball or rounders. (Fig. 129.)

Many sports were associated with hunting and military training. Wrestling and stick fighting are two examples of training that involved close engagement between opponents. Foot races and archery were also popular, and after the introduction of the horse and chariot, royalty and the elite enjoyed chariot races. There is little evidence of riding until the Late period, when Near Easterners and their divinities were shown on the back of horses. For relaxation, the elite in particular hunted wild game, often in special parks established for the purpose, and went fishing and fowling in the marshes with their families. Swimming, although not depicted frequently, was also a pleasurable pastime, especially in the heat of the day.

Board games such as *senet*, the snake game, and jackal and hounds (also known as the shield game) provided less energetic and more relaxing entertainment. Unfortunately, although the boards and the pieces for these games have come down to us intact, the rules have not, and we can only guess as to

Figure 129. Egyptians often played sports or watched them. These jousting boatmen are from the tomb of Nefer at Saqqara. Those boatmen who fell into the water had to be rescued from the threat of crocodiles. The register above shows people dancing. Photo Salima Ikram.

how they were played. They bear some resemblance to Ludo and Parcheesi. Gaming pieces and their boards were made of stone, bone, ivory, wood, or faience. (Fig. 130.)

Musicians, singers, dancers, and story-tellers provided professional entertainment. Story-tellers may have travelled from village to village, telling traditional tales, as well as passing on news. Large households might have had performers attached to them; certainly, the court and temples would have, for both sacred and secular music and dance. Unfortunately, no musical notation has been identified so it is impossible to tell what ancient Egyptian music sounded like, although it is possible that Nubian music, as well as Coptic liturgical music, can provide some clues. The number of drums, *sistra* (rattles), clappers, and other percussion instruments suggests that the music had a strong beat. Melodies were created with flutes, harps, and lyres. (Fig. 131.) Both men and women played instruments and sang, while certain dances were the purview of men, and others of women. From tomb scenes, it seems that secular dancing in particular was fairly acrobatic, involving lots of

Figure 130. Here, Queen Nefertari is shown in her tomb in the Valley of the Queens playing the board game senet. This game was a bit like Parcheesi or Ludo. It is frequently depicted in funerary contexts, perhaps as a representation of the different steps the deceased has to go through to reach eternal life. Photo T. M. Ramadan.

Figure 131. As can be seen in these images from the tomb of Rekhmire at Thebes, musicians often performed at banquets. Both women and men sang and played the harp, drums, and ukelele-like instruments as entertainment. Photo Salima Ikram.

fluid movement and backbends. Music was a large part of everyday life and was often used to relieve the tedium of work. Tomb scenes depict drummers and flautists playing their instruments to encourage the harvest and the processing of the grain. Even today, manual labourers sing to establish a rhythm to their work.

9

The Living
and the Dead
Mummies, Tombs,
and Mortuary Cults

Because the Egyptians believed that life continued after death (see Chapter 5), they mummified their bodies so that their souls (particularly the *ka*) would always have a form to animate and enjoy the Afterlife. Also, when possible, the Egyptians constructed their tombs from stone so that they could shelter the deceased forever. In addition to a burial place, Egyptian tombs, or 'houses for eternity', provided a physical location for the maintenance of family ties through the celebration of the mortuary cult, and a place where the dead and the living could interact.

Mummification

In order to be presented to Osiris for judgement, and to live eternally, the body of the deceased had to be transformed into a mummy. (Fig. 132.) A mummy is the artificially preserved body of a human being or an animal. (Fig. 133.) (Fig. 134.) Egyptians mummified their dead to preserve the body so that it could be reanimated by the soul and enjoy the delights of the Afterworld, which they believed was very similar to this world, except more pleasant.

Figure 132. This scene, from a papyrus in Berlin, shows the weighing of the heart against the feather of truth in the presence of Osiris and other gods. If the heart is heavier than the feather, the deceased is devoured by Ammit; if not, he can enter the Afterlife. Photo Nicholas Warner.

Figure 133. This mummy of a man was excavated in Theban Tomb 11/12 by a Spanish team directed by Jose Galan. Tomb robbers had plundered the tomb and left the mummy on top of a pile of rubble with its face exposed, perhaps as a warning to other thieves. The mummy might date to the 21st Dynasty. Photo Salima Ikram.

Figure 134. Egyptians mummified many kinds of animals. There were four main types of animal mummies: pets, sacred creatures, votive offerings, and food offerings. This crocodile, originally coming from Kom Ombo, was a votive offering to Sobek and was mummified simply, using natron and resins. Photo Anna-Marie Kellen.

The basis of mummification is preservation through dehydration using natron. Natron, a naturally deposited material found particularly in Wadi Natrun, located some 40 kilometres from Cairo, is basically a combination of salt and baking soda. Natron desiccates and inhibits bacterial activity. Removing the liquid from a body left the skin, hair, and sinew well preserved, and any ancient Egyptian who could afford even a basic method of mummification arranged for it. Those who were too poor to pay for this service were buried in the dry desert sand, which had a similar dehydrating effect as long as the body was not wrapped or placed in a coffin. The Egyptians believed that as long as the right spells were read and offerings made to the *ka*, the deceased could achieve an enjoyable Afterlife even without elaborate mummification.

Methods of mummification evolved over time, and often a variety of methods was used at a particular period, in different areas or by different embalming houses. The most 'classic' form of mummification was practised in the 18th Dynasty. The initial step was to remove from the body both its internal organs and its fluids in order to avoid decay. First the embalmers extracted the brain by inserting a sharp, pointed instrument into the left nostril, pushing through the ethmoid bone and poking into the cranium to break up the brain. The Egyptians favoured the left side, as this was where

The Destruction of Mummies

Many mummies have been destroyed over time for a variety of reasons: for their adornments, as souvenirs, for medicine (see box on the mummy trade in Chapter 2), and for other practical purposes. When people could not find sufficient firewood they would burn mummies as fuel. Mummies were allegedly used to make a paint marketed in Europe under the name 'Mummy Brown'. During the American Civil War, when cotton was scarce, mummy bandages were taken to Maine and turned into brown paper in which butchers would wrap joints of meat and other commodities. Animal mummies did not escape destruction either. In addition to being burned for fuel, cat mummies in particular were used as ballast for ships returning to Europe from Egypt. Once a ship was in port, the 'ballast' was either tossed overboard or crushed and sold to farmers as fertilizer.

the heart was located. Because they believed that the heart the seat of the soul and the essence of a person, they considered the left the important side. The embalmers then used a flexible tool to whip up the brain and liquefy it, finally teasing it out via the nostrils using an instrument with a hooked end. Once the brain had been extracted, molten resin was poured through the nostrils into the cranium, and the head was manipulated so that its interior was coated by the resin. The resin, which inhibited bacterial growth, served to disinfect and deodorize the head. The nostrils were plugged with small linen rolls to keep the resin in place.

The next step in the process was to remove the internal organs. A small cut was made in the lower left side of the abdomen. The lungs, liver, intestines, and stomach were removed through the incision and mummified separately, before being stored in vessels called canopic jars. The heart was never removed from the body as it was key to the resurrection of the deceased and had to be weighed against the feather of *maat* for a successful rebirth.

Each of the four internal organs was protected by a different demi-god, known collectively as the 'Four Sons of Horus'. Originally, these dieties were shown with human heads, but from the New Kingdom on, the divinities were more personalised. Imseti was shown with the head of a man and was responsible for protecting the liver; he was associated with the goddess Isis. Hapy had the head of a baboon and was in charge of the lungs; he was associated with Nephthys. Duamutef was canid-headed and protected the stomach; he was associated with the goddess Neith. Qebehsenuef was hawk-headed

Figure 135.   Canopic jars, such as these in New York's Metropolitan Museum of Art, were used to contain mummified viscera. Each head represents a specific deity responsible for a particular organ: human-headed Imseti, the liver; jackal-headed Duamutef, the stomach; hawk-headed Qebehsenuef, the intestines, and baboon-headed Hapy, the lungs. Prior to the Late Period, canopic jars had either plain lids or human-headed ones, although the association with these four gods, also known as the Four Sons of Horus, was already established in the Old Kingdom. Photo Salima Ikram.

and cared for the intestines; he was associated with Selqet. These protective demi-gods appeared on canopic jars, coffins, sarcophagi, and other funerary equipment. (Fig. 135.)

After evisceration, the body was washed out with cleansing palm wine, dried with linen towels, and filled with small linen bags containing natron. The whole body was immersed in powdered natron. The natron served to suck out the bodily fluids and had to be changed intermittently during the first few weeks of desiccation. Desiccation took forty days.

The second half of the mummification process took thirty days, during which time the body of the deceased was transformed into that of a semi-divine being. The embalmers dusted the natron from the body, wiped it with wine, and anointed it with seven sacred oils. The oils served not only a ritual purpose but also a practical one: they returned some flexibility to the body so that the limbs would not snap while it was being wrapped. Often the body was painted with resin, imparting a golden hue. The resin, which protected the body from bacteria, insects, and vermin, also referred to the Egyptian belief that the dead were transformed into divine beings, and that the flesh of the gods was made of gold, their bones of silver, and their

Figure 136.   Starting in the Middle Kingdom, masks made of cartonnage were placed over the head and sometimes over the shoulders of the mummy. This mask, in Hildesheim Museum (No. 1258), shows a woman wearing an elaborate wig, and dates to the end of the Ptolemaic period. Real beads adorn her neck and crown her head. Her face is gilded to emphasize her metamorphosis into a divine being after her death, as the flesh of the gods was thought to be of gold, their bones of silver, and their hair of lapis lazuli. Photo Salima Ikram.

hair of lapis lazuli. Then the body was wrapped in linen bandages interspersed with protective amulets while priests read prayers over the corpse and burnt incense prior to escorting it to the tomb. The bandages provided physical protection for the mummy, while the prayers wove a metaphysical

protection around the body. Royal and elite mummies were often further enhanced by a mask that fit over the head and sometimes over the shoulders of the body. (Fig. 136.)

The seventy days of mummification were associated with the Osiris as they paralleled the length of time the star Sothis (Sirius), identified with Osiris, was absent from the sky. Obviously, actual desiccation might take a longer or shorter time, depending on the stoutness of the deceased; fatter people took longer to desiccate than thinner ones. However, for religious reasons, embalmers tried to maintain a seventy-day total for the preparation of the body, although we have examples of individuals whose mummification took much longer, such as Queen Meresankh III at Giza, whose embalming took 272 days. Whether this was due to her girth or to the fact that her tomb was unfinished at the time is unknown.

Amulets

An amulet is generally defined as a protective piece of jewellery. All classes of ancient Egyptian wore amulets to protect themselves against disease, misfortune, and attacks by snakes and scorpions, and to encourage good fortune, good health, fertility, and wealth. Certain amulets were worn to prevent specific diseases or were a part of a medical cure. Some amulets were made of precious materials, such as gold or semi-precious stones; the more mundane were of faience, and clay, or such natural objects as shells or pebbles.

The efficacy of an amulet at times depended on what it was made of or on its colour. Thus, if a red stone amulet were unavailable, a red faience one would suffice, as the emphasis was on its being red, symbolic of the sun, fire, and blood. Special amulets were placed on the mummy as aids on the journey to the Afterlife and to ensure a safe arrival. Thus, *djed* pillars, the symbol of Osiris and his vertebral column, were placed at the mummy's back; a headrest was placed under the neck to prevent the head from rolling off; and *wadjet* eyes of Horus were placed all over the body to protect it. The chief amongst these amulets was the heart scarab. This large scarab was placed over the deceased's heart and inscribed with a spell from the Book of the Dead that would ensure that the deceased safely arrived in the Afterworld. The favoured inscription was Spell 30: 'Oh my heart I have from my mother, O my heart that I had on earth, do not rise up against me as a witness in the presence of the Lord of Things; do not speak against me concerning what I have done, do not bring up against me anything I have done in the presence of the Great God, Lord of the West.' (Fig. 137.)

Figure 137. Both the living and the dead wore amulets for protection. These funerary amulets made out of faience, now in Leipzig Museum, include a winged scarab; several djed *pillars, symbols of Osiris, indicating stability;* tyt *amulets associated with Isis and the flow of the blood;* wadjet *eyes to protect and resurrect;* ib, *or heart, amulets in the shape of a jar; and images of different divinities. Photo Salima Ikram.*

Funerals, Funerary Processions, and Tomb Equipment

Once the seventy days of mummification were completed, the body, laid on a sled, was transported to the tomb in a funeral procession. At its most basic, the procession consisted of family members and friends, carrying grave goods, as well as of priests to perform the final rites. Elaborate funerals included not only friends and family but also hired mourners, who would wail, rend their garments, and heap dust on their heads; in addition, there were several priests in the procession who burnt incense and recited prayers along the route. The plentiful grave goods that were to accompany the deceased to the hereafter were carried by a host of bearers. A curious object

Figure 138. In addition to a coffin that was pulled on a sledge, funerary processions such as that of Ramose at Thebes included mourners, people bearing grave goods, and ritual items like the tekenu, *an obscure object resembling a kneeling person that was wrapped in cloth or an animal-skin and dragged on a sledge before the coffin. Photo Salima Ikram.*

called the *tekenu* also was part of this procession from the Middle Kingdom onward. In the Middle Kingdom, it appears to have been either a wrapped figure that was crouching or that was in the foetal position, with only its head visible. In the New Kingdom the *tekenu* was shown as an entirely wrapped bundle, or with its head and sometimes an arm showing. Its precise identity and role in the funerary ritual is enigmatic. (Fig. 138.)

At the tomb, priests, assisted by the eldest son and heir (or daughter, if there were no sons), performed the necessary funerary rituals. The most important of these was the Opening of the Mouth (*wepet-r*) ritual. The eldest son, wearing the special leopard-skin of the *sem*, or funerary priest, performed this ceremony on the (sometimes encoffined) corpse, touching the eyes, nose, mouth, ears, and face of the mummy with sacred implements, including an adze, while reciting appropriate prayers and burning incense. This ceremony restored the five senses to the body and readied it to make the journey to the land of Osiris and eternal life. A funerary dance, associated with the city of Buto, performed by two men wearing basketry headdresses reminiscent of Osiris's *atef* crown, formed a part of the ritual for rejuvenation. In the presence of the deceased, the priests and mourners consumed a final funerary banquet consisting of meat, bread, beer, wine, and other foods. Once the banquet was over, the body was placed in a coffin. (Fig. 139.)

Coffins were made of wood or cartonnage, and sometimes of pottery. The form of the coffins changed over time, varying between rectangular boxes and anthropomorphic containers; the latter first became popular in the New Kingdom, with the form surviving until the end of Pharaonic pagan history.

Figure 139. The Opening of the Mouth ceremony, carried out by the deceased's heir or close relative in the role of the sem *priest (wearing a leopard-skin), restored the five senses to the mummy. This was one of the most important parts of the funerary ritual, and even elite youngsters, such as the one in this coffin now in Munich, were accorded elaborate funerary rites. Photo Salima Ikram.*

Most Old Kingdom coffins were relatively plain, enhanced only by images of the palace façade and a pair of eyes through which the mummy could look out. During the Middle Kingdom, coffins became elaborately inscribed with the Coffin Texts (see Chapter 5), which provided a map and a set of instructions for the deceased's journey to reach the hereafter. Anthropomorphic coffins of the 18th Dynasty were decorated with fewer texts; occasionally, they were enhanced with images of funerary deities. During the New Kingdom, in some instances, the mummy was not placed just in one coffin, but in a series of coffins, one inside the other, similar to nested Russian dolls. Coffins from Dynasty 19 onward were elaborately painted with images of many different deities and were also heavily inscribed with funerary texts to help the deceased achieve a fulfilled Afterlife. From Dynasty 21, the coffins, rather than the tombs, provided the deceased with the requisite spells necessary for survival in the hereafter. Late period coffins varied in their complexity, and those from the Graeco-Roman period often just consisted of a painted cartonnage case that closely followed the form of the body, almost like another shroud. (Fig. 140.)

The coffins of royalty and of the wealthy were placed in yet another final container: a sarcophagus. The word *sarcophagus* is derived from the Greek

Figure 140. The mummy was placed in a series of coffins, such as these belonging to Nany and now in the Metropolitan Museum of Art, New York, before being interred in a tomb or in a stone sarcophagus in a tomb. Coffin style changed greatly over time; these yellow coffins are typical of the 21st and early 22nd Dynasties. Photo Salima Ikram.

for 'flesh-eater', apparently because of a (mistaken) Hellenic belief that certain stones that were used to make these containers actually consumed the body. Sarcophagi, generally made of stone, provided further protection for the body. Owing to its bulk the sarcophagus was placed in the burial

Figure 141. Stone sarcophagi often contained a coffin or a cartonnage-wrapped mummy. This granite example, from the Old Kingdom cemetery at Giza, now in Hildesheim (No. 3177), is enhanced with a façade reminiscent of the niched walls of houses. The bosses on either end of the lid were used to move it around and are a feature of many large stone objects. Ideally, these were removed once the sarcophagus was in place, although this did not always happen. Photo Salima Ikram.

chamber prior to the funeral, and the encoffined body placed within it. Stone sarcophagi were used by royalty and nobility from the Old Kingdom until the New Kingdom; at that juncture, stone became almost exclusively reserved for royalty until the 26th Dynasty. (Fig. 141.)

In addition to the enclosed body, the burial chamber was filled with the grave goods that would be used by the deceased in the Afterworld. Grave goods included food and drink, furniture, clothing, shoes, toilette boxes, jewellery, cosmetics, perfumes, games, tools, weapons, funerary texts, inscribed on papyrus, *shabtis* (*ushabtis*) or servant figures that served the dead and would work in their place should any labour be required by the gods, and statues of the deceased. Once the burial chamber had been filled, it was hermetically sealed. Ideally, the door was closed forever, although generally tomb robbers breached the sealed doors and plundered the tomb not too long after the burial had taken place.

Although robbing a tomb was regarded as a heinous crime, it was a fairly common practice in antiquity, and was probably carried out by the very people who had helped construct the tomb, or by the priests that were supposed to care for it. However, if tomb robbers were apprehended, they were severely punished, particularly if they had desecrated a royal tomb, the final resting place of a god. A papyrus dating to the 21st Dynasty details the trial and convictions of thieves who desecrated the tombs in the Valley of the Kings – they were sentenced to death by impalement.

Cemeteries and Tombs

Cemeteries were generally situated on the west bank of the Nile, identified with the setting sun and death. When this was impractical owing to the course of the river and the associated arable land, tombs' locations were changed. However, the grammar of a tomb's internal decoration provided a clue as to which way was supposed to represent east and the rising sun that symbolised resurrection. Some sites were regarded as especially sacred, such as Abydos, which was associated with mythological events (the Osiris myth), or Saqqara, which was connected to the blessed tombs of Djoser and Imhotep, and often people chose to be buried at such a location so that they could benefit from the site's holiness.

Tombs were houses for the dead and the final repository of the mummy. (Fig. 142.) The main function of the tomb was to protect the body of the deceased, provide a place for the funerary cult, and act as a magical machine that recreated the cosmos and helped the deceased enjoy eternal life. Ideally, they were made of stone so that they could last forever. However, this was feasible only for royalty and the elite. Poorer people made do with what they could afford, aided by religious texts to achieve an eternal existence (see Chapter 5). Throughout Egyptian history, the most basic tomb consisted of a hole dug into the desert surface that was marked by a mound or tumulus, a mud-brick or stone stela, and an offering place.

In dynastic times, tombs consisted of two parts: a super-structure where the deceased's cult was celebrated, the site of prayers and offerings (*huwt aat* or *shepes*), and a sub-structure where the deceased was buried (*khenet*). (Fig. 143.) The underground chamber was the equivalent of the Underworld, the realm of Osiris; the shaft or passage leading from the surface – often within or close to the tomb chapel – was a liminal area of transition, akin to the passage to the Underworld. The tomb chapel was in the land of the living, where the *ka* and *ba* could interface with the living, and its decoration associated it with solar imagery. Thus, the deceased was linked with the sun god Re and with

Figure 142. *The tomb of Niankhnum and Khnumhotep at Saqqara typifies the idea of tomb as house. This structure has a courtyard in front and an internal one around which rooms are organized. Light enters the chambers through small slits high up in the wall, thus keeping the rooms cool. Photo Salima Ikram.*

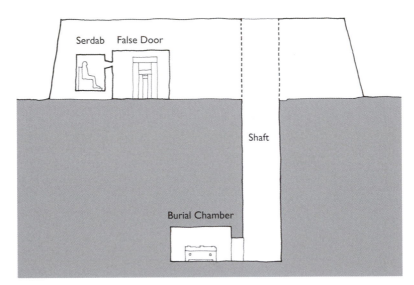

Figure 143. *This mastaba illustrates the two main portions of a tomb, the super- and sub-structures. It also shows a false door, and the* serdab, *containing a statue of the deceased. Drawing Nicholas Warner.*

Figure 144. The rock-cut tombs at Beni Hasan give a sense of tomb-as-house, with courtyards and columned porticoes carved out of the living rock. The proto-Doric columns support a stone roof that is carved to imitate a wooden one. Photo Salima Ikram.

Osiris, both divinities who were involved with rebirth, resurrection, and eternal life. The chapels were the portion of the tombs that could be visited and still are today; in antiquity, the burial chambers were sealed to protect the dead at rest, as well as their funerary goods.

Tombs were generally of two types: rock cut and free standing, although there are plenty of examples that have elements of both kinds of architecture, depending on the tomb owner's wealth and the geography and geology of the cemetery. Rock-cut tombs were cut straight into stone and were more common in the limestone and sandstone cliffs of Upper Egypt. These were carved horizontally into cliff faces and consisted of one or more chambers, sometimes columned. (Fig. 144.) More elaborate tombs had exterior courtyards and porticoes. Shaft tombs were simpler, consisting of vertical shafts culminating in one or more chambers. The cult place of these tombs was a simple offering emplacement at the mouth of the shaft, bearing the name and titles of the deceased. Such tombs were used throughout ancient Egyptian history. Tombs from the Graeco-Roman period followed more classical models and consisted of *loculi* (*sing.* loculus), basically a series of human-sized

Figure 145.   Graeco-Roman burials were most commonly placed in loculi, *such as these at Kom el-Shugafa at Alexandria. These slots were sealed with a stone slab, with the tomb owner's name painted or carved on it. Some mausolea belonged to a single family, although other larger tombs acted more as a general cemetery and contained the bodies of several different groups. Photo Salima Ikram.*

rectangular slots carved into solid rock into which the mummified bodies were inserted. (Fig. 145.)

Owing to the absence of solid rock, built tombs were most common in Lower Egypt, although examples of this type also exist in the south. Ideally, such tombs were stone constructions, but during Egypt's early history, prior to the 3rd Dynasty and the construction of Djoser's Step Pyramid, they were made of mud brick. Poorer people have used mud-brick constructions throughout Egyptian history. (Fig. 146.)

Amongst constructed tombs, the most common tomb shape was that of the *mastaba* (Arabic for 'bench', reflecting the similarity between the tomb's shape and the benches found outside traditional Arab homes). In the early

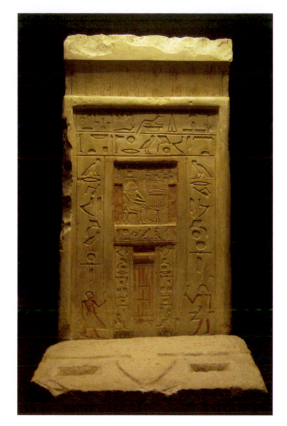

Figure 146. A false door, such as this one belonging to Khesi at Saqqara, was a crucial component of a tomb, for it was the point at which the spirit of the dead could move between the worlds of the living and the dead. False doors were crowned by a cavetto cornice and consisted of a tablet at the top showing an image of the deceased before a table of offerings, and a series of lintels and door-jambs inscribed with the name and titles of the deceased along with an offering formula and images of family members. Offerings to the dead were placed on an altar before the false door. Photo Salima Ikram.

Old Kingdom, these were solid constructions with niches containing offering slabs or stelae and statues on the east side of the building. However, they were soon constructed as if they were houses, with a series of rooms including what might be a lavatory. Mastabas (and some pyramids) also had a room called a *serdab*, Arabic for 'cellar'. These rooms generally contained statues of the deceased and were either closed entirely or had small slits through which the deceased could watch activities taking place in the tomb.

Later on, in the New Kingdom, most free-standing tombs of the nobility took the shape of scaled-down temples, complete with pylons, courts, and

Figure 147. Before he was king, Horemheb began building a tomb at Saqqara. After ascending the throne, he started a new tomb in the Valley of the Kings and also added the royal uraeus to the foreheads of his images in his Saqqara tomb to indicate the change in his status. Ultimately, he was buried in the Valley of the Kings and his Saqqara tomb was used for his wife and other family members. Photo Salima Ikram.

colonnades; mini-pyramids capped a portion of the structure. Graeco-Roman tombs were very variable in their form. Some, particularly those at Tuna el-Gebel, were shaped like houses, complete with false windows, picket fences, and drain pipes. A curious group of tombs in Dakhla Oasis consisted of a series of vaulted burial chambers and chapels, topped by a mud-brick pyramid – the last pyramids made in Egypt.

Royal tombs always differed in architecture and decoration from the tombs of commoners. Kings' tombs were regarded as highly sacred sites as they were the burial places of deities. In the Old and Middle Kingdoms, their super-structures took the form of enormous pyramids, and they had simple sub-structures, often a single room that held the body and the grave goods that accompanied the deceased into the hereafter. Kings' mortuary cults were celebrated in a series of temples that were part of the funerary complex that was physically attached to the pyramid (see Chapter 5). The New Kingdom saw a significant change in this arrangement: the substructure was separated from the super-structure or cult place. This may have been due to an increased desire to ensure the security of the royal burials, as well as a result of changes in state religion as Thebes and the god Amun replaced the supremacy of Re and the Memphite region. From Dynasty 18 until the Third Intermediate period, kings were interred in a remote desert valley, now known as the Valley of the Kings. Their burial chambers consisted of long passageways with chambers coming off of them cut deep into the rock. The cult places for the rulers of this period, their memorial temples or Temples of Millions of Years, were located at the desert margins (see Chapter 5). These were where the active worship of the kings and their royal *ka* took place. In addition to the tombs where they were buried, kings (and occasionally elites) sometimes had cenotaphs, or tombs that did not contain the body of the deceased but provided a focal point for the continuation of their memory.

Decorating the tomb was a very important part of constructing a magical space that recreated the cosmos, thereby permitting the deceased to live in an eternal and perfect world. Images and text were charged with power, as the Egyptians believed that they both had the ability to come to life and be reified, and they were a crucial component of the tomb. If the tomb were robbed and the mummy was destroyed, the images on the tomb walls would provide the soul with an alternative source of sustenance and a body to reanimate. Including statues of the deceased in the tomb was also crucial for this reason. (Fig. 147.)

Royal and private tombs were differently decorated, reflecting the dissimilar roles of their owners. The Afterlife was far more serious for a king than for anyone else. Even in the hereafter the king was responsible to the gods and charged with maintaining the cosmos and control over Egypt, and with helping the sun god Re vanquish his enemies so that the world could continue to exist. The Afterlife of the non-royals was a more idyllic version of life on earth, with few responsibilities.

Initially, the burial chambers of pyramids were unadorned; however, from the end of the 5th Dynasty to the end of the Old Kingdom they were inscribed with Pyramid Texts that helped the king achieve eternal existence and aided him in his battles to maintain *maat*. Middle Kingdom burial chambers were undecorated; perhaps royal funerary texts of this period were written on papyrus and placed in the tomb. The temples associated with royal burials tended to be well decorated from the 5th Dynasty onward. Prior to that, only the

Figure 148. Hatshepsut's funerary temple at Deir el-Bahari illustrated several events specific to her reign, such as the expedition that she sent to Punt to acquire incense trees that she then dedicated to Amun. Images of this exotic land, perhaps located on the East African coast, show houses on stilts and the turtles and fish that inhabited the sea (probably the Red Sea) that bordered Punt. Photo Salima Ikram.

causeways connecting the temples were adorned, often with images reflecting daily life or particular events from the king's reign. The decorative themes in the mortuary temples from the 5th Dynasty onward focussed on the role of divine kingship, with the king shown enacting various rituals, such as the slaying of the hippopotamus, symbol of chaos, running the *heb-sed*, and erecting pillars that alluded to the enduring nature of Osiris and kingship. Images of gods supporting the king were also a crucial part of the decoration.

New Kingdom burial chambers were enhanced by texts from a variety of funerary books (see Chapter 5), and by images of the gods assisting the king in his quest for an eternal existence amongst them. The accompanying temples continued to be decorated with images of gods and kings, as well as with significant events from the king's reign. Thus, Hatshepsut recorded an expedition to Punt at Deir el-Bahari, Ramesses II celebrated his victory at Qadesh in the Ramesseum, and Ramesses III showed himself repelling the attacks of the Sea Peoples. (Fig. 148.) Depictions of more prosaic activities, such as market scenes, or scenes showing the changing seasons such as were found on Old Kingdom causeways, were virtually non-existent by the New Kingdom.

Figure 149. The hunting of animals that represented chaos, such as the hippopotamus, ensured that maat *was being upheld and that the forces of* isfet *were not in the ascendancy. This scene in the tomb of Mereruka at Saqqara depicts a group of men harpooning the animals, with the tomb owner in the background. The artist who carved this scene made a mistake in the position of the crocodile's feet, and they were re-carved. When the tomb was completed the error would have been covered with a thin layer of plaster and paint, but that is now missing. Photo Salima Ikram.*

Royal tombs of the Third Intermediate period at Tanis were inscribed with images of the king and gods, as well as with a plethora of texts designed to ensure eternal life and the unification of the king with the gods. No royal tombs from the Late period onward have been discovered thus far.

From the Old Kingdom until the Ramesside era private tomb chapels were enhanced with scenes of daily life: farmers at work in the fields, the tomb owner hunting and fishing, butchers and bakers at work, people dining at banquets, and other activities. These images can be interpreted both literally, as records of what was necessary for an ideal eternal existence, and on a metaphoric level. Thus, in a scene of the tomb owner hunting in the desert or on the Nile, the deceased was not only enjoying a sporting activity but was also routing chaos and maintaining *maat*. (Fig. 149.) Other images involving agricultural activities were allusions to funerary texts that describe the

Figure 150. The royal tomb of Horemheb in the Valley of the Kings (KV57) was decorated traditionally with images of the king making offerings to different gods and being blessed by them in return. Photo T. M. Ramadan.

pleasures and riches of the hereafter. For the most part, few funerary texts appeared in tombs until the Middle Kingdom, when prayers and invocations to the gods such as Osiris became common. As time passed, images that were used by kings in an earlier period were adopted by the elite after the kings had moved on to new sets of images and texts. Thus, some Middle Kingdom tombs displayed portions of the Pyramid Texts that were no longer to be found in royal sepulchres.

From the Ramesside period on, the number of images of daily life decreased dramatically in private tombs. These were replaced by images of the gods, as well as by many more prayers and invocations to the deities. Throughout their history, non-royal burial chambers were rarely decorated, and when they were, the images reflected the offerings buried with the dead. In some rare cases, late New Kingdom burial chambers were inscribed with religious texts to aid the deceased's journey to the Afterlife. (Fig. 150.)

During the Third Intermediate period few Egyptians constructed elaborate sepulchres; their focus was on their heavily inscribed coffins. The decoration of Late Period elite tombs, particularly those dating to the 25th and 26th Dynasties, followed the ideals of the Old and Middle Kingdoms.

Graeco-Roman tomb decoration varied depending on where the tomb was located. Some tombs followed a classical scheme of decoration with images of Greek and Roman divinities juxtaposed with Egyptian ones, while other tombs showed scenes of daily life, but the people in them were carved or painted in an Egyptian Hellenistic style, an amusing blend of the classical and Egyptian traditions.

Members of ancient Egypt's royalty and nobility started building their tombs quite early in their lives, as such elaborate constructions required time, money, and attention. According to Herodotus, a pyramid took twenty years to build. No doubt this was the case for certain pyramids, but the length of time actually varied depending on the size of the construction and the number of people needed to build it. Many tombs, both royal and private, were unfinished at the time of their owners' death, and they were often left thus as heirs were loath to continue to pay for them.

Mortuary Cults

The funerary cults of the wealthy were sustained through offerings and prayers provided by loyal family members and, more important, through endowments made by the deceased. During his or her lifetime, the tomb owner dedicated lands or produce to pay the priests who looked after the tomb and the cult. Hepdjefa, a noble from Asyut, inscribed instructions in his tomb for the division of his estate and the payment of his mortuary priests. These mortuary priests, who worked in rotation, were called the *hemu-ka*, or servants of the *ka*. Their duties involved making offerings (which reverted to them after consecration) to the soul of the tomb owner, maintaining the tomb, offering up prayers, and safeguarding the burial. Royal cults were much larger and more complex, and the maintenance of those cults was often affiliated with divine cult temples, particularly in the New Kingdom. Ultimately, regardless of whether a cult was royal or private, the descendants of the deceased would divert the income to their own cults or to other uses. This is why decorating and equipping the tomb was vital: the images and offerings would provide the soul of the deceased with sustenance and prayers throughout eternity.

Tombs were inscribed with the name and titles of the deceased, together with a series of standard offering formulae to be read by priests, family members, and passers-by to invoke the spirit of the dead and to ensure that his or her soul would continue to flourish in the hereafter. The most ancient and common offering formulae was the *hetep-di-nisw* formula, translated as 'a gift or boon that the king gives', and it was inscribed on lintels, false doors, and offering tables. The formula ensured that the deceased was remembered, blessed by gods, and provided with the standard offerings of a thousand loaves of bread, a thousand jars of beer, oxen, fowl, linen, natron, and all things good and pure. Other prayers, such as the 'Admonitions to the Living', were inscribed in tombs and asked visitors to the tomb to recite the offering fomulas for the deceased; in exchange, the *akh* form of the tomb owner would praise the visitors to the divine king and the gods, and ensure their safety within the necropolis.

Curses

Much fuss has been made about curses inscribed in tombs. Only a few of these exist; most were aimed at those who descrated the tomb by entering it in an unclean state or who intended to harm its occupant. The inscription on the mastaba of Khentika, called Ikhekhi (6th Dynasty), at Saqqara reads:

> All who enter my tomb in an impure state, having eaten abominations ... they shall not be pure to enter into [it] or there will be judgement against them in the Council [of gods] ... I shall seize his neck like a bird ... I shall put fear of myself in him ... so that the living may fear the [beings] who go to the West ...

The inscription in the First Intermediate period tomb of Tefibi at Asyut was more severe: the son of the desecrator would not live to inherit, no one would carry out the thief's funerary ceremonies, the thief's spirit would be deprived of libations and offerings, and the spirit would perish in the Afterworld. Such texts, however, were few and far between, and none has been found in a royal tomb.

The Living and the Dead

Being dead and inhabiting Amenti, the Afterworld, did not mean that the Egyptians ceased to be connected to the world of the living. In addition to funerary priests, family members regularly visited their dead ancestors, giving offerings, reciting prayers, and relating current family news. This custom continues in modern Egypt. Special attention was paid to ancestral tombs during religious festivals, such as the Theban Festival of the Valley.

These cemetery visits also provided an opportunity for the living to ask the dead for their supernatural assistance and advice or, in some instances, to demand that unquiet ghosts stop troubling the living. In addition to making verbal requests, supplicants left letters to the dead, which have been found in several cemeteries and date to all periods. These letters were inscribed on papyri, on linen fragments, and, most often, on pottery bowls that held offerings to tempt the deceased's spirit to help the living. One letter written by a widow and her children to her deceased husband asks his aid in obtaining justice and wreaking vengeance on the person who was attempting to defraud them of their inheritance. Other letters requested help in curing disease, as well as in obtaining further assistance from Osiris and other gods. For the Egyptians, the connection between the dead and the living was strong, and death was not really an end, but a beginning.

Glossary

Please note that the glossary does not provide names of divinities or sites as these are represented in the text and can be accessed through the index.

absolute dating Carbon 14 (C-14) and dendrochrology dating for organic materials; potassium-argon dating for ancient minerals; and thermoluminescence (TL) and archaeomagnetic dating for ceramics

akh an element of the soul that can be likened to the 'divine spark'

Amentet 'The West'; the dwelling place of the dead

Apis bull a bull revered particularly at Memphis and seen as a physical manifestation of the god Ptah. The Egyptians believed that a fragment of Ptah's divine essence entered the animal during its lifetime and upon its death was born into another similarly marked creature.

ba the aspect of the soul depicted as a human-headed bird that can detach itself from the body and has independence of movement

barrel vault semi-circular vaulting used throughout Egyptian history

BC/BCE Traditionally, BC indicates before the birth of Christ; some scholars believe that it is more politically correct to use BCE, meaning 'before the common era'. However, many cultures toward which Western scholars are trying to express cultural sensitivity consider this usage to be hypocritical and prefer the more traditional BC.

ben-ben sacred stone of Heliopolis, perhaps a meteorite, believed to take a roughly pyramidal shape

bitumen mineral pitch; any natural hydrocarbon

block statue stone statue showing a squatting individual with knees drawn up to the chin, and frequently inscribed with texts

BP 'before the present', meaning before 1950, the date chosen to represent the present when this concept was introduced. The term is most commonly used in geological dating.

canopic jar or container one of four vessels that contained the internal organs of the mummified deceased

cartonnage material made of linen, glue, papyrus, and plaster. Often refers to painted whole-body casings made of this material.

cartouche a sign resembling a knotted rope formed into an oval (*shenu*, in Egyptian) containing the royal name and symbolising its eternal existence. Napoleon's soldiers and savants thought that the symbol resembled a gun cartridge, or *cartouche* in French.

cenotaph grave marker or a tomb that does not contain a corpse

corvée a period of work required by the state in lieu of taxes

cosmogony the nature of the divine creation of the cosmos

cosmology an interpretation of the nature of the cosmos

epigraphy study of inscriptions, often involving copying them using different methods

false door a stone doorway in a tomb inscribed with offerings and the name and titles of the deceased; a focus for the mortuary cult

Frölich's (Froelich's) Syndrome a mixture of endocrine abnormalities believed to result from damage to the hypothalamus, the part of the brain where certain functions such as sleep cycles and body temperature are regulated. This syndrome appears to affect males primarily. Its most obvious and common characteristics are delayed puberty, small testes, and obesity.

funerary books a series of texts that aid the deceased in journeying safely through the Underworld (e.g., The Book of Gates, The Book of What Is in the Underworld, and The Book of the Heavenly Cow)

gebel 'mountain', in Arabic

geophysical survey using special equipment such as ground-penetrating radar or magnetometry to locate subsurface archaeological remains

gezira (pl. *guzur*) 'island', in Arabic; also used to describe turtlebacks

glacis defensive sloping area surrounding fortifications

htp-di-nsw funerary formula for the provision of offerings to the deceased

hypostyle hall chamber with its room supported by a number of columns

ka aspect of the soul that is created together with the body; it is symbolised by a pair of upraised arms.

khedive a viceroy; a title frequently used for local rulers within the Ottoman Empire

Marfan's Syndrome a heritable condition that affects the connective tissue. The primary purpose of connective tissue is to hold the body together and provide a framework for growth and development. In Marfan's sufferers, the connective tissue is defective. Because connective tissue is found throughout the body, the syndrome can affect many of the body's systems, including the skeleton, eyes, heart, blood vessels, nerves, skin, and lungs. Marfan's sufferers may be taller than average and have loose joints, elongated limbs, flat feet, and curved spines.

mastaba a type of tomb common from the Archaic period onward. The word *mastaba* is derived from the Arabic word for a mud-brick bench, which the tomb resembles.

mortuary cult also known as funerary cult; cult of the deceased celebrated by priests and family members and sustained by endowed estates

mummy artificially preserved human or animal corpse. The word is derived from the Persian *mum*, meaning 'wax' or 'bitumen'.

naos the holy of holies; the sanctuary

natron a combination of sodium carbonate and bicarbonate used to desiccate and purify corpses; occurs naturally in Egypt, especially in the Wadi Natrun, near Cairo

nome from the Greek word for a province, administered by a nomarch; *sepat* in Egyptian. By the time of the New Kingdom, Egypt had forty-two nomes.

obelisk a tall, rectangular pillar hewn from a single block of stone surmounted by a pyramidion. It was a symbol of the sun cult. The word comes from the Greek, *obol*, meaning '(roasting) spit'.

Osirid column a pillar fronted by a human figure shown with its feet together and garbed like Osiris

ostrakon (*pl.* ostraka) fragment of pottery or limestone that is used for writing

papyrus column column with a papyrus capitol and often having triangular sections resembling those found in real papyrus stems

peristyle court courtyard with a row of columns around its edges

pillar a rectangular column

portico a covered entrance to a building, supported by pillars or columns

pylon a massive ceremonial gateway made up of two tapering massifs joined over a doorway, and thought to symbolise the horizon (*akhet*)

Pyramid Texts texts inscribed in the burial chambers of pyramids from the end of the 5th Dynasty until the First Intermediate period when their use was usurped by the elite and abandoned by royalty

relief (sunk) a sunken two-dimensional design carved into a surface

relief (raised/bas) a two-dimensional design where the background is carved away, leaving the standing image

sarcophagus rectangular or quasi-rectangular outermost container intended to hold a coffin of a different form or material. It can be made of stone or wood.

serdab from the Arabic for 'cellar', a sealed room that contains statues, located within a tomb

serekh rectangular frame, with panelled lower section, used to enclose the Horus name of a king, and representing the palace façade and enclosure

shabti (also *ushabti*) magical servant figure found in tombs from the middle of the Middle Kingdom onward that would work for, or in place of, the deceased. Large numbers, at least one for each day of the year as well as extras, are often found in a single burial, starting in the mid-8th Dynasty.

skeuomorph object imitating the form of another in a different medium (e.g., stone vessels carved into the shape of a basket)

stela (*pl.* stelae) a stone slab that is either rectangular or semi-circular on top and is erected in either a tomb or a temple. Frequently, the topmost area (lunette, if curved) contains images and the rest of the slab is inscribed with text. Stelae either commemorate historic events, are inscribed with prayers, or serve as markers of events or people.

wadi Arabic for 'valley'

Notes

Chapter 2 Travellers, Thieves, and Scholars: The History of Egyptology and Egyptomania

1. Okasha El-Daly, *Egyptology: The Missing Millennium* (London: University College, 2005): 57–73.
2. Sir John Mandeville, *The travels of Sir John Mandeville: with three narratives in illustration of it: The voyage of Johannes de Plano Carpini; The journal of Friar William de Rubruquis' The Journal of Friar Odoric* (New York: Dover, 1964); J. W. Bennett, *The Rediscovery of Sir John Mandeville* (New York: Modern Language Association of America, 1954); G. Milton, *The Riddle and the Knight: In Search of Sir John Mandeville* (London: Hodder and Stoughton, 1996).
3. L. Greener, *The Discovery of Egypt* (New York: Dorset, 1966): 85.
4. D. M. Reid, *Whose Pharaohs? Archaeology, Museums, and Egyptian National Identity from Napoleon to World War I* (Cairo: AUC, 2002): 50–109.
5. C. Sheikholeslami and M. Saleh, 'A Short History of the Egyptian Museum', in *The Egyptian Museum at the Millennium* (Cairo: Supreme Council of Antiquities, 2000): 85.
6. F. Tiradritti, 'The History of the Egyptian Museum', in *Treasures of the Egyptian Museum*, ed. F. Tiradritti (London: Thames and Hudson, 1999): 16–17.
7. Greener, *The Discovery of Egypt*, 196.
8. A. Edwards, *A Thousand Miles Up the Nile* (London: Darf, 1993): 307–9.
9. M. S. Drower, *Flinders Petrie: A Life in Archaeology* (Madison: University of Wisconsin Press, 1995): 424.

Chapter 4 Shadows in the Sand: Egypt's Past

1. For the whole text of this story and others in the Westcar Papyrus, see M. Lichtheim, *Ancient Egyptian Literature* 1 (Berkeley: University of California Press, 1973): 215–22, and W. K. Simpson, ed., *The Literature of Ancient Egypt* (Cairo: AUC, 2003): 16–30.
2. To read the texts from Harkhuf's tomb in full, see Lichtheim, *Ancient Egyptian Literature* 1, 23–27, or Simpson (ed.), *Literature of Ancient Egypt*, 410–12.
3. Current scholarship is divided between including the 14th Dynasty in the Middle Kingdom or in the Second Intermediate period. This book follows Aidan Dodson's chronology as set out in A. M. Dodson and D. Hilton, *The Complete Royal Families of Ancient Egypt* (London: Thames and Hudson, 2004).

Chapter 5 Maintaining Egypt: Religion

1. Although these creatures are not all technically canids, they resemble one another phenotypically and in the taxonomy of ancient Egypt would have been grouped together.
2. In other versions of the tale, Isis revives Osiris and couples with him after she retrieves his body from Byblos. Seth comes upon the once-again inanimate body of his brother and chops it into pieces. The pregnant Isis gathers the pieces together, erecting shrines at each find-spot, and makes Osiris whole again. Then, she, together with Nephthys, Thoth, and Anubis, mummifies Osiris.

Chapter 7 Town Life and Country Life

1. M. Lichtheim, 'The Instruction of Ptahhotep', *Ancient Egyptian Literature* 1 (Berkeley: University of California Press, 1975): 69.

Chapter 8 From Sunrise to Sunset: Daily Life of the Ancient Egyptians

1. A fine translation of the entire text can be found in M. Lichtheim, *Ancient Egyptian Literature* 1 (Berkeley: University of California Press, 1973): 184–92.
2. W. K. Simpson, 'The Instruction of Amenemope', in *The Literature of Ancient Egypt*, ed. W. K. Simpson (Cairo: AUC Press, 2003): 226.
3. Simpson, 'The Instruction of Amenemope', 240.
4. V. A. Tobin, 'The Maxims of Ptahhotep', in *The Literature of Ancient Egypt*, ed. W. K. Simpson (Cairo: AUC Press, 2003): 136.
5. V. A. Tobin, 'The Cairo Love Songs', in *The Literature of Ancient Egypt*, ed. W. K. Simpson (Cairo: AUC Press, 2003): 319.
6. V. A. Tobin, 'The Love Songs of Papyrus Chester Beatty I', in *The Literature of Ancient Egypt*, ed. W. K. Simpson (Cairo: AUC Press, 2003): 326.
7. M. Lehner, 'Rediscovering Egypt's Bread Baking Technology', *National Geographic*, January 1995: 32–5.
8. It should be remembered that the definition of art is a difficult subject and has changed over time. The definitions that are common in the twenty-first century AD are probably not the same as those of people living in the twenty-first century BC.
9. V. Davies and R. Friedman, 'The Narmer Palette: A Forgotten Member', *Nekhen News* (1998) 10: 22.
10. Sylvie Cauville, 'Les inscriptions dédicatoires du temple d'Hathor à Dendera', *Bulletin de l'Institut Français d'Archéologie Orientale* 90 (1990): 83–114; Sylvie Cauville and Didier Devauchelle, 'Les mesures réelles du temple d'Edfou', *Bulletin de l'Institut Français d'Archéologie Orientale* 84 (1984): 23–34.

Further Reading

Abbreviations

AUC	American University in Cairo
EEF/S	Egypt Exploration Fund/Society
IFAO	Institut Français d'Archéologie Orientale
JARCE	*Journal of the American Research Center in Egypt*
JEA	*Journal of Egyptian Archaeology*
JNES	*Journal of Near Eastern Studies*
MMA	Metropolitan Museum of Art, New York

Books Used in More Than One Chapter

Freed, R. E., Y. J. Markowitz, and S. H. D'Auria, eds. 1999. *Pharaohs of the Sun: Akhenaten – Nefertiti – Tutankhamen.* Boston: Museum of Fine Arts.

Lichtheim, M. 1973–80. *Ancient Egyptian Literature,* 1–3. Berkeley: University of California Press.

Simpson, W. K., ed. 2003. *The Literature of Ancient Egypt.* Cairo: AUC Press.

Trigger, B. G., B. J. Kemp, D. O'Connor, and A. B. Lloyd. 1983. *Ancient Egypt: A Social History.* Cambridge: Cambridge University Press.

Chapter 1

Butzer, K. 1960. Archeology and geology in ancient Egypt. *Science* 132: 1617–24.

Butzer, K. 1976. *Early Hydraulic Civilization in Egypt: A Study in Cultural Ecology.* Chicago: University of Chicago Press.

Said, R. 1981. *The Geological Evolution of the River Nile.* New York: Springer.

Said, R., ed. 1990. *The Geology of Egypt.* Rotterdam: A. A. Balkema.

Said, R. 1997. The role of the desert in the rise and fall of ancient Egypt. *Sahara* 9: 7–22.

Sampsell, B. M. 2003. *A Traveler's Guide to the Geology of Egypt.* Cairo: AUC Press.

Chapter 2

Adkins, L., and R. Adkins. 2000. *The Keys of Egypt: The Race to Read the Hieroglyphs*. London: HarperCollins.

Bennett, J. W. 1954. *The Rediscovery of Sir John Mandeville*. New York: Modern Language Association of America.

Breasted, C. 1943. *Pioneer to the Past: The Story of James Henry Breasted*. New York: Charles Scribner.

Colla, E. 2007. *Conflicted Antiquities: Egyptology, Egyptomania, Egyptian Modernity*. Durham, NC; Duke University Press.

Curl, James S. 1994. *Egyptomania: The Egyptian Revival, a Recurring Theme in the History of Taste*. Manchester: Manchester University Press.

Dawson, W. R., E. Uphill, and M. L. Bierbrier. 1995. *Who Was Who in Egyptology*. London: EES.

Drower, M. S. 1995. *Flinders Petrie: A Life in Archaeology*. Madison: University of Wisconsin Press.

Dunham, D. 1942. George Anrew Reisner. *American Journal of Archaeology* 46: 410–12.

Dunham, D. 1972. *Recollections of an Egyptologist*. Boston: Museum of Fine Arts.

Edwards, A. 1993. *A Thousand Miles Up the Nile*. London: Darf.

El-Daly, Okasha. 2005. *Egyptology: The Missing Millennium*. London: University College Press.

Frayling, C. 1992. *The Face of Tutankhamun*. London: Faber and Faber.

Greener, L. 1966. *The Discovery of Egypt*. New York: Dorset.

Haarmann, U. 1980. Regional sentiment in medieval Islamic Egypt. *Bulletin of the School of Oriental and African Studies* 43: 55–66.

Herold, C. 1962. *Bonaparte in Egypt*. London: Unwin.

Iversen, E. 1993. *The Myth of Egypt and Its Hieroglyphs in European Tradition*. Princeton, NJ: Princeton University Press.

James, T. G. H., ed. 1982. *Excavating in Egypt*. Chicago: University of Chicago Press.

Mandeville, Sir John. 1964. *The Travels of Sir John Mandeville*. New York: Dover.

Milton, G. 1996. *The Riddle and the Knight: In Search of Sir John Mandeville*. London: Hodder and Stoughton.

Petrie, W. M. F. 1969. *Seventy Years in Archaeology*. New York: Greenwood.

Petrie, W. M. F. 1976. *Ten Years' Digging in Egypt*. Chicago: Ares. Reprint of 1900 publication.

Reeves, N. 2000. *Ancient Egypt: The Great Discoveries*. London: Thames and Hudson.

Reid, D. M. 2002. *Whose Pharaohs? Archaeology, Museums, and Egyptian National Identity from Napoleon to World War I*. Cairo: AUC Press.

Sallam, H. 2000. Ahmed Kamal Pasha (1851–1923): A family of Egyptologists. In *Proceedings of the 8th International Congress of Egyptologists*. Edited by Z. Hawass and L. Pinch-Brock. Cairo: AUC Press: 1015–19.

Sheikholeslami, C., and M. Saleh. 2000. A short history of the Egyptian museum. In *The Egyptian Museum at the Millennium*. Edited by C. Sheikholeslami. Cairo: Supreme Council of Antiquities: 85.

Thompson, J. 1992. *Sir Gardner Wilkinson and His Circle*. Austin: University of Texas Press.

Tiradritti, F., ed. 1999. *Treasures of the Egyptian Museum*. London: Thames and Hudson.

Further Reading

Vercoutter, J. 1992. *The Search for Ancient Egypt*. New York: Harry Abrams.

Wortham, J. D. 1971. *British Egyptology, 1549–1906*. Newton Abbot, UK: David and Charles.

Chapter 3

Ellis, L., ed. 2000. *Archaeological Method and Theory: An Encyclopedia*. London: Garland.

Chapter 4

Aldred, C. 1988. *Akhenaten: Pharaoh of Egypt*. New York: Thames and Hudson.

Arnold, D. 1996. *The Royal Women of Amarna*. New York: MMA.

Balout, L., and C. Roubet. 1985. *La Momie de Ramses II*. Paris: Musée de l'Homme.

Bowman, A. K. 1986. *Egypt after the Pharaohs*. London: British Museum.

Breasted, J. H. 2001. *Ancient Records of Egypt 1–5*. Urbana: University of Illinois Press.

Burridge, A. 1996. Did Akhenaten suffer from Marfan's Syndrome? *The Biblical Archaeologist* 59.2: 127–28.

Clayton, P. 1994. *Chronicle of the Pharaohs*. London: Thames and Hudson.

Dodson, A. M. 1995, 2000. *Monarchs of the Nile*. Cairo: AUC Press.

Dodson, A. M., and D. Hilton. 2004. *The Complete Royal Families of Ancient Egypt*. London: Thames and Hudson.

Förster, F. 2007. The Abu Ballas trail: A Pharaonic donkey-caravan route in the Libyan Desert (SW-Egypt). In *Atlas of Cultural and Environmental Change in Arid Africa*. Edited by O. Bubenzer, A. Bolten, and F. Darius. Africa Praehistorica 21. Cologne: Heinrich-Barth-Institut: 130–33.

Grajetzki, W. 2006. *The Middle Kingdom of Ancient Egypt: History, Archaeology and Society*. London: Duckworth.

Grimal, N.-C. 1992. *A History of Ancient Egypt*. Oxford: Blackwell.

Hölbl, G. A. *History of the Ptolemaic Empire*. Translated by T. Saavedra. London: Routledge.

Kemp, B. J. 1989, 2006. *Ancient Egypt: Anatomy of a Civilisation*. London: Routledge.

Kitchen, K. A. 1973. *The Third Intermediate Period in Egypt*. Warminster: Aris and Phillips.

Kitchen, K. A. 1982. *Pharaoh Triumphant*. Warminster: Aris and Phillips.

Kuhlmann, K. P. 2002. The 'oasis bypath' or the issue of desert trade in Pharaonic times. Edited by Jennerstrasse 8. *Tides of the Desert – Gezeiten der Wüste*. Köln: Heinrich-Barth-Institut: 125–70.

Kuper, R., and Förster, F. 2003. Khufu's 'mefat' expeditions into the Libyan desert. *Egyptian Archaeology* 23: 25–28.

Midant-Reynes, B. 2000. *The Prehistory of Egypt from the First Egyptians to the First Pharaohs*. Oxford: Blackwell.

Moeller, N. 2005. The First Intermediate period: A time of famine and climate change? *Ägypten und Levante/Egypt and the Levant* 15: 153–67.

Morkot, R. 2000. *The Black Pharaohs: Egypt's Nubian Rulers*. London: Rubicon.

Murnane, W. J. 1995. *Texts from the Amarna Period in Egypt*. Atlanta, GA: Scholars.

Paulshock, B. Z. 1980. Tutankhamun and his brothers: Familial gynecomastia in the Eighteenth Dynasty. *Journal of the American Medical Association* 244.2: 160–64.

Redford, D. 1984. *Akhenaten: The Heretic King*. Princeton, NJ: Princeton University Press.

Ryholt, K. 1997. *The Political Situation in Egypt During the Second Intermediate Period*. Copenhagen: Museum Tusculanum Press.

Shaw, I., ed. 2000. *The Oxford History of Ancient Egypt*. Oxford: Oxford University Press.

Spencer, A. J. 1993. *Early Egypt*. London: British Museum.

Chapter 5

Andrews, C. 1994. *Amulets of Ancient Egypt*. London: British Museum.

Bleeker, C. J. 1967. *Egyptian Festivals: Enactments of Religious Renewal*. Leiden: E. J. Brill.

El-Shabban, S. 2000. *Temple Festival Calendars of Ancient Egypt*. Liverpool: Liverpool University Press.

Frankfort, H. 1961. *Ancient Egyptian Religion: An Interpretation*. New York: Harper and Row.

Frankfort, H., H. A. Frankfort, J. A. Wilson, T. Jacobson, and W. A. Irwin. 1946. *The Intellectual Adventure of Ancient Man*. Chicago: University of Chicago Press.

Hart, G. 1990. *Egyptian Myths*. London: British Museum.

Hornung, E. 1982. *Conceptions of God in Ancient Egypt: The One and the Many*. Translated by J. Baines. Ithaca, NY: Cornell University Press.

Hornung, E. 1999. *The Ancient Egyptian Books of the Afterlife*. Translated by D. Lorton. Ithaca, NY: Cornell University Press.

Meeks, D., and C. Favard-Meeks. 1997. *Daily Life of the Egyptian Gods*. Translated by G. M. Goshgarian. Ithaca, NY: Cornell University Press.

Pinch, G. 1993. *Votive Offerings to Hathor*. Oxford: Griffith Institute.

Pinch, G. 2002. *Egyptian Mythology*. Oxford: Oxford University Press.

Pinch, G. 2006. *Magic in Ancient Egypt*. London: British Museum.

Quirke, S. 1992. *Ancient Egyptian Religion*. London: British Museum.

Quirke, S., ed. 1997. *The Temple in Ancient Egypt: New Discoveries and Recent Research*. London: British Museum.

Sauneron, S. 2000. *The Priests of Ancient Egypt*. Translated by D. Lorton. Ithaca, NY: Cornell University Press.

Shafer, B., ed. 1991. *Religion in Ancient Egypt*. Ithaca, NY: Cornell University Press.

Shafer, B., ed. 1997. *Temples of Ancient Egypt*. Ithaca, NY: Cornell University Press.

Stevens, A. 2006. *Private Religion at Amarna*. Oxford: British Archaeological Reports.

Wilkinson, R. 2000. *The Complete Temples of Ancient Egypt*. London: Thames and Hudson.

Wilkinson, R. 2003. *The Complete Gods and Goddesses of Ancient Egypt*. London: Thames and Hudson.

Chapter 6

Baer, K. 1960. *Rank and Title in the Old Kingdom*. Chicago: University of Chicago Press.

Bakir, Abd el-Mohsen. 1952. *Slavery in Pharaonic Egypt*. Cairo: Government Press.

Bierbrier, M. 1982. *The Tomb Builders of the Pharaohs*. London: British Museum.

Cerny, J. 1973. *A Community of Workmen at Thebes in the Ramesside Period*. Cairo: IFAO.

Donadoni, S., ed. 1997. *The Egyptians*. Chicago: University of Chicago Press.

Edgerton, W. 1951. The strikes in Ramesses III's twenty-ninth year. *JNES* 10: 137–45.

Eyre, C. J. 1979. A 'strike' text from the Theban necropolis. In *Orbis Aegyptiorum Speculum, Glimpses of Ancient Egypt: Studies in Honour of H. W. Fairman*. Edited by J. Ruffle, G. A. Gaballa, and K. Kitchen. Warminster: Aris and Phillips: 80–91.

Fischer, H. G. 1954. Four provincial administrators at the Memphite cemetery. *Journal of the American Oriental Society* 74.1: 26–34.

Gardiner, A. 1948. *Ramesside Administrative Documents*. London: Oxford University Press.

Hayes, W. C. 1953. Notes on the government of Egypt in the Late Middle Kingdom. *JNES* 12: 31–39.

Hayes, W. C. 1955. *A Papyrus of the Late Middle Kingdom in the Brooklyn Museum*. New York: Brooklyn Museum.

James, T. G. H. 2003. *Pharaoh's People: Scenes from Life in Imperial Egypt*. New York: Tauris Parke.

Kanawati, N. 1980. *Governmental Reforms in Old Kingdom Egypt*. Warminster: Aris and Phillips.

Lichtheim, M. 1988. *Ancient Egyptian Autobiographies Chiefly of the Middle Kingdom*. Freiburg: Universitatsverlag Freiburg Schwiez.

Lorton, D. 1977. The treatment of criminals in ancient Egypt. *Journal of the Economic and Social History of the Orient* 20: 2–64.

Martin, G. 1971. *Egyptian Administration and Private Name Seals*. Oxford: Oxford University Press.

McDowell, A. 2001. *Village Life in Ancient Egypt: Laundry Lists and Love Songs*. Oxford: Oxford University Press.

Quirke, S. 1990. *The Administration of Egypt in the Late Middle Kingdom*. Whitstable: Sia.

Quirke, S. 1991. Royal power in the 13th Dynasty. In *Middle Kingdom Studies*. Edited by S. Quirke. Whitstable: Sia: 123–39.

Richards, J. 2005. *Society and Death in Ancient Egypt: Mortuary Landscapes of the Middle Kingdom*. Cambridge: Cambridge University Press.

Robins, G. 1993. *Women in Ancient Egypt*, London: British Museum.

Strudwick, N. 1985. *The Administration of Egypt in the Old Kingdom*, London: Kegan Paul.

Valbelle, D. 1985. *Les Ouvriers de la Tombe: Deir el-Medinéh a l'Époque Ramesside*. Cairo: IFAO.

Van den Boorn, G. P. F. 1988. *The Duties of the Vizier*. London: Kegan Paul.

Ward, W. 1982. *Index of Egyptian Administrative and Religious Titles of the Middle Kingdom*. Beirut: American University of Beirut Press.

Wente, E. F. 1990. *Letters from Ancient Egypt*. Atlanta, GA: Scholar's.

Chapter 7

Adams, M. D. 1998. The Abydos settlement site project: Investigation of a major provincial town in the Old Kingdom and First Intermediate period. In *Proceedings of the Seventh International Congress of Egyptologists, 1995*. Edited by C. Eyre. Leuven: Peeters: 19–30.

Allen, J. P. 2002. *The Heqanakht Papyri*. New York: MMA.

Badawy, A. 1966, 1968. *A History of Egyptian Architecture* 2–3. Berkeley: University of California Press.

Badawy, A. 1990. *A History of Egyptian Architecture* 1. London: Histories and Mysteries of Man. Originally published 1954.

Baer, K. 1956. A note on Egyptian units of area in the OK. *JNES* 15: 113–17.

Baer, K. 1962. The low cost of land in ancient Egypt. *JARCE* 1: 25–45.

Bard, K. A. 1987. The geography of excavated Predynastic sites and the rise of complex society. *JARCE* 24: 81–94.

Eyre, C. J. 1994. The water regimes for orchards and plantations in Pharaonic Egypt. *JEA* 80: 57–80.

Gardiner, A. 1948. *The Wilbour Papyrus* 1–4. Oxford: Griffith Institute.

Hoffman, M. A., H. Hamroush and R. O. Allen. 1986. A Model of Urban Development for the Hierakonpolis Region from Predynastic through Old Kingdom Times, *JARCE* 23: 175–187.

Katary, S. L. D. 1989. *Land Tenure in the Ramesside Period*. London: Kegan Paul.

Kemp, B. J. 1977. The early development of towns in Egypt. *Antiquity* 51: 185–200.

Kemp, B. J., ed. 1984–89. *Amarna Reports* 1–5. London: EES.

Lacovara, P. 1997. *The New Kingdom Royal City*. London: Kegan Paul.

Lavovara, P. 1999. The city of Amarna. In *Pharaohs of the Sun*. Edited by R. E. Freed, Y. J. Markowitz, and S. H. D'Auria. Boston: Museum of Fine Arts: 61–71.

Mallinson, M. 1999. The sacred landscape. In *Pharaohs of the Sun*. Edited by R. E. Freed, Y. J. Markowitz, and S. H. D'Auria. Boston: Museum of Fine Arts: 72–80.

Menu, B. 1970. *Le regime juridique des terres et du personnel attache a la terre dans le P. Wilbour*. Paris: University of Lille Press.

Menu, B. 2004. *Égypte pharaonique: nouvelles recherches sur l'histoire juridique, économiqueet sociale de l'ancienne Égypte*. Paris: L'Harmattan.

Miller, R. 1990. Hogs and hygiene. *JEA* 76: 125–40.

O'Connor, D. 1972. The geography of settlement in ancient Egypt. In *Man, Settlement, and Urbanism*. Edited by P. J. Ucko, R. Tringham, and G. W. Dimbleby. London: Duckworth: 681–98.

O'Connor, D. 1979. The university museum excavations at the palace-city of Malkata. *Expedition* 21: 52–3.

O'Connor, D. 1989. City and palace in New Kingdom Egypt. *Cahiers de Recherches de l'Institut de Papyrologie et d'Égyptologie de Lille* 11: 73–87.

Peet, T. E., and C. L. Woolley. 1923. *The City of Akhenaten* 1. London: EES.

Shaw, I. 1998. Egyptian patterns of urbanism: A comparison of three New Kingdom settlement sites. In *Proceedings of the Seventh International Congress of Egyptologists, 1995*. Edited by C. Eyre. Leuven: Peeters: 1049–60

Smith, H. S. 1985. Settlements in the Nile Valley. In *Mélanges Gamal E. Mokhtar*. Cairo: IFAO: 287–94.

Stadelman, R. 1994. Royal palaces of the Late New Kingdom in Thebes. In *Essays in Honor of Hans Goedicke*. Edited by B. M. Bryan and D. Lorton. San Antonio, TX: Van Siclen Books: 309–16.

Chapter 8

Aldred, C. 1971. *Jewels of the Pharaohs*. London: Thames and Hudson.

Allam, S. 1991. Egyptian law courts in Pharaonic and Hellenistic times. *JEA* 77: 109–27.

Allen, J. P. 2005. *The Art of Medicine in Ancient Egypt*, New York: MMA.

Andrews, C. 1991. *Ancient Egyptian Jewelery*. New York: H. N. Abrams.

Arnold, D. 1991. *Building in Egypt*. Oxford: Oxford University Press.

Blackman, A. M. 1945. The king of Egypt's grace before meat. *JEA* 31: 57–73.

Breasted, J. H. 1930. *The Edwin Smith Surgical Papyrus*. Chicago: University of Chicago Press.

Brewer, D. J., and R. F. Friedman. 1989. *Fish and Fishing in Ancient Egypt*. Warminster: Aris and Phillips. Cambridge: Cambridge University Press, 2004.

Cerny, J. 1973. *A Community of Workmen at Thebes in the Ramesside Period*. Cairo: IFAO.

Darby, W. P., and Ghalioungui, L. Grivetti. 1977. *Food: the Gift of Osiris* 1–2. London: Academic.

Davies, N. de G. 1935. The king as sportsman. *Bulletin of the MMA* 30.2: 49–53.

Davies, V., and R. Friedman. 1998. The Narmer Palette: A forgotten member. *Nekhen News* 10: 22.

Decker, W. 1993. *Sports and Games in Ancient Egypt*. Cairo: AUC Press.

Eyre, C. J. 1987. Work and the organisation of work in the Old Kingdom. In *Labor in the Ancient Near East*. Edited by M. Powell. New Haven, CT: Yale University Press: 5–47.

Ghalioungi, P. 1963. *Magic and Medical Science in Ancient Egypt*. London: Hodder and Stoughton.

Hall, R. 1986. *Egyptian Textiles*. Princes Risborough, UK: Shire.

Hepper, F. N. 1990. *Pharaoh's Flowers*. London: British Museum.

Ikram, S. 1994. Food for eternity I, II. *KMT: A Modern Journal of Egyptology* 5.1: 25–33; 5.2: 53–60, 75–77.

Ikram, S. 1996. *Choice Cuts: Meat Production in Ancient Egypt*. Leuven: Peeters.

James, T. G. H. 1962. *The Hekanakhte Papers and Other Early Middle Kingdom Documents*. New York: MMA.

Janssen, J., and R. Janssen. 2007. *Growing Up and Getting Old in Ancient Egypt*. London: Golden House Publications.

Janssen, J., and P. W. Pestman. 1968. Burial and inheritance in the community of necropolis workmen at Thebes (P. Boulaq X and O. Petrie 16). *Journal of the Economic and Social History of the Orient* 11: 137–70.

Jones, D. 1995. *Boats*. Austin: University of Texas Press.

Kendall, T. 1978. *Passing Through the Netherworld. The Meaning and Play of Senet, and Ancient Egyptian Funerary Games*. Boston: Museum of Fine Art and the Kirk Game Company.

Killen, G. 1994. *Egyptian Woodworking and Furniture*. Princes Risborough, UK: Shire.

Lesko, L. L. 1977. *King Tut's Wine Cellar*. Berkeley: University of California Press.

Lucas, A., and J. Harris. 1962. *Ancient Egyptian Materials and Industries*. London: E. Arnold.

Manniche, L. 1989. *An Ancient Egyptian Herbal*. London: British Museum.

Manniche, L. 1999. *Sacred Luxuries: Fragrance, Aromatherapy and Cosmetics in Ancient Egypt*. London: Opus.

McDowell, A. 1990. *Jurisdiction in the Workmen's Community of Deir el Medina*. Leiden: Nederlands Instituut voor het nabije Oosten.

Nicholson, P., and I. Shaw, eds. 2000. *Ancient Egyptian Materials and Technologies*. Cambridge: Cambridge University Press.

Further Reading

Nunn, J. F. 1996. *Ancient Egyptian Medicine*. London: British Museum.

Peet, T. E. 1923. *The Rhind Mathematical Papyrus, British Museum, 10057 and 10058*. Liverpool: Liverpool University.

Peet, T. E. 1930. *The Great Tomb Robberies of the 20th Egyptian Dynasty*. Oxford: Oxford University Press.

Pestman, P. W. 1961. *Marriage and Matrimonial Property in Ancient Egypt: A Contribution to Establishing the Legal Position of the Woman*. Leiden: Brill.

Poo, Mu-chou. 1995. *Wine and Wine Offering in the Religion of Ancient Egypt*. London: Kegan Paul. Originally published London: Hodder and Stoughton, 1923.

Robins, G. 1993. *Women in Ancient Egypt*. Cambridge, MA: Harvard University Press.

Robins, G. 1994. *Proportion and Style in Ancient Egyptian Art*. Austin: University of Texas Press.

Robins, G. 1997. *The Art of Ancient Egypt*. Cambridge, MA: Harvard University Press.

Robins, G. 1993. *Women in Ancient Egypt*. Cambridge, MA: Harvard University Press.

Rossi, C., 2004. *Architecture and Mathematics in Ancient Egypt*. Cambridge: Cambridge University Press.

Russmann, E. R. 1989. *Egyptian Sculpture: Cairo and Luxor*. Austin: University of Texas Press.

Samuel, D. 1989. Their staff of life. In *Amarna Reports 5*. Edited by B. J. Kemp. London: EES: 253–90.

Säve-Söderbergh, T. 1946. *The Navy of the Eighteenth Egyptian Dynasty*. Uppsala: Uppsala University.

Scheel, B. 1989. *Egyptian Metalworking and Tools*. Princes Risborough, UK: Shire.

Shaw, I. 1991. *Egyptian Warfare and Weapons*. Princes Risborough, UK: Shire.

Silverman, D. 1990. *Language and Writing in Ancient Egypt*. Pittsburgh: Carnegie Museum of Natural History.

Spalinger, A. J. 2005. *War in Ancient Egypt*. Oxford: Blackwell.

Vinson, S. 1994. *Egyptian Boats and Ships*. Princes Risborough, UK: Shire.

Whale, S. 1989. *The Family in the Eighteenth Dynasty of Egypt*. Sydney: Australian Centre for Egyptology.

Williams, R. J. 1972. Scribal training in ancient Egypt. *Journal of the American Oriental Society* 92.2: 214–21.

Chapter 9

D'Auria, S., P. Lacovara and C. Roehrig. 1988. *Mummies and Magic: The Funerary Arts of Ancient Egypt*. Boston: Museum of Fine Arts.

Dodson, A., and S. Ikram. 2008. *The Tomb in Ancient Egypt*. London: Thames and Hudson.

Gardiner, A., and K. Sethe. 1928. *Egyptian Letters to the Dead*. London: EES.

Ikram, S. 2003. *Death and Burial in Ancient Egypt*. London: Longman/Pearson.

Ikram, S., and A. Dodson. 1998. *The Mummy in Ancient Egypt*. London: Thames and Hudson.

Kamrin, J. 1999. *The Cosmos of Khnumhotep II at Beni Hasan*. London: Kegan Paul.

Kanawati, N. 2001. *The Tomb and Beyond: Burial Customs of Ancient Egyptian Officials*. Warminster: Aris and Phillips.

Lehner, M. 1997. *The Complete Pyramids*. London: Thames and Hudson.

Stewart, H. M. 1995. *Egyptian Shabtis*. Princes Risborough, UK: Shire.

Taylor, J. H. 2001. *Death and the Afterlife in Ancient Egypt*. London: British Museum.

Taylor, J. 1989. *Egyptian Coffins*. Princes Risborough, UK: Shire.

Egyptological Resources

The Web

There are a great many Egyptological resources online. Some of these are unreliable, but others, particularly the Web sites of museums and excavations, are excellent. The most useful site is www.newton.cam.ac.uk/egypt, which provides connections to reliable sites (and clearly marks those that are personal pages) dealing with all aspects of ancient Egypt. Another helpful site is Thesaurus linguae Aegyptiae, http://aaew2.bbaw.de/tla/. This provides a searchable corpus of Egyptian texts with translations.

Books

General Reference Books

Baines, J., and J. Malek. 2002. *Atlas of Ancient Egypt*. Cairo: AUC Press. *This excellent work lists major sites and what can be found at each and provides a basic overview of Egyptian culture and history.*

Bard, K. A., ed. 1999. *The Encylopedia of the Archaeology of Ancient Egypt*. London: Routledge. *Overview articles on main chronological periods are followed by signed entries covering sites, topics, archaeology, and geography, with bibliographies.*

Faulkner, R. O. 1976. *A Concise Dictionary of Middle Egyptian*. Oxford: Griffith Institute.

Helck, W., and E. Otto. 1972–92. *Lexikon der Ägyptologie* 1–7. Wiesbaden: Harrassowitz. (Abbrev.: LÄ.) *A thorough encyclopaedia of ancient Egypt. Each article has an extensive bibliography; the articles are in several languages. A cornerstone of the study of ancient Egypt.*

Porter, B., and R. Moss. 1934–81. *Topographical Bibliography of Ancient Egyptian Hieroglyphic Texts, Reliefs and Paintings* 1–7. Oxford: Griffith Institute. *Lists sites and what they contain in detail, together with references and plans.* Volume 8 (1999ff.), by J. Malek et al., *deals with unprovenanced objects in museums.*

Redford, D. 2001. *The Oxford Encyclopedia of Ancient Egypt* 1–3. New York: Oxford University Press. *Similar to the Helck and Otto Lexikon, but its entries are less detailed; all entries are in English.*

Shaw, I., and Nicholson, P. 1995. *British Museum Dictionary of Ancient Egypt*. London: British Museum. *Short articles (with some bibliographical references) on sites and topics.*

Texts in Translation

Breasted, J. H. 2001. *Ancient Records of Egypt* 1–5. Urbana: University of Illinois Press.

Kitchen, K. 1993–2000. *Ramesside Inscriptions* 1–4. Oxford: Blackwell.

Lichtheim, M. 1973–80. *Ancient Egyptian Literature*, 1–3. Berkeley: University of California Press.

Parkinson, R. B. 1991. *Voices from Ancient Egypt*. London: British Museum.

Simpson, W. K., ed. 2003. *The Literature of Ancient Egypt*. Cairo: AUC Press.

Hieroglyphics

Allen, J. P. 2001. *Middle Egyptian: An Introduction to the Language and Culture of Hieroglyphs*. Cambridge: Cambridge University Press. *For the more serious student.*

Collier, M., and B. Manley. 1998. *How to Read Egyptian Hieroglyphs*. Berkeley: University of California Press. *A good introduction to the study of hieroglyphics.*

Faulkner, R. 1962. *Concise Dictionary of Middle Egyptian*. Oxford: Griffith Institute. *The basic Egyptian dictionary.*

Gardiner, Sir A. 1950. *Egyptian Grammar*. Oxford: Oxford University Press. *A standard textbook.*

History

Clayton, P. 1994. *Chronicle of the Pharaohs*. London: Thames and Hudson. *Major pharaohs and facts concerning them.*

Dodson, A., and D. Hilton. 2004. *The Complete Royal Families*. London: Thames and Hudson. *Family connections of all Egyptian dynasties.*

Shaw, I., ed. 2000. *The Oxford History of Ancient Egypt*. Oxford: Oxford University Press. *Basic overview of Egyptian history.*

Art, Architecture, and Materials

Arnold, D. 2003. *The Encyclopedia of Ancient Egyptian Architecture*. Edited and translated by S. Gardiner, N. Strudwick, and H. Strudwick. Princeton, NJ: Princeton University Press. *Short articles, with bibliography, plans, and illustrations, on sites, structures, and terminology.*

Badawy, A. 1966, 1968. *A History of Egyptian Architecture* 2–3. Berkeley: University of California Press. *Basic overview of Egyptian architecture.*

Badawy, A. 1990. *A History of Egyptian Architecture* 1. London: Histories and Mysteries of Man. (Orig. pub. 1954.) *Basic overview of Egyptian architecture.*

Lucas, A., and J. Harris. 1962. *Ancient Egyptian Materials and Industries*. London: E. Arnold. *An overview of manufacturing materials and methods used to produce a variety of objects.*

Nicholson, P. T., and I. Shaw. 2000. *Ancient Egyptian Materials and Technology*. Cambridge: Cambridge University Press. *Articles on different materials and technologies used by the Egyptians.*

Schäfer, H. 1986. *Principles of Egyptian Art.* Translated and edited by J. Baines. Oxford: Griffith Institute.

Smith, W. S. 1998. *The Art and Architecture of Ancient Egypt*. New Haven, CT: Yale University Press. *Standard introductory text for Egyptian art.*

Vandier, J. 1952–78. *Manuel d'Archéologie Égyptienne* 1–6. Paris: A. and J. Picard.

Index